S0-BNB-405

Studies in Marxism and social theory

Capitalism and social democracy

Studies in Marxism and Social Theory

Edited by G. A. Cohen, Jon Elster and John Roemer

The series is jointly published by the Cambridge University Press and the Editions de la Maison des Sciences de l'Homme, in close collaboration with the Laboratoire Européen de Psychologie Sociale of the Maison, as part of the joint publishing agreement established in 1977 between the Fondation de la Maison des Sciences de l'Homme and the Syndics of the Cambridge University Press.

The books in the series are intended to exemplify a new paradigm in the study of Marxist social theory. They will not be dogmatic or purely exegetical in approach. Rather, they will examine and develop the theory pioneered by Marx, in the light of the intervening history, and with the tools of non-Marxist social science and philosophy. It is hoped that Marxist thought will thereby be freed from the increasingly discredited methods and presuppositions which are still widely regarded as essential to it, and that what is true and important in Marxism will be more firmly established.

Also in the series
Jon Elster *Making Sense of Marx*

Capitalism and social democracy

Adam Przeworski
University of Chicago

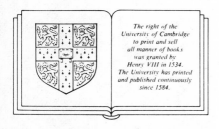

The right of the
University of Cambridge
to print and sell
all manner of books
was granted by
Henry VIII in 1534.
The University has printed
and published continuously
since 1584.

Cambridge University Press
Cambridge
New York   New Rochelle
Melbourne   Sydney

Editions de la Maison des Sciences de l'Homme
Paris

Published by the Press Syndicate of the University of Cambridge
The Pitt Building, Trumpington Street, Cambridge CB2 1RP
32 East 57th Street, New York, NY 10022, USA
10 Stamford Road, Oakleigh, Melbourne 3166, Australia
and Editions de la Maison des Sciences de l'Homme
54 Boulevard Raspail, 75270 Paris Cedex 06

First published 1985
First paperback edition 1986
Reprinted 1987, 1988

Printed in Great Britain at the University Press, Cambridge

British Library Cataloguing in Publication Data

Przeworski, Adam
Capitalism and social democracy.—
(Studies in Marxism and social theory)
1. Socialism   2. Democracy
I. Title   II. Series
335.5   HX73

ISBN 0 521 26742 0 hard cover
ISBN 2 7351 0105 3 (France only)

ISBN 0 521 33656 2 paperback
ISBN 2 7351 0172 X (France only)

SE

Contents

Acknowledgments

This book grew out of a conspiracy between Joanne Fox Przeworski and Michael Burawoy, who decided some eight years ago that they had enough listening to me and that I must write down on paper everything about which I sought to convince them. My luck continued even since then. John Sprague and Michael Wallerstein collaborated with me in working out problems with which I could not have coped on my own. John Kautsky and Philippe Schmitter insisted over the years in disagreeing with almost every word I ever gave them to read. They are largely responsible for my endless rewriting of the same ideas. Jane Jenson and Erik Olin Wright forced me repeatedly to search for new arguments and new data, just to persuade them. I have benefited from expressions of interest, suggestions, and disagreements from David Abraham, Ike Balbus, Pierre Birnbaum, Fernando Cortés, Jon Elster, Gösta Esping-Anderson, J. David Greenstone, Douglas Hibbs, Elisabeth Jelin, Ira Katznelson, Mark Kesselman, Norbert Lechner, Margaret Levi, Colin Leys, Guillermo O'Donnell, Leo Panitch, Göran Therborn, Ernest Underhill, Jerzy Wiatr, Maurice Zeitlin, and, I am certain, many others whose thoughts I internalized so thoroughly that I no longer remember the origins.

If I dared go public with my ideas, even to objectivize them in print, it is only because I had the opportunity to test them first with my students, and even colleagues, at the University of Chicago. Anyone who survives this ordeal has lost all fear.

My institutional debts are equally extensive. Several parts of the book were written under grants from the National Science Foundation, SOC75-17906 and SOC78-04595. At various moments I received sabbatical leave from the University of Chicago. Finally, recent revisions were made while I was under a grant from the German Marshall Fund of the United States. Without their support this book would not have been written.

I feel exceptionally privileged to have received so many reactions while this book was in the making. I hope that its appearance will be treated as just another round in recurring discussions.

Chapter One is an extended and revised version of an article which appeared originally in the *New Left Review*, 122 (1980).

vii

Chapter Two is a revised version of an article which appeared originally in *Politics and Society*, 7 (1977): 343–401. The Postscript is based on an article entitled "The Ethical Materialism of John Roemer," *Politics and Society*, 11 (1982): 289–313.

Chapter Three was co-authored with John Sprague and written originally for this volume.

Chapter Four is a revised version of an article which appeared originally in *Political Power and Social Theory*, 1 (1980): 21–66.

Parts of Chapter Five were published in an article entitled "Material Interests, Class Compromise and the Transition to Socialism," *Politics and Society*, 10 (1980): 125–53. Other parts were co-authored with Michael Wallerstein and were published originally under the title "The Structure of Class Conflict in Democratic Capitalist Societies," *American Political Science Review*, 76 (1982): 215–38.

Chapter Six was co-authored with Michael Wallerstein. It is reprinted here from *Democracy*, 2 (1982): 52–68.

Chapter Seven appeared originally in *Politics and Society*, 11 (1982): 289–313.

Introduction

Not to repeat past mistakes: the sudden resurgence of a sympathetic interest in social democracy is a response to the urgent need to draw lessons from the history of the socialist movement. After several decades of analyses worthy of an ostrich, some rudimentary facts are being finally admitted. Social democracy has been the prevalent manner of organization of workers under democratic capitalism. Reformist parties have enjoyed the support of workers. Perhaps even more: for better or worse social democracy is the only political force of the Left that can demonstrate a record of reforms in favor of workers.

Is there anything to be learned from the social democratic experience? The answer is by no means apparent, as years of a *tout court* rejection testify. One may reject, as the revolutionary Left of various shades has done during one hundred years, the electoral alternative. But if insurrection by a minority is rejected — either because it is unfeasible or because it does not lead to socialism — then social democracy is the only historical laboratory where lessons can be sought. The cost of repeating past mistakes cannot be ignored: we continue to live under capitalism.

But what is a "mistake"? The very possibility of committing mistakes presupposes simultaneously a political project, some choice among strategies, and objective conditions that are independent with regard to the particular movement. If the strategy of a party is uniquely determined, then the notion of "mistakes" is meaningless: the party can only pursue the inevitable. "We consider the breakdown of the present social system to be unavoidable," Karl Kautsky wrote in his commentary on the Erfurt Programme of the *Sozialdemokratische Partei Deutschlands* in 1891, "because we know that the economic evolution inevitably brings on the conditions that will compel the exploited classes to rise against this system of private ownership." (1971: 90) Socialism was seen as an inevitable consequence of economic development, and the party, while necessary, was itself a determined link in the chain of causality. Plekhanov provided the most explicit formulation of this view: "Social Democracy views historical development from the standpoint of necessity, and its own activities as a necessary link in the chain of those necessary conditions

1

which combined make the victory of socialism inevitable." (1965: vol. XI, 77) In this model of history, economic factors were thought to determine simultaneously the conditions for the revolution and the actions of people under these conditions. The activity of the party was thus predetermined. There was no room for errors. In a world of necessity the question of errors cannot even be posed.

It is perhaps less apparent that the notion of mistakes is also rendered meaningless within the context of a radically voluntaristic understanding of historical possibilities. Critics of social democracy often adopted a voluntaristic posture. For them, the deterministic model of history was destroyed by the Soviet Revolution. Since a revolution had occurred where economic conditions were not "ripe," suddenly it became possible under all circumstances. Hence Lukacs, writing in 1924, asserted that "The theory of historical materialism therefore presupposes the universal actuality of the proletarian revolution." (1971: 11–12) Trotsky, who thought that objective conditions "have not only 'ripened'; they have begun to get somewhat rotten," claimed in 1938 that "All now depends upon the proletariat, i.e., *chiefly* on its revolutionary vanguard. The historical crisis of mankind is *reduced* to the crisis of the revolutionary leadership." (Claudin, 1975: 79) Horkheimer despaired in 1940 that the "present talk of inadequate conditions is a cover for the tolerance of oppression. For the revolutionary, conditions have always been ripe." (1973: 11) But if everything is always possible, then only motives explain the course of history. For an error is a relation between projects and conditions; mistakes are possible if and only if some strategies are ineffective in advancing the realization of a given project under existing conditions while other strategies would have advanced it under the same conditions. If everything is possible, then the choice of strategy is only a matter of will; it is the same as the choice of the project itself. Hence biographical factors become the key to the understanding of social democracy. MacDonald's addiction to the King's tea becomes the cause of his betrayal; understanding of the movement is reduced to discoveries of deceptions, scandals, and betrayals. "Betrayal" is indeed the proper way of understanding social democratic strategies in a world free of objective constraints. But accusations of betrayal are not particularly illuminating in the real world.

Accidents may be the motor of history, but somehow it seems implausible that so many political leaders of workers would by mere chance happen to be "traitors." And even if they were, Claudin is right in observing that "This explanation calls out for another to be given: why did the workers follow these 'traitor' leaders?" (1975: 56) We must admit the fact that, as Arato put it,

a version of the theory that hardly exhausts, and in part falsifies, the theoretical project of Karl Marx managed to express the immediate interests of the industrial working class —

the social stratum to which all political Marxisms have been inevitably drawn – and . . . the philosophy of praxis that projected a link between the objective possibilities of the present and a liberated future almost always has been politically irrelevant. (1973: 2)

Neither "ideological domination" nor repression is sufficient to account for the manner in which workers organize and act under capitalism. The working class has been neither a perpetual dupe nor a passive victim: workers did organize in unions and in most countries as political parties; these organizations have had political projects of their own; they chose strategies and pursued them to victories as well as defeats. Even if itself molded by capitalist relations, the working class has been an active force in transforming capitalism. We will never understand the resilience of capitalism unless we seek the explanation in the interests and in the actions of workers themselves.

If we are to draw lessons from historical experience, we can assume neither that the practice of political movements is uniquely determined by any objective conditions nor that such movements are free to act at will, independently of the conditions they seek to transform. These conditions constitute at each moment the structure of choice: the structure within which actors deliberate upon goals, perceive alternatives, evaluate them, choose courses of action, and pursue them to create new conditions.

Any movement that seeks to transform historical conditions operates under these very conditions. The movement for socialism developed within capitalist societies and faced definite choices that arise from this particular organization of society. These choices have been threefold: (1) whether to seek the advancement of socialism within the existing institutions of the capitalist society or outside of them; (2) whether to seek the agent of socialist transformation exclusively in the working class or to rely on multi- or even non-class support; and (3) whether to seek reforms, partial improvements, or to dedicate all efforts and energies to the complete abolition of capitalism.

These choices constitute the subject of the book. While the issue of participation is discussed only briefly, as a prologue to the story, the questions of the relation between the socialist movement and the working class and of the strategy of socialist transformation are formulated systematically, analyzed empirically, and applied to the analysis of concrete historical events. Although a collection of articles written over the span of six years, the book is narrowly directed to the analysis of two principal theses: (1) in the process of electoral competition socialist parties are forced to undermine the organization of workers as a class, and (2) compromises over economic issues between workers and capitalists are possible under capitalism and at times preferred by workers over more radical strategies. These two hypotheses explain why in many democratic capitalist countries workers were and continue to be organized by multi-class-oriented, economically reformist electoral parties — "social democratic" parties, whether or not they wear the label. These hypotheses imply at the same time that reforms are not irreversible and cumulative and thus provide the basis for a critique of social democracy.

The book consists of four parts. The first chapter, "Social Democracy as a Historical Phenomenon," provides the overall theoretical and historical framework for the entire analysis. The next two chapters analyze the role of political parties in the process of organization of workers into a class. Chapter Two, "Proletariat into a Class," provides a review of the marxist historiography of the processes of class formation. The central argument is that the organization of politics in terms of class should be seen as a contingent historical outcome of continual conflicts, in the course of which classes become organized, disorganized, and reorganized. This theoretical approach is applied in the subsequent chapter to analyze the strategies of electoral socialist parties and their effect on the voting behavior of individual workers in seven European countries since the turn of the century. The analysis demonstrates that socialist parties faced a choice between pursuing votes and organizing workers as a class and that an overwhelming mandate for socialist transformations is not a likely outcome of elections regardless of strategies parties adopt.

The next three chapters are devoted to the choice of economic strategies facing workers under democratic capitalism. Chapter Four, "Material Bases of Consent," presents those elements of the economic structure and the political institutions of democratic capitalism which mold the terms of choice available to workers. This chapter sets the general theoretical framework within which strategic questions can be analyzed. The argument in Chapter Five demonstrates that a compromise which entails the perpetuation of capitalist forms of property is under some circumstances preferable for workers who seek to maximize their material welfare. Even if socialism were superior in satisfying material needs, the threat of disinvestment may prevent workers from supporting a strategy of transition. Chapter Six emphasizes that the combination of private ownership of the means of production with political democracy is a compromise and highlights the threat to democracy embodied in the current right-wing offensive.

The theoretical principles which underlie the entire book are reviewed in the last chapter. In a polemic with a theory of exploitation and class offered by John Roemer, this chapter provides a statement of theoretical issues that remain unresolved. Finally, the Postscript returns to the prospects for socialism and the question of the transformative capacity of social democracy.

This book is a result of a gnawing obsession that forsaken possibilities are hiding somewhere behind the veil of our everyday experiences. A search for possibilities must reconstruct the logic of choices faced by the movement for socialism within the capitalist society; it must recreate the historical possibilities that were opened and closed as each choice was made and find which of the past decisions constrain our present alternatives.

These tasks call for a particular methodology. Social relations are treated here as structures of choices available to the historical actors, individual and collective, at each moment of history, and in turn as the outcomes of strategies adopted earlier by some political forces. Behavior is thus analyzed as strategic action, oriented toward goals, based on deliberations, responding to perceived alternatives, resulting from decisions. Some of the alternatives appear rather clear, at least in retrospect — so clear that they can be analyzed with the aid of mathematical models. This is the case of both electoral and economic strategies. Some other choices are well understood but difficult to calculate, for the actors involved as well as for observers, because the consequences of alternative courses of action are highly unpredictable. But there must also exist alternatives of which we are not aware. Particularly today, when it seems that the Left has lost not only its promise as a force of liberation but even its originality as an alternative for the next election, it remains difficult to believe that nothing else is possible. It is to uncover these forsaken possibilities that we need look back at the historical experience.

1. Social Democracy as a Historical Phenomenon

The Decision to Participate

The crucial choice was whether to participate. Earlier events resulted in establishing the principle of democracy in the political realm. Yet political rights were merely formal when accompanied by the compulsion and inequality that reigned in the social realm. As it emerged around 1850, socialism was thus a movement that would complete the revolution started by the bourgeoisie by wresting from it "social power" just as the bourgeoisie had conquered political power. The recurrent theme of the socialist movement ever since has been this notion of "extending" the democratic principle from the political to the social, in effect primarily economic, realm.

Yet precisely because the principle of democracy was already present in the political institutions, the means by which socialism would be achieved appeared as a choice. The project of the early, communitarian, socialists was to build a society within the society, a community of immediate producers associated in workshops and manufactures, cooperating as consumers and administering their own affairs. This society of associated producers was to be built in complete independence of the bourgeois world; it was simply to by-pass the emerging capitalist, and to a great extent industrial, order. Yet as soon as the new bourgeois society developed its political institutions – first the bureaucracy and the standing army and then the popularly elected parliament – the posture of aloof independence could not be sustained. One could no longer maintain, as had Proudhon, that social reform cannot result from political change. Even if political action were indeed ineffective in bringing about social reform, once established, the new political institutions had to be treated either as an enemy or a potential instrument. The choice had become one between "direct" and "political" action: a direct confrontation between the world of workers and the world of capital or a struggle through political institutions. Building a society within the society was not enough: conquest of political power was necessary. As Marx argued in his Inaugural Address to the First International in 1864, "To be able to emancipate the working class, the cooperative system must be developed at the national level, which implies that it must dispose of national means. . . . Under these conditions, the great duty of the working class is to conquer political power." (1974: 80) Hence Marx claimed that workers must organize as a political party and this party must conquer power on the road to establishing the socialist society. But the tormenting question was whether this party should avail itself of the already existing institutions in its quest for political power. Political democracy, specifically suffrage, was a ready-made weapon for the working class. Was this weapon to be discarded or was it to be wielded on the road from "political to social emancipation"?

The anarchist response was resoundingly negative. What anarchists feared and what they claimed was not only that political action is unnecessary and ineffective but that any involvement in bourgeois institutions, whatever its purpose and whatever its form, would destroy the very movement for socialism. The Anarchist Congress at Chaud-de-Fonds warned in 1870 that "all workers' participation in bourgeois governmental politics cannot have other results than the consolidation of the existing state of affairs and thus would paralyze socialist revolutionary action of the proletariat." (Droz, 1966: 33) The very consideration of an improvement of workers' situation within capitalist society — a discussion of international codes for the protection of labor at the founding meeting of the Second International in 1889 — brought anarchists to exclaim immediately that whoever accepts reforms is not a true socialist (Joll, 1966: 45). Alex Danielsson, one of the founders of the Swedish Social Democracy, maintained in 1888 that electoral participation would change socialism "from a new theory of society and the world to a paltry program for a purely parliamentary party, and at that instant the enthusiasm in the workers' core will be extinguished and the ideal of social revolution degenerate into a pursuit of 'reforms' that will consume all the workers' interests." (Tingsten, 1973: 352) As Errico Malatesta observed in retrospect, "Anarchists have always kept themselves pure, and remain the revolutionary party par excellence, the party of the future, because they have been able to resist the siren song of elections." (Guerin, 1970: 19)

Those who became socialists were the ones who decided to utilize political rights of workers in those societies where workers had them and to struggle for these rights where they were still to be won. The abstentionist current lost its support within the First International after 1873 and the newly formed socialist parties, most founded between 1884 and 1892, embraced the principles of political action and of workers' autonomy (Haupt, 1980).

Yet the attitude of socialist parties toward electoral participation was ambivalent at best. This ambivalence was not theoretical: little is to be gained by interpreting and reinterpreting every word Marx wrote about bourgeois democracy for the simple reason that Marx himself and the men and women who led the newly formed parties into electoral battles were not quite certain what to expect of electoral competition. The main question – one which history never resolved because it cannot be resolved once and for all – was whether the bourgeoisie would respect its own legal order in case of an electoral triumph of socialism. If socialists were to use the institution of suffrage – established by the bourgeoisie in its struggle against absolutism – to win elections and to legislate a society toward socialism, would the bourgeoisie not revert to illegal means to defend its interests? This is what had happened in France in 1851, and it seemed likely that it would happen again.

Thus the essential question facing socialist parties was whether, as Hjalmar Branting posed it in 1886, "the upper class [would] respect popular will *even if it demanded the abolition of its privileges.*" (Tingsten, 1973: 361) Sterky, the leader of the left wing of the Swedish Social Democrats, was among those who took a clearly negative view: "Suppose that . . . the working class could send a majority to the legislature; not even by doing this would it obtain power. One can be sure that the capitalist class would then take care not to continue along a parliamentary course but instead resort to bayonets." (Ibid.) No one could be completely certain: Austrian Socialists, for example, promised in their Linz program of 1926 to "govern in strict accordance with the rules of the democratic state," but they felt compelled to warn that "should the bourgeoisie by boycotting revolutionary forces attempt to obstruct the social change which the labour movement in assuming power is pledged to carry out, then social democracy will be forced to employ dictatorial means to break such resistance." (Lesser, 1976: 145) The main doubt about electoral participation was whether revolution would not be necessary anyway, as August Bebel put it in 1905, "as a purely defensive measure, designed to safeguard the exercise of power legitimately acquired through the ballot." (Schorske, 1955: 43)

Under these conditions the attitude toward electoral participation was understandably cautious. Socialists entered electoral politics gingerly, "only to utilize them for propaganda purposes," and vowed "not to enter any alliances with other parties or to accept any compromises" (Resolution of the Eisenach Congress of the S.P.D. in 1870). At best, many thought, universal suffrage was one instrument among others, albeit one that had "the incomparably higher merit of unchaining the class struggle . . .," as Marx put it in 1850 (1952a: 47). Elections were to be used only as a ready-made forum for organization, agitation, and propaganda. The typical posture is well illustrated by this motion offered in 1889: "Since Sweden's Social Democratic Workers' Party is a propaganda party, i.e., [it considers] its main objective to be the dissemination of information about Social Democracy, and since participation in elections is a good vehicle for agitation, the Congress recommends participation." (Tingsten, 1973: 357)

Elections were also useful in providing the leadership with a reading of the "revolutionary fervor of the masses." But this is all they seemed to promise at the moment when socialists decided to participate. The last edition of *The Origins of Private Property, Family, and the State* which appeared during Engels' lifetime still contained in 1891 the assertion that universal suffrage is merely "the gauge of the maturity of the working class. It cannot and never will be anything more in the present-day state." (1942: 158)

Each step toward participation rekindled controversies. The German Social Democratic Party argued whether to allow one of its members to become the Deputy Speaker of the Reichstag, whether to vote on the budget, even whether to trade votes in the second round of elections (Schorske, 1955). The Norwegian Labor Party refused in 1906 to trade votes in the second round even though no compromise was implied (Lafferty, 1971: 127). In 1898, a survey of the opinions of prominent leaders of the Second International showed that while interventions into bourgeois politics were thought to be at times advisable, six of the respondents voted *"jamais"* with regard to participating in a government, eleven admitted it was possible only *très exceptionnellement*, and a minority of twelve thought that such participation is either always desirable or at least it was in the case of Millerand (Fiechtier, 1965: 69–75). Of the sixty-nine Swedish Social Democrats polled by telegram whether the party should join the Liberal government in 1911, sixty-three responded against participating (Tingsten, 1973: 418). While some parties "suspended" class struggle and entered into coalition governments before the end of World War I, even in Great Britain the decision to form the first Labour government in 1924 was a subject of intense polemics and had to be rationalized as an opportunity to acquire experience necessary for the socialist era (Lyman, 1957).

Opponents of participation seem to hold a permanent place in the political spectrum. As established parties take each step toward full participation, new voices emerge to continue the tradition according to which the belief in the parliamentary battles "between frogs and mice" (Luxemburg, 1967: 37) is a manifestation of what Marx called under very special circumstances "parliamentary cretinism." (1952a: 77) "Integration is the price," Horkheimer repeated in the 1940 Anarchist *memento*, "which individuals and groups must pay in order to flourish under capitalism." (1973: 5) "Elections, a trap for fools," was a title of an article by Sartre on the eve of the 1973 French parliamentary elections. *"Voter, c'est abdiquer"*, shouted the walls of Paris in 1968.

Democratic Capitalism and Political Participation

Electoral abstention has never been a feasible option for political parties of workers. Nor could participation remain merely symbolic. As long as democratic competition offers to various groups an opportunity to advance some of their interests in the short run, any political party that seeks to mobilize workers must avail itself of this opportunity.

Capitalism is a particular form of social organization of production and exchange. Based on an advanced division of labor, capitalism is a system in which production is oriented toward the needs of others, toward exchange. It is therefore a system in which even the people who directly participate in transforming nature into useful products — the immediate producers — cannot physically survive on their own. Furthermore, capitalism is a system in which those who do not own the instruments of production must sell their capacity to work. Workers obtain a wage, which is not a title to any part of the specific product which they generate but an abstract medium for acquisition of any goods and services. They must produce profit as a condition of their continued employment.

The product is appropriated privately in the sense that workers have no institutional claim to its allocation or distribution in their role as immediate producers. Capitalists, who are profit-takers, decide under multiple constraints how to allocate the product, in particular what part of it to invest, where, how, and when. These allocations are constrained by the fact that capitalists compete with each other and that they can be influenced by the political system. The ownership of the means of production also endows the proprietors with the right to organize (or to delegate the organization of) production. Capitalists, as employers, regulate the organization of work, although they may be again constrained by rules originating from the political system. As immediate producers, workers have no institutional claim to directing the productive activities in which they participate.

Under these conditions, political democracy constitutes the opportunity for workers to pursue some of their interests. Electoral politics constitutes the mechanism through which anyone can as a citizen express claims to goods and services. While as immediate producers workers have no institutional claim to the product, as citizens they can process such claims through the political system. Moreover, again as citizens as distinguished from immediate producers, they can intervene in the very organization of production and allocation of profit.

Capitalists are able to seek the realization of their interests in the course of everyday activity within the system of production. Capitalists continually "vote" for allocation of societal resources as they decide to invest or not, to employ or dismiss labor, to purchase state obligations, to export or to import. By contrast, workers can process their claims only collectively and only indirectly, through organizations which are embedded in systems of representation, principally trade-unions and political parties. Participation is hence necessary for the realization of interests of workers. Revolutionary ideals may move history, but they neither nourish nor shelter. As Schumpeter observed:

a wholly negative attitude, though quite satisfactory in principle, would have been impossible for any party of more than negligible importance to keep. It would have inevitably collided with most of the real desiderata of organized labor and, if persisted in for any length of time, would have reduced the followers to a small group of political ascetics . . . No party can live without a program that holds out the promise of immediate benefits. (1942: 316–17)

If they are to utilize the opportunity offered by democracy, workers must organize as participants. And even if this opportunity is limited, it is the only one that is institutionalized, the only one that is available to workers as a collectivity. Participation in democratic politics is necessary if workers are to be able to conduct other forms of struggle, including direct confrontation with capitalists. Socialists faced a hostile state, in which the permanently organized forces of repression were in the hands of landowners or the bourgeoisie. In the situation in which armed insurrections were made unfeasible by technological changes in the art of warfare — the point emphasized by Engels in 1895 — parliamentary participation was the only recourse available to workers. It is important that the turning point in the tactics of several socialist parties occurred after the failures of general strikes which were organized around economic issues. While strikes oriented toward extensions of suffrage were successful in Belgium and Sweden, the use of mass strikes for economic goals invariably resulted in political disasters: in Belgium in 1902 (Landauer, 1959, I; 472–73), Sweden in 1909 (Schiller, 1975: 208–17), France in 1920 (Maier, 1975: 158), Norway in 1921 (Lafferty, 1971: 191), and Great Britain in 1926 (Miliband, 1975: 148). All these strikes were defeated; in the aftermath trade-unions were decimated and repressive legislation was passed. These common experiences of defeat and repression had a decisive effect in directing socialist parties toward electoral tactics. Parliamentary representation was necessary to protect the movement from repression: this was the lesson drawn by socialist leaders. As Kautsky wrote already in 1891, "The economic struggle demands political rights and these will not fall from heaven." (1971: 186)

Moreover, participation was necessary because as an effect of universal suffrage masses of individuals can have political effects without being organized. Unless workers are organized as a class, they are likely to vote on the basis of other sources of collective identification, as Catholics, Bavarians, women, Francophones, consumers, and so forth. Once elections were organized and workers obtained the right to vote, they had to be organized to vote as workers.

The fact is that the only durable organizations are those that chose to participate in bourgeois institutions. For unless a participation is totally ineffective in advancing interests of workers in the short run, all organizations of workers must either join or vanish.

Electoral Participation and Class Organization

The reason why involvement in representative politics of the bourgeois society has never ceased to evoke controversy is that the very act of "taking part" in this particular system shapes the movement for socialism and its relation to workers as a class. The recurrent question is whether involvement in electoral politics can result in socialism or must strengthen the existing, that is capitalist, social order. Is it possible for the socialist movement to find a passage between the "two reefs" charted by Rosa Luxemburg: "abandonment of the mass character or abandonment of the final goals"? (Howard, 1973: 93) Participation in electoral politics is necessary if the movement for socialism is to find mass support among workers, yet this very participation appears to obstruct the attainment of final goals. Working for today and working toward tomorrow appear as horns of a dilemma.

Participation imprints a particular structure upon the organization of workers as a class. The effect of participation upon internal class relations has been best analyzed by Luxemburg:

the division between political struggle and economic struggle and their separation is but an artificial product, even if historically understandable, of the parliamentary period. On the one hand, in the peaceful development, "normal" for the bourgeois society, the economic struggle is fractionalized, disaggregated into a multitude of partial struggles limited to each firm, to each branch of production. On the other hand, the political struggle is conducted not by the masses through direct action, but in conformity with the structure of the bourgeois state, in the representative fashion, by the pressure exercised upon the legislative body. (1970a: 202)

The first effect of "the structure of the bourgeois state" is thus that wage-earners are formed as a class in a number of independent and often competitive organizations, most frequently as trade-unions and political parties, but also as cooperatives, neighborhood associations, clubs, etc. One characteristic feature of capitalist democracy is the individualization of class relations at the level of politics and ideology (Lukacs, 1971: 65–6; Poulantzas, 1973). People who are capitalists or wage-earners within the system of production all appear in politics as undifferentiated "individuals" or "citizens." Hence, even if a political party succeeds in forming a class on the terrain of political institutions, economic and political organizations never coincide. Multiple unions and parties often represent different interests and compete with each other. Moreover, while the class base of unions is confined to certain groups of people more or less permanently employed, political parties which organize wage-earners must also mobilize people who are not members of unions. Hence there is a permanent tension between the narrower interests of unions and the broader interests represented by parties. Class organized as a participant does not appear as a single actor in concrete historical conflicts (Miliband, 1977: 129).

The second effect is that relations within the class become structured as relations of representation. The parliament is a representative institution: it seats individuals, not masses. A relation of representation is thus imposed upon the class by the very nature of capitalist democratic institutions. Masses do not act directly in defense of their interests; they delegate this defense. This is true of unions as much as of parties: the process of collective bargaining is as distant from the daily experience of the masses as elections. Leaders become representatives. Masses represented by leaders: this is the mode of organization of the working class within capitalist institutions. In this manner participation demobilizes the masses.

The organizational dilemma extends even further. The struggle for socialism inevitably results in the *embourgeoisement* of the socialist movement: this is the gist of Roberto Michels' classical analysis. The struggle requires organization; it demands a permanent apparatus, a salaried bureaucracy; it calls for the movement to engage in economic activities of its own. Hence socialist militants inevitably become bureaucrats, newspaper editors, managers of insurance companies, directors of funeral parlours, and even *Parteibudiger* – party bar keepers. All of these are petty bourgeois occupations. "They impress," Michels concluded, ". . . a markedly petty bourgeois stamp." (1962: 270) As a French dissident wrote recently, "The working class is lost in administering its imaginary bastions. Comrades disguised as notables occupy themselves with municipal garbage dumps and school cafeterias. Or are these notables disguised as comrades? I no longer know." (Konopnicki, 1979: 53)

A party that participates in elections must forsake some alternative tactics: this is the frequently diagnosed tactical dilemma. As long as workers did not have full political rights, no choice between insurrectionary and parliamentary tactics was necessary. Indeed, political rights could be conquered by those who did not have them only through extra-parliamentary activities. César de Paepe, the founder of the *Parti Socialiste Brabançon*, wrote in 1877 that "in using our constitutional right and legal means at our disposal we do not renounce the right to revolution." (Landauer, 1959, 1: 457) This statement was echoed frequently, notably by Engels in 1895. Alex Danielsson, a Swedish left-wing socialist, maintained in a more pragmatic vein that Social Democrats should not commit themselves to "a dogma regarding tactics that would bind the party to act according to the same routine under all circumstances." (Tingsten, 1973: 362) That a mass strike should be used to achieve universal (and that meant male) suffrage was not questioned, and both the Belgian and Swedish parties led successful mass strikes that resulted in extensions of suffrage.

Yet as soon as universal suffrage was obtained, the choice between the "legal" and the "extra-parliamentary" tactics had to be made. J. McGurk, the chairman of the Labour Party, put it sharply in 1919:

We are either constitutionalists or we are not constitutionalists. If we are constitutional-ists, if we believe in the efficacy of the political weapon (and we do, or why do we have a Labour Party?) then it is both unwise and undemocratic because we fail to get a majority at the polls to turn around and demand that we should substitute industrial action. (Miliband, 1975: 69)

To win votes of people other than workers, particularly the petite bourgeoisie, to form alliances and coalitions, to administer the government in the interest of workers, a party cannot appear to be "irresponsible," to give any indication of being less than whole-hearted about its commitment to the rules and the limits of the parliamentary game. At times the party must even restrain its own followers from actions that would jeopardize electoral progress. Moreover, a party oriented toward partial improvements, a party in which leaders-representatives lead a petit-bourgeois life-style, a party that for years has shied away from the streets cannot "pour through the hole in the trenches," as Gramsci put it, even when this opening is forged by a crisis. "The trouble about the revolutionary left in stable industrial societies," observed Eric Hobsbawm (1973: 14–15), "is not that its opportunities never came, but that the normal conditions in which it must operate prevent it from developing the movements likely to seize the rare moments when they are called upon to behave as revolutionaries . . . Being a revolutionary in countries such as ours just happens to be difficult."

This dilemma became even more acute when democracy – representative democracy characteristic of bourgeois society – ceased to be merely a tactic and was embraced as the basic tenet of the future socialist society. Social democratic parties recognized in political democracy a value that transcends different forms of organization of production. Jean Jaures (1971: 71) claimed that "The triumph of socialism will not be a break with the French Revolution but the fulfillment of the French Revolution in new economic conditions." Eduard Bernstein (1961) saw in socialism simply "democracy brought to its logical conclusion." Representative democracy became for social democrats simultaneously the means and the goal, the vehicle for socialism and the political form of the future socialist society, simultaneously the strategy and the program, instrumental and prefigurative. (For the views of Kautsky and Luxemburg, who were somewhat more cautious, see respectively Salvadori, 1971, and Geras, 1976.)

Hence social democrats faced a dilemma, dramatized by Gay in his biography of Bernstein.

Is democratic socialism, then, impossible? Or can it be achieved only if the party is willing to abandon the democratic method temporarily to attain power by violence in the hope that it may return to parliamentarism as soon as control is secure? Surely this second alternative contains tragic possibilities: a democratic movement that resorts to authoritarian methods to gain its objective may not remain a democratic movement for long. Still, the first alternative − to cling to democratic procedures under all circumstances − may doom the party to continual political impotence. (1970: 7)

The Promise of Elections

In spite of all the ambivalence, in spite of the pressure of short-term preoccupations, socialists entered into bourgeois politics to win elections, to obtain an overwhelming mandate for revolutionary transformations, and to legislate the society into socialism. This was their aim and this was their expectation.

Electoral participation was based on the belief that democracy is not only necessary but that it is sufficient for reaching socialism. "If one thing is certain," Engels wrote in 1891 in a letter that was to meet with Lenin's acute displeasure, "it is that our Party and the working class can only come to power under the form of a democratic republic. This is even the specific form of the dictatorship of the proletariat." (1935: 486) Jaures saw in democracy "the largest and most solid terrain on which the working class can stand . . . the bed rock that the reactionary bourgeoisie cannot dissolve without opening fissures in the earth and throwing itself into them" (Derfler, 1973: 59) Millerand was, as always, most incisive: "To realize the immediate reforms capable of relieving the lot of the working class, and thus fitting it to win its own freedom, and to begin, as conditioned by the nature of things, the socialization of the means of production, it is necessary and sufficient for the socialist party to endeavor to capture the government through universal suffrage." (Ensor, 1908: 54)

Socialists entered into elections because they had to be concerned about immediate improvements of workers' conditions. Yet they entered in order to bring about socialism. Is this divergence between cause and purpose a symptom of rationalization? Was the pathos of final goals just a form of self-deception?

Such questions are best left for psychologists to resolve. But one thing is certain. Those who led socialist parties into electoral battles believed that dominant classes can be "beaten at their own game." Socialists were deeply persuaded that they would win elections, that they would obtain for socialism the support of an overwhelming numerical majority. They put all of their hopes and their efforts into electoral competition because they were certain that electoral victory was within reach. Their strength was in numbers, and elections are an expression of numerical strength. Hence, universal suffrage seemed to guarantee socialist victory, if not immediately then certainly within the near future. Revolution would be made at the ballot box. Among the many expressions of this conviction is the striking apologia delivered by Engels in 1895:

The German workers . . . showed the comrades in all countries how to make use of universal suffrage. . . . With the successful utilization of universal suffrage . . . an entirely new method of proletarian struggle came into operation, and this method quickly developed even further. It was found that state institutions, in which the rule of the bourgeoisie is organized, offer the working class still further opportunities to fight these very state institutions.

And Engels offered a forecast: "If it [electoral progress] continues in this fashion, by the end of the century we shall . . . grow into the decisive power in the land, before which all other powers will have to bow, whether they like it or not." (1960: 22)

The grounds for this conviction were both theoretical and practical. Already in *The Communist Manifesto*, Marx and Engels described socialism as the movement of "the immense majority." (1967: 147) In an 1850 article on "The Chartists" in the New York *Daily Tribune* and then again in 1867 in the Polish émigré newspaper *Glos Wolny*, Marx repeated that "universal suffrage is the equivalent of political power for the working class of England, where the proletariat forms the large majority of the population . . ." Kautsky's *The Class Struggle*, probably the most influential theoretical statement of the early socialist movement, maintained that the proletariat already constituted the largest class "in all civilized countries." (1971: 43) And even if the first electoral battles would not end in triumph, even if the proletariat was not yet the majority, electoral victory seemed only a matter of time because capitalism was swelling the ranks of the proletarians. The development of factory production and its corollary concentration of capital and land were to lead rapidly to proletarianization of craftsmen, artisans, merchants, and small agricultural proprietors. Even "the physician, the lawyer, the priest, the poet, the man of science" were being converted into proletarians, according to *The Communist Manifesto*. This growth of the number of people who sell their labor power for a wage was not accidental, temporary, or reversible: it was viewed as a necessary feature of capitalist development. Hence, it was just a question of time before almost everyone, "all but a handful of exploiters," would become proletarians. Socialism would be in the interest of almost everyone, and the overwhelming majority of the people would electorally express their will for socialism. A young Swedish theoretician formulated this syllogism as follows in 1919:

The struggle for the state is political. Its outcome is therefore to a very great extent contingent upon the possibility open to society's members — whose proletarianism has been brought about by the capitalist process — to exercise their proper influence on political decision-making. If democracy is achieved, the growth of capitalism means a corresponding mobilization of voices *against* the capitalist system itself. Democracy therefore contains an automatically operative device that heightens the opposition to capitalism in proportion to the development of capitalism. (Tingsten, 1973: 402)

Indeed, while those who eventually became communists saw in the Russian Revolution the proof that successful insurrection is always possible, for social democrats the necessity to rely on an insurrection of a minority meant only that conditions for socialism were not yet mature (Kautsky, 1919). While Branting, for example, shared Gramsci's first reaction to the October Revolution (see Fiori, 1973: 112) when he maintained that "the whole developmental idea of socialism is discarded in Bolshevism," he drew precisely the conclusion that socialists should wait until conditions ripen to the point that an overwhelming majority of the people would electorally express their will for socialist transformations (Tingsten, 1973: 405). Since they were thoroughly persuaded that such conditions would be brought about by the development of capitalism, social democrats were not chagrined by electoral reversals, which were interpreted only to mean that the point had not yet arrived. Even when they had to relinquish control over the government, social democrats were not tempted to hasten the course of history. History spoke through the people, people spoke in elections, and no one doubted that history would make people express their will for socialism.

These expectations, based on the conviction about the future course of history, were almost immediately vindicated by the electoral progress of socialist parties. The German party — posed by Engels as the model to be followed — despite years of depression grew from 125,000 votes in 1871 to 312,000 in 1881, to 1,427,000 in 1890, to 4,250,000 on the eve of World War I. Indeed, as soon as the Anti-Socialist laws were allowed to lapse, S.P.D. became in 1890 the largest party in Germany with 19.7 percent of the vote. By 1912 their share of 34.8 percent was more than twice that of the next largest party. No wonder that Bebel in 1905 could make "explicit the widely held assumption of his fellow socialists that the working class would continue to grow and that the party would one day embrace a majority of the population . . ." (Schorske, 1955: 43) Several parties entered even more spectacularly into the competition for votes. In 1907, Finnish Social Democrats won the plurality, 37 percent, in the first election under universal suffrage. The Austrian Social Democrats won 21.0 percent after male franchise was made universal in 1907, 25.4 in 1911, and the plurality of 40.8 percent in 1919. The Belgian *Parti Ouvrier* won 13.2 percent when the *régime censitaire* was abolished in 1894 and kept growing in jumps to win in 1925 the plurality of 39.4 percent, a success which "stimulated them to hope that continuing industrialization would produce an increasing socialist working-class electorate." (Mabille and Lorwin, 1977: 392) Even in those countries where the first steps were not equally dramatic, electoral progress seemed inexorable. In the religiously politicized Netherlands, socialism marched in big steps, from 3 percent in 1896 to 9.5, 11.2, 13.9, and 18.5 in 1913. The Danish party obtained 4.9 in 1884, the first election it contested, only 3.5 percent in 1889; from this moment on the party never failed to increase the share of the vote until 1935 when it won 46.1 percent. There again, "there was a general expectation that as the sole party representing the labour movement, it would achieve power through an absolute majority of the electorate." (Thomas, 1977: 240) The Swedish party began meekly, offering candidates on joint lists with Liberals; it won 3.5 percent in 1902, 9.5 in 1905, 14.6 in 1908, jumped to 28.5 percent in 1911 after suffrage was extended, increased its share to 30.1 and 36.4 in the two successive elections of 1914, and together with its left-wing off-shoot won the plurality of the vote, 39.1 percent, in 1917. The Norwegian Labor Party grew about 5 percent in each election from 1897 when it obtained 0.6 percent onward to 1915 when its share reached 32.1 percent.

Practice was confirming the theory. From election to election the forces of socialism were growing in strength. Each round was a new success. A few thousand at best during the first difficult moments, socialists saw their electorate extend to millions. The progress seemed inexorable; the majority and the mandate for socialism embodied therein were just a matter of a few years, a couple of elections. One more effort and humanity would be ushered into a new era by the overwhelming expression of popular will. "I am convinced," Bebel said at the Erfurt Congress, "that the fulfillment of our aims is so close that there are few in this hall who will not live to see the day." (Derfler, 1973: 58)

Social Democracy and the Working Class

The socialist party was to be the working class organized. As Bergounioux and Manin (1979: 27) observed, "workers' autonomy outside politics or a political emancipation that would not be specifically workers', such were the two tendencies at the moment when Marx and Engels contributed to the founding of the International Workingmen's Association." Marx's decisive influence was a synthesis of these two positions: socialism as a movement of the working class in politics. The orientation Marx advocated was new: to organize a "party" but one that would be distinctly of workers, independent from and opposed to all other classes. The organization of workers "into a class, and consequently into a political party" (Marx and Engels, 1967: 144) was necessary for workers to conquer political power and, in Marx's view, it should not and would not affect the autonomy of the working class as a political force. "The emancipation of the working class should be," in the celebrated phrase, "the task of the working class itself."

We know why Marx expected workers to become the moving force for socialism: by virtue of their position within the capitalist society, workers were simultaneously the class that was exploited in the specifically capitalist manner and the only class that had the capacity to organize production on its own once capitalist relations were abolished (Mandel, 1971: 23). Yet this emphasis on the "organic relation" between socialism and the working class − the relation conceived of as one between the historical mission and the historical agent − does not explain by itself why socialists sought during the initial period to organize only workers and all the workers. The reasons for this privileged relation between socialist parties and the working class were more immediate and more practical than those that could be found in Marx's theory of history.

First, capitalism is a system in which workers compete with each other unless they are organized as a class. Similarity of class position does not necessarily result in solidarity since the interests which workers share are precisely those which put them in competition with one another, primarily as they bid down wages in quest of employment. Class interest is something attached to workers as a collectivity rather than as a collection of individuals, their "group" rather than "serial" interest (Sartre, 1960). A general increase of wages is in the interest of all workers, but it does not affect relations among them. In turn, a law establishing a minimal level of wages, extending compulsory education, advancing the age of retirement, or limiting working hours affects the relation among workers without being necessarily in the interest of each of them. Indeed, some workers would prefer to work beyond their normal retirement age even if they were excluding other workers from work; some people who do not find employment would be willing to be hired for less than the minimal wage even if it lowered the general level of wages; some would be willing to replace striking workers even if it resulted in a defeat of a strike. Class interest does not necessarily correspond with the interests of each worker as an individual. Individual workers as well as those of a specific firm or sector have a powerful

incentive to pursue their particularistic interest at the cost of other workers unless some organization – a union, a party, or the state directly – has the means to
enforce collective discipline. Hence, in order to overcome competition, workers
must organize and act as a collective force. As Marx put it, "combination always
has a double aim, that of stopping competition among workers, so that they can
carry on general competition with the capitalist." (n.d.: 194) Socialist parties
were to be the organizations that would limit competition within the class as it
confronted class enemies. Mobilization of the entire class was essential precisely
to prevent particular groups of workers from eroding class solidarity by
competing with organized members of the class.

Secondly, the emphasis on the distinct interests of the working class was
necessary to prevent the integration of workers as individuals into bourgeois
society. Under capitalism, capitalists naturally appear to be the bearers of future
universal interests while the interests of all other groups appear as inimical to
future development and hence particularistic. Universalism is the natural
ideology of the bourgeoisie since, as long as people living in the same society
are thought to have some "general," "common," or "public" economic interests,
capitalists as a class represent these interests.

The new society which became institutionalized in Western Europe in the
aftermath of the industrial revolution was the embodiment of this universalism.
For the first time in history the economically dominant class portrayed itself as
the future of the entire society: this was the revolution which the bourgeoisie
introduced in the realm of ideology (Gramsci, 1971: 260). Bourgeois legal norms
established the universal status of "individuals" who were equal in their relations
to things – regardless whether these were means of production or of
consumption – and equal in their relation with each other – again regardless
whether they appeared contractually as sellers or buyers of labor power (Balibar,
1970). At the same time, bourgeois ideology postulated a basic harmony of
interests of individuals–citizens.

Bourgeois political institutions express this vision of society. The parliament
was to be the forum of rational deliberation in pursuit of the general good. While
economics was viewed as the realm of passion generated by narrow self-interest,
politics was to be the autonomous realm of reason. Parties, as well as other
divisions based on groupings of interests, were regarded as evil and dangerous.
Politics was to stand above economic divisions of society.

If the movement for socialism was not to be absorbed within this ideology
and these institutions, it was necessary to transform the very vision of politics.
To the abstract rationalism of "pure politics" socialists juxtaposed an image
reflecting the conflict of interests of a society divided into classes. In place of the
ideal of rational individuals seeking the common good, socialists put forth the

"reality" of men who were carriers of their class interests. The very conception of society based on harmony of interests was sharply denied by the ideology of class conflict.

Socialists claimed that the bourgeoisie not only has particularistic interests but also that these are in conflict with interests of workers. Workers are not "individuals" of the bourgeois society; they are a distinct class in a society divided into classes. If their interests appear as particularistic within the capitalist society, it is because this society is built upon the conflict of particularistic interests of different classes. Only by separating themselves from other classes could workers pursue their interests and thereby fulfill their historical mission of emancipating the entire society. In his *Address to the Communist League* in 1850 (Marx and Engels, 1969, I: 117), Marx emphasized that workers "must themselves do the utmost for their final victory by clarifying their minds as to what their class interests are, by taking their position as an independent party as soon as possible and by not allowing themselves to be seduced for a single moment by the hypocritical phrases of the democratic petty bourgeoisie into refraining from the independent organization of the party of the proletariat." Rosenberg (1965: 161) reports the tendency of German socialism in the 1860s to "isolate itself and to emphasize these qualities that differentiated it from all the groups and tendencies of the wealthy classes. At this stage the radical proletarian movement tended particularly to see the nobility and the peasants, the manufacturers and the intellectuals as 'a uniform reactionary mass.'" The same was true of the first labor candidates who competed in the Paris election of 1863 (Ibid.: 165). The notion of "one single reactionary mass" underlay the Gotha Programme of 1875 and reappeared in the Swedish program of 1889 (Tingsten, 1973: 357). Still in 1891, when Engels was asked to comment on a draft of the Erfurt Programme, he objected to a reference to "the people in general" by asking "who is that?" (n.d.: 56) And with his typical eloquence, Jules Guesde argued in Lille in 1890: "The Revolution which is incumbent upon you is possible only to the extent that you will remain yourselves, class against class, not knowing and not wanting to know the divisions that may exist in the capitalist world." (Fiechtier, 1965: 258)

Indeed, the initial difficulty which socialists faced was that workers were distrustful of any influences originating outside their class. Socialism seemed an abstract and an alien ideology in relation to daily experience. It was not apparent to workers that an improvement of their conditions required that the very system of wage labor must be abolished. Bergounioux and Manin report that according to a study of the French workers at the beginning of the Third Republic there was a resistance among workers to the socialist message, an emphasis on the direct conflict between workers and employers, and a neglect of politics (1979: 25). In Belgium, a party bearing a socialist label, *Parti Socialiste Belge*, was founded in 1879 but had difficulty persuading workers' associations to affiliate. According to Landauer (1959, I; 457–8) workers were mistrustful of socialist propaganda and de Paepe argued that "the word 'socialist' frightens many workers." Thus was born in 1885 *Parti Ouvrier Belge*: a workers' party in place of a socialist one. In Great Britain, trade-unionists objected to and until 1918 were successful in preventing the Labour Party from admitting members of other classes on individual bases. If socialists were to be successful, theirs had to be a workers' party. In Sweden, the first local cells of the Social Democratic Party were in fact called *Arbetarekommuner*, Workers' Communes (Fusilier, 1954: 29). Socialists were anxious to emphasize the class character of the movement and were willing to make doctrinal compromises to implant socialism among workers.

The Electoral Dilemma

The majority which socialists expected to win in elections was to be formed by workers. The proletariat – acting upon its interests and conscious of its mission – was to be the social force precipitating the society into socialism. But this proletariat was not and never became a numerical majority of voting members of any society. The prediction that the displaced members of the old middle classes would either become proletarians or join the army of the unemployed did not materialize.

The old middle classes, particularly the independent agricultural proprietors, almost vanished as a group in most Western European countries, but their sons and daughters were more likely to find employment in an office or a store than in a factory. Moreover, while the proportion of adult population engaged in any activity outside the household drastically fell in the course of capitalist development, those excluded from gainful activities did not become a reserve proletariat. Extended compulsory education, forced retirement, large standing armies, effective barriers to economic participation of women – all had the effect of reducing the entry into the proletariat. As the result, from 1890 to 1980 the proletariat continued to be a minority of the electorate. In Belgium, the first European country to have built substantial industry, the proportion of workers did break the magic number of the majority when it reached 50.1 percent in 1912. Since then it has declined systematically, down to 19.1 percent in 1971. In Denmark, the proportion of workers in the electorate never exceeded 29 percent. In Finland, it never surpassed 24 percent. In France, this proportion declined from 39.4 percent in 1893 to 24.8 in 1968. In Germany, workers increased as a proportion of the electorate from 25.5 percent in 1871 to 36.9 in 1903 and since then have constituted about one-third of the electorate. In Norway, workers constituted 33 percent of the electorate in 1894 and their proportion peaked in 1900 at 34.1 percent. In Sweden, the proportion of workers in the electorate grew from 28.9 percent in 1908 to 40.4 percent in 1952; then it declined to 38.5 in 1964.

The rules of the democratic game, while universal and at times fair, show no compassion. If a party is to govern alone, unburdened by the moderating influence of alliances and the debts of compromise, it must obtain some specific proportion of the vote, not much different from 50 percent. Electoral institutions preceded the birth of parties which seek to use them as the vehicle toward socialism, and those institutions carry within themselves the fundamental rule which makes the victory of an isolated minority impossible. A party representing a class which has fewer members than the other classes combined cannot win electoral battles.

The combination of minority status with majority rule constitutes the historical condition under which socialists have to act. This objective condition imposes upon socialist parties a choice: socialists must choose between a party homogeneous in its class appeal but sentenced to perpetual electoral defeats and a party that struggles for electoral success at the cost of diluting its class character. This choice is not between revolution and reform. There is no a-priori reason and no historical evidence to suppose that an electoral class-pure party of workers would be any more revolutionary than a party heterogeneous in its class base. Indeed, class-pure electoral parties of workers, of which the S.P.D. during the Weimar period is probably the prime example (Hunt, 1970), can be totally committed to the defense of particularistic interests of workers within the confines of capitalist society. Such class parties can easily become mere electoral interest groups, pressuring for a larger share of the national product without any concern for the manner in which it is produced. A pure party of workers who constituted a majority of the electorate would perhaps have maintained its ultimate commitment without a compromise, as socialists said they would when they saw the working class as majoritarian. But to continue as a minority party dedicated exclusively to ultimate goals in a game in which one needs a majority – more, an overwhelming mandate – to realize these goals would have been absurd. To gain electoral influence for whatever aims, from the ultimate to the most immediate, working-class parties must seek support from members of other classes.

Given the minority status of workers within the class structure of capitalist societies, the decision to participate in elections thus alters the very logic of the problem of revolutionary transformation. The democratic system played a perverse trick on socialist intentions: the emancipation of the working class could not be the task of workers themselves if this emancipation was to be realized through elections. The only question left was whether a majority for socialism could be recruited by seeking electoral support beyond the working class.

There is a peculiar tendency among contemporary observers to see the strategy of appealing to a heterogeneous class base as a relatively recent effect of the "deradicalization" of socialist movements. The German *Mittleklass Strategie* is seen as the prototype of this new orientation and Kurt Schumacher as its architect (Paterson, 1977). In this interpretation socialist parties begin to enlist support from groups other than workers only after they have given up their socialist goals.

This view is simply inaccurate. Socialist parties sought support beyond the working class as soon as the prospect of electoral victory became real and ever since they continued to go back and forth between a search for allies and the emphasis on the working class. That triumphant forecast made by Engels in 1895 which predicated that socialists would become a force before which "all powers will have to bow" was conditional in his view upon the success of the party in "conquering the greater part of the middle strata of society, petty bourgeoisie and small peasants." His advice to the French party – advice the French did not need since they were already doing it (Landauer, 1961) – was the same: recruit the small peasants. The Erfurt Programme of 1891 set the tone in which appeals to "the middle classes" were couched: their interests "paralleled" those of the proletariat; they were the "natural allies" of the proletariat (Kautsky, 1971). Guesdists in France began to advocate alliances as soon as Guesde was elected to the Parliament in 1893 (Derfler, 1973: 48). In Belgium, the first program adopted in 1894 by the *Parti Ouvrier* appealed to the lower-middle class and the intelligentsia (Landauer, 1959, I: 468). In Sweden, a multi-class strategy was debated as early as 1889, and the party kept moving toward a heterogeneous class orientation until its full acceptance in 1920 (Tingsten, 1973). The British Labour Party did defeat in 1912 a proposal to open the membership, on an individual basis, to "managers, foremen, [and] persons engaged in commercial pursuits on their own account." (McKibbin, 1974: 95) But in 1918, as it took a programmatic turn to the Left, Labour opened its ranks to "workers by brain." Indeed, in his polemic with Beer (1969), McKibbin interprets the very emphasis on socialism in the 1918 program as an attempt to capture the "professional middle classes." (1974: 97) Revisionists everywhere asserted that workers were not a majority and that the party must seek support beyond the working class. Bernstein, Jaures, and MacDonald came to this conclusion independently: once a party committed itself to electoral competition they had to embrace this conclusion. By 1915, Michels could already characterize social democratic strategy as follows:

For motives predominantly electoral, the party of the workers seeks support from the petty bourgeois elements of society, and this gives rise to more or less extensive reactions upon the party itself. The Labour Party becomes the party of the "people." Its appeals are no longer addressed to the manual workers, but to "all producers," to the "entire working population," these phrases being applied to all the classes and all the strata of society except the idlers who live upon the income from investments. (1962: 254)

The post-war orientation of several social democratic parties toward broadly understood middle strata is not a result of a new strategic posture but rather a reflection of the changing class structure of Western Europe. The proportion of the population engaged in agriculture declined during the twentieth century, more rapidly during the 1950s than during any of the preceding decades. The "new middle classes" almost replaced the "old" ones numerically. Party strategies reflected, albeit with some lag, the numerical evolution of class structure. What is relatively new, therefore, is only the explicit indication of salaried employees as the pool of potential socialist support. It was Bernstein after all who introduced the notion of the *Volkspartei*, not Schumacher or Brandt. The search for allies is inherent to electoralism.

Once they decided to compete for votes of "natural allies," whether these were the old or the new middle classes, socialists were appealing to the overwhelming majority of the population. Branting's estimate in 1889 that the "people" constituted 95 percent of the Swedish society was probably only slightly exaggerated, given his definition of "the people." (Tingsten, 1973: 135) Seeking an equitable distribution of the burden of World War I debt, *Labour and the New Social Order*, a programmatic document of the party, asserted that "In this manner the Labour Party claims the support of four fifths of the whole nation." (Henderson, 1918: 125) There is no reason to doubt that today the working class together with its allies comprise around 80 percent of the population of France (*Parti Communiste Français*, 1971) or of the United States (Wright, 1976). If to industrial workers we add white-collar employees, petits bourgeois, housewives, retirees, and students, almost no one is left to represent interests antagonistic to socialism. Exploiters remain but a handful: "the business man with a tax-free expense account, the speculator with tax-free capital gains and the retiring company director with a tax-free redundancy payment," in the words of the 1959 Labour Party electoral manifesto (Craig, 1969: 130).

Yet social democratic parties never obtained the votes of four-fifths of the electorate in any country. Only in a few instances have they won the support of the one-half of the people who actually went to the polls. They are far from obtaining the votes of all whom they claim to represent. Moreover, they cannot even win the votes of all workers – the proletariat in the classical sense of the word. In several countries as many as one-third of manual workers vote for bourgeois parties. In Belgium as many as one-half of the workers do not vote socialist (Hill, 1974: 83). In the United Kingdom, the Labour Party lost 49 percent of the working-class vote in the 1979 election. Social democrats appear condemned to minority status when they are a class party, and they seem equally relegated when they seek to be the party of the masses, of the entire nation. As a pure party of workers they cannot win the mandate for socialism, but as a party of the entire nation they have not won it either.

Some of the reasons why no political party ever won a majority with a program of socialist transformation are undoubtedly external to the electoral system. Yet social democratic parties face a purely electoral dilemma. Class shapes political behavior of individuals only as long as people who are workers are organized politically as workers. If political parties do not mobilize people qua workers but as "the masses," "the people," "consumers," "taxpayers," or simply "citizens," then workers are less likely to identify themselves as class members and, eventually, less likely to vote as workers. By broadening their appeal to the "masses," social democrats weaken the general salience of class as a determinant of political behavior of individuals.

The strategies oriented toward broad electoral support have an effect not only upon the relation between workers and other classes but primarily within the class, upon the relations among workers. In order to be successful in electoral competition, social democratic parties must present themselves to different groups as an instrument for the realization of their immediate economic interest, immediate in the sense that these interests can be realized when the party is victorious in the forthcoming election. Supra-class alliances must be based on a convergence of immediate economic interests of the working class and of other groups. Social democrats must offer credits to the petite bourgeoisie, pensions to salaried employees, minimal wages to workers, protection to consumers, education to the young, family allowances to families. This convergence cannot be found in measures that strengthen the cohesion and combativeness of workers against other classes. When social democrats extend their appeal, they must promise to struggle not for objectives specific to workers as a collectivity — those that constitute the public goods for workers as a class — but only those which workers share as individuals with members of other classes. The common grounds can be found in a shift of tax burden from indirect to direct taxation, in consumer protection laws, in spending on public transportation, and the like. These are concerns which workers as individuals share with others who receive low incomes, who purchase consumer products, who commute to work. They are not interests of workers as a class but of the poor, of consumers, commuters, etc.

None of this implies that the party no longer represents workers when it appeals to the masses. Although the convergence is never perfect and some interests of workers are often compromised, the party continues to represent those interests which workers as individuals share with other people. Hence social democratic parties oriented toward "the people" continue to be parties of workers as individuals. What they cease to be is the organization of workers as a class which disciplines individuals in their competition with each other by posing them against other classes. It is the very principle of class conflict – the conflict between internally cohesive collectivities – that becomes compromised as parties of workers become parties of the masses.

Differentiation of the class appeal, however, affects not only the organization of workers as a class. It has a fundamental effect on the form of political conflicts in capitalist societies since it reinstates a classless vision of politics. When social democratic parties become parties "of the entire nation," they reinforce the vision of politics as a process of defining the collective welfare of "all members of the society." Politics once again is defined on the dimension individual–nation, not in terms of class.

This de-emphasis of class conflict in turn affects workers. As class identification becomes less salient, socialist parties lose their unique appeal to workers. Social democratic parties are no longer qualitatively different from other parties; class loyalty is no longer the strongest base of self-identification. Workers see society as composed of individuals; they view themselves as members of collectivities other than class; they behave politically on the basis of religious, ethnic, regional, or some other affinity. They become Catholics, Southerners, Francophones, or simply "citizens."

It is now clear that the dilemma comes back with a vengeance within the very system of electoral competition. The choice between class purity and broad support must be lived continually by social democratic parties because when they attempt to increase their electoral support beyond the working class these parties reduce their capacity to mobilize workers. This choice was not made once and for all by any party; nor does it represent a unidirectional evolution. Indeed, if there exists an electoral trade-off between appealing to the masses and recruiting workers, then strategic shifts are imperative from the purely electoral point of view. Histories of particular parties are replete with strategic reversals, with major changes of direction, controversies, schisms, and scissions. S.P.D. returned to an emphasis on class in 1905; Swedish Social Democrats temporarily abandoned their attempt to become a multi-class party once in 1926 and then again in 1953; the Norwegian Labor Party emphasized its class orientation in 1918; German young socialists launched a serious attack on the *Mittleklass Strategie* a decade ago; conflicts between an *ouvrierist* and a multi-class tendency today wrench several parties. In terms of purely electoral considerations social democrats face a dilemma. They are forced to go back and forth between an emphasis on class and an appeal to the nation. They seem unable to win either way, and they behave the way rational people do when confronted with dilemmas: they bemoan and regret, change their strategies, and once again bemoan and regret.

Social democrats have not succeeded in turning elections into an instrument of socialist transformation. To be effective in elections they have to seek allies who would join workers under the socialist banner, yet at the same time they erode exactly that ideology which is the source of their strength among workers. They cannot remain a party of workers alone and yet they can never cease to be a workers' party.

Reform and Revolution

Socialists entered into elections with ultimate goals. The Hague Congress of the First International proclaimed that the "organization of the proletariat into a political party is necessary to insure the victory of social revolution and its ultimate goal – the abolishment of classes." (Chodak, 1962: 39) The first Swedish program specified that "Social Democracy differs from other parties in that it aspires to completely transform the economic organization of bourgeois society and bring about the social liberation of the working class. . . ." (Tingsten, 1973: 118–19) Even the most reformist among revisionists, Millerand, admonished that "whoever does not admit the necessary and progressive replacement of capitalist property by social property is not a socialist." (Ensor, 1908: 51)

These were the goals that were to be reached through legislation, upon a mandate of an electorally expressed majority, as the will of universal suffrage. Socialists were going to abolish exploitation, to destroy the division of society into classes, to remove all economic and political inequalities, to finish the wastefulness and anarchy of capitalist production, to eradicate all sources of injustice and prejudice. They were going to emancipate not only workers but humanity, to build a society based on cooperation, to rationally orient energies and resources toward satisfaction of human needs, to create social conditions for an unlimited development of personality. Rationality, justice, and freedom were the guiding goals of the social democratic movement.

These were ultimate goals: they could not be realized immediately, for economic as well as political reasons. And social democrats were unwilling to wait for the day when these aims could finally be accomplished. They claimed to represent interests of workers and of other groups not only in the future but as well within "present-day," that is capitalist, society. The *Parti Socialiste Français*, led by Jaures, proclaimed at its Tours Congress of 1902 that "The Socialist Party, rejecting the policy of all or nothing, has a program of reforms whose realization it pursues forthwith," and listed fifty-four specific demands concerning democraticization, secularization, organization of justice, family, education, taxation, protection of labor, social insurance, nationalization of industries, and foreign policy (Ensor, 1908: 345ff.). The first program of the Swedish Social Democrats in 1897 demanded direct taxation, development of state and municipal productive activities, public credit including direct state control of credit for farmers, legislation concerning work conditions, old age, sickness, and accident insurance, legal equality, and freedoms of organization, assembly, speech, and press (Tingsten, 1973: 119–20).

This orientation toward immediate improvements was never seen by its architects as a departure from ultimate goals. Since socialism was thought to be inevitable, there would be no reason why immediate measures should not be advocated by socialist parties: there was no danger, not even a possibility, that such measures could prevent the advent of the inescapable. As Kautsky put it, "it would be a profound error to imagine that such reforms could delay the social revolution." (1971: 93) Ultimate goals were going to be realized because history was on the side of socialism. Revisionists within the movement were, if anything, even more deterministic than those who advocated insurrectionary tactics. Millerand argued, for example, in the Saint-Mandé speech that "Men do not and will not set up collectivism; it is setting itself up daily; it is, if I may be allowed so to phrase it, being secreted by the capitalist regime." (Ensor, 1908: 50)

Even when social democratic movements left the protection of history to rediscover justification of socialism in ethical values, no dilemma appeared in the consciousness of socialist leaders. Bernstein's famous renunciation of final goals did not imply that they would remain unfulfilled, but only that the way to realize them was to concentrate on proximate aims. Jaures, speaking about the conquest of political power by workers, provided the classical image: "I do not believe, either, that there will necessarily be an abrupt leap, the crossing of the abyss; perhaps we shall be aware of having entered the zone of the Socialistic State as navigators are aware of having crossed the line of a hemisphere – not that they have been able to see as they crossed a cord stretched over the ocean warning them of their passage, but that little by little they have been led into a new hemisphere by the progress of their ship." (Ensor, 1908: 171) Indeed, for social democrats immediate reforms constitute "steps" in the sense that gradually they accumulate toward a complete restructuring of society. Anticipating Bernstein's argumentation, Georg von Vollmar, the leader of the Bavarian wing of the S.P.D., declared at the Erfurt Congress: "Beside the general or ultimate goal we see a nearer aim: the advancement of the most immediate needs of the people. For me, the achievement of the most immediate demands is the main thing, not only because they are of great propagandist value and serve to enlist the masses, but also because, in my opinion, this gradual progress, this gradual socialization, is the method strongly indicated for a progressive transition." (Gay , 1970: 258)

Reform and revolution do not require a choice within the social democratic view of the world. To bring about "social revolution" – the phrase which before 1917 connoted transformation of social relations but not necessarily an insurrection – it is sufficient to follow the path of reforms. Reforms are thought to be cumulative and irreversible: there was nothing strange in Jaures' argument that "Precisely because it is a party of revolution . . . the Socialist Party is the most actively reformist. . . ." (Fiechtier, 1965: 163) The more reforms, the faster they are introduced, the nearer the social revolution, the sooner the socialist ship would sail into the new world. And even when times are not auspicious for new steps to be made, even when political or economic circumstances require that reforms be postponed, eventually each new reform would build upon past accomplishments. Mitigating the effects of capitalism and transforming it piece by piece would eventually lead to a complete restructuring of society. Reviewing Miliband's (1969) book, Benjamin Barber best expressed this perspective: "surely at some point mitigation becomes transformation, attenuation becomes abolition; at some point capitalism's 'concessions' annihilate capitalism. . . . This is not to say that such a point has been reached, only that there must be such a point." (1970: 929)

Economic Projects and Political Realities

The "social revolution" envisioned by social democrats was necessary because capitalism was irrational and unjust. And the fundamental cause of this inefficiency and inequity was private property of the means of production. While private property was occasionally seen as the source of most disparate evils – from prostitution and alcoholism to wars – it was always held directly responsible for the irrationality of the capitalist system and for the injustice and poverty that it generated.

Already in *"Socialism: Utopian and Scientific"*, one of the most important theoretical sources of the socialist movement, Engels emphasized that the increasing rationality of capitalist production within each firm is accompanied, and must be accompanied, by the chaos and anarchy of production at the societal scale. "The contradiction between socialized production and capitalist appropriation," Engels wrote, "now presents itself as *an antagonism* between the organization of production in the individual workshop and the anarchy of production in society generally." (1959: 97–8) Speaking in 1920, Branting repeated that "In the basic premises of the present social order there are no satisfactory guarantees either that production as an entity is given the most rational orientation possible, or that profit in the various branches is used in the way that is best from the national economic and social point of view." (Tingsten, 1973: 239)

The second effect of private property is the unjust distribution of material rewards which it generates. "The economic case for socialism," wrote a Labour Party theoretician, "is largely based on the inability of capitalism to bring about any equitable or even practicable distribution of commodities in an age of mechanisation and mass-production." (Cripps, 1933: 475) Even the most decisive break with the marxist tradition, the Bad Godesberg program of 1959, maintained that the "Market economy does not assure of itself a just distribution of income and property."

Given this analysis, socialization or nationalization of the means of production was the principal method for realizing socialist goals and hence the first task to be accomplished by social democrats after the conquest of power. "Social revolution," writes Tingsten (1973: 131), "was always understood to mean systematic, deliberate socialization under the leadership of the Social Democratic working class." Socialization or nationalization — a terminological ambiguity which was significant — was the manner by which socialist revolution would be realized.

Until World War I, as socialist parties concentrated their efforts on winning suffrage and organizing workers as a class, little if any concrete thought was devoted to the means by which socialization was to be accomplished. The very possibility of actually being in a position to pursue a program of socialization caught all socialist parties by surprise when the war destroyed the established order, unleashed spontaneous movements of factory occupations, and opened the doors to governmental participation. Indeed, the wave of factory occupations which occurred in Austria, Germany Finland, Italy, and Sweden appeared to the established socialist parties and trade-unions almost as much a threat to their own authority and organization as to the capitalist order (Maier, 1975: 63; Spriano, 1967: 50–63; Williams, 1975: 121–45: Wigforss, 1924: 672).

As these spontaneous movements were repressed or exhausted, the logic of parliamentarism re-established its grip on the social democratic movement. Nationalization efforts turned out to be so similar in several countries that their story can be summarized briefly. The issue of socialization was immediately placed on the agenda of social democratic parties in Austria, Finland, Germany, Great Britain, Holland, Italy, and Sweden and of the C.G.T. in France. In several countries, notably Germany, Great Britain, and Sweden, "socialization committees" were established by respective parliaments, while in France Léon Blum introduced in the Chamber a bill to nationalize the railway industry. The commissions were supposed to prepare detailed programs of socialization – in some cases for all basic industries and in others for specific ones, typically coal. The British commission finished its career quickly as Lloyd George simply ignored its recommendations; in Germany the issue of coal nationalization lingered after the resignation of the first commission; and in Sweden the socialization committee worked sixteen years, spending most of its time studying similar efforts elsewhere, and expired without making any recommendations. Although social democrats formed or entered governments in several countries, the global result of these first attempts at socialization was null: with the exception of the French armament industry in 1936, not a single company was nationalized in Western Europe by a social democratic government during the entire inter-war period.

How did it happen that the movement that set itself to revolutionize society by changing the very base of its productive organization ended the period of integration into the political institutions of capitalism without even touching its fundaments? When Marx described in 1850 the anatomy of capitalist democracy, he was certain that, unless withdrawn, universal suffrage would lead from "political to social emancipation"; that, once endowed with political rights, workers would proceed immediately to destroy the "social power" of capitalists by socializing the means of production (1952a: 62). Still in 1928, Wigforss saw this outcome as inevitable: "The universal suffrage is incompatible with a society divided into a small class of owners and a large class of unpropertied. Either the rich and the propertied will take away universal suffrage, or the poor, with the help of their right to vote, will procure for themselves a part of the accumulated riches." (Tingsten, 1973: 274–5) And yet while social democrats held power in Austria, Belgium, Denmark, Finland, France, Germany, Great Britain, Norway, and Sweden, the riches remained nearly intact, and certainly private property of the means of production was not disturbed.

One can cite a number of reasons. Not negligible was the theoretical ambiguity of the very project of the "expropriation of expropriators." One difficulty lay in that ambiguous relation between "socialization" – the turning over of industries to their employees – and "nationalization" – their general direction by the state. On the one hand, as Korsch (1975: 68), Wigforss (Tingsten, 1973: 208), and others pointed out, direct control of particular firms by the immediate producers would not remove the antagonism between producers and consumers, that is, workers in other firms. On the other hand, transfer to centralized control of the state would have the effect of replacing the private authority of capital by the bureaucratic authority of the government, and the Soviet example loomed large as a negative one. The *gestionnaire* tendency dominated in Germany, where the principle was even incorporated into the constitution, and Sweden; the *planiste* tendency found its most important articulation in Belgium and France under the influence of Henri de Man. A veritable wave of constitution-writing ensued immediately in the aftermath of World War I: Otto Bauer in Austria (1919), Karl Kautsky in Germany (1925), G. D. H. Cole in Great Britain (1919), Henri de Man in Belgium – all rushed to devise some ways of combining rationality at the level of the society as a whole with the control of the immediate producers over their own activities.

Yet this burst of theoretical activity came rather belatedly in relation to the demands of practical politics. The fact, frequently admitted by social democratic politicians, was that they did not know how to proceed to the realization of their program. The choice of industries which were to be nationalized, methods of financing, techniques of management, and the mutual relations among sectors turned out to be technical problems for which social democrats were unprepared. Hence they formed study commissions and waited.

Nevertheless, the cause of the social democratic inertia was much more profound than the ambiguity of their plans. Socialists nowhere won a sufficient number of votes to obtain a parliamentary majority and hence to be able to legislate anything without support or at least consent of other parties. Remarkably, and quite to their surprise, socialist parties in several countries were invited to take office as minority governments or to enter governments as members of multi-party coalitions. And the question of what to do as a minority government presented itself as the following choice: either the party would pursue its socialist objectives and be promptly defeated or it would behave like any other party, administering the system and introducing only those few reforms for which it could obtain a parliamentary majority.

Each strategy was viewed in terms of its long-term effects. Proponents of the maximalist strategy argued that the party would educate the electorate about its socialist program and would expose the reactionary character of the bourgeois parties. They claimed that the people would then return the party to office with a majority and the mandate to pursue its socialist program. Only in Norway was this strategy adopted; the government lasted three days in 1928; and the party was returned to office four years later only after it had moderated its socialist objectives.

Proponents of a minimal program argued that the most important task a party could accomplish was to demonstrate that it is "fit to govern," that it is a governmental party. "We are not going to undertake office to prepare for a General Election," said MacDonald in 1924, "we are going to take office in order to work." (Miliband, 1975: 101) Their expectation, in turn, rested on the belief that reforms were irreversible and cumulative. As Lyman put it,

Gradualists imagined that socialism could be achieved by instalments, each instalment being accepted with no more serious obstruction on the part of the Conservatives than Labour opposition generally gave to Tory governments. Each instalment would then remain, unharmed by interludes of Tory rule, and ready to serve as the foundation on which the next Labour government would resume construction of the socialist commonwealth. (1965: 142–3)

Hence the party would come into office, introduce those reforms and only those reforms for which it could muster the support of a parliamentary majority, and then leave to return when a new mandate issued from the electorate. "We hope to continue only as long in office, but certainly as long in office as will enable us to do some good work that will remove many obstacles which would have hampered future governments if they found the problems that we know how to face": this was the intention of the Labour Party in 1924 (MacDonald cited by Lyman, 1957: 106; for a similar statement by Branting in 1920 see Tingsten, 1973: 238). Hence Blum introduced a distinction between the "exercise of power" and the "conquest of power": as a minority socialists could only exercise it, but they should exercise it in such a way that would eventually lead to its conquest (Colton, 1953).

The Compromise

If socialists could not pursue an immediate program of nationalization, what could they do in the meantime? They could and did pursue ad-hoc measures designed to improve the conditions of workers: develop housing programs, introduce minimal wage laws, institute some protection from unemployment, income and inheritance taxes, old age pensions. Such measures, although they favored workers, were neither politically unfeasible nor economically shocking – they continued the tradition of reforms of Bismarck, Disraeli, and Giolitti. These measures modified neither the structure of the economy nor the political balance of forces.

The fact is that until the 1930s social democrats did not have any kind of an economic policy of their own. The economic theory of the Left was the theory that criticized capitalism, claimed the superiority of socialism, and led to a program of nationalization of the means of production. Once this program was suspended – it was not yet abandoned – no socialist economic policy was left (Bergounioux and Manin, 1979: 110). Socialists behaved like all other parties: with some distributional bias toward their constituency but full of respect for the golden principles of the balanced budget, deflationary anti-crisis policies, gold standard, and so on. Skidelsky's characterization of the Labour Party is of general validity: "The English political culture was relatively homogeneous. There were certain leading ideas, or patterns of thought, which all sensible men accepted. This applied particularly to economic thinking. Politicians in the 1920s deployed a stock of economic wisdom which was a kind of codification of what they assumed to be the successful practice of the 19th century. . . ." (1970: 6) Of Blum it is said that he "could envisage no intermediate stage between pure doctrinaire socialism and the free play of capitalism . . ." (Wall, 1970: 541), and it seems that neither could anyone else. The only known theory of reforms was that which called for nationalization; no other coherent alternative existed.

Such an alternative did emerge in response to the Great Depression. In Sweden, Norway, and to a lesser extent France, socialist governments responded to unemployment with a series of anti-cyclical policies that broke the existing economic orthodoxy. It remains a matter of controversy whether the Swedish policies were developed autonomously, from Marx via Wicksell, or were an application of the already circulating ideas of Keynes (Gustafsson, 1973). The fact is that social democrats everywhere soon discovered in Keynes' ideas, particularly after the appearance of his *General Theory*, something they urgently needed: a distinct policy for administering capitalist economies. The Keynesian revolution — and this is what it was — provided social democrats with a goal and hence the justification of their governmental role, and simultaneously transformed the ideological significance of distributive policies that favored the working class.

From the passive victim of economic cycles, the state became transformed almost overnight into an institution by which society could regulate crises to maintain full employment. Describing the policies of the Swedish government of 1932, Gustav Möller, the architect of the unemployment program, emphasized that previously unemployment relief was a "system meant only to supply bare necessities to the unemployed, and did not have the purpose of counteracting the depression . . . Economic cycles, it was said, follow natural economic laws, and governmental interference with them is, by and large, purposeless and, from a financial point of view, even dangerous in the long run." (1938: 49) Both Möller and Wigforss (1938) described how the Swedish Social Democrats discovered that unemployment can be reduced and the entire economy invigorated if the state follows anti-cyclical policies, allowing deficits to finance productive public works during depressions and paying back the debts during periods of expansion. Society is not helpless against the whims of the capitalist market, the economy can be controlled, and the welfare of citizens can be continually enhanced by the active role of the state: this was the new discovery of social democrats.

And this was not yet all: Keynesianism was not only a theory that justified socialist participation in government but, even more fortuitously from the social democratic point of view, it was a theory that suddenly granted a universalistic status to the interests of workers. Earlier, all demands for increased consumption were viewed as inimical to the national interest: higher wages meant lower profits and hence a reduced opportunity for investment and future development. The only conceivable response to crisis was to cut costs of production, that is, wages. This was still the view of the Labour Party in 1929. But in the logic of Keynes' theory higher wages, particularly if the wage fund was increased by raising employment rather than the wage rate (which did not rise in Sweden until 1936), meant an increase of aggregate demand, which implied increased expectations of profit, increased investment, and hence economic stimulation. Although it is again unclear whether this policy was indeed influenced by Keynes' writings (Colton, 1969: 198), the French *Front Populaire* introduced in 1936 a policy whereby "Through wage increases, a shorter work week, a public works program, and travel and vacation expenditures . . . purchasing power and consumer demand would be raised, industry would increase production to meet the rising demand . . . and the depression would be overcome." (Colton, 1969: 190) The significance of increasing wages changed from being viewed as an impediment to national economic development to its stimulus. Short-term particularistic interests of workers and of other people who consumed most of their income could now be held to coincide with the long-term interest of society as a whole. Corporatist defense of the interests of workers, a policy social democrats pursued during the twenties, and the electoral strategy toward the "people" now found ideological justification in a technical economic theory. The very terms of ideological discourse became transformed; "the costs of the health service," wrote Bertil Ohlin in 1938 (1938: 5), "represented an *investment* in the most valuable productive instrument of all, the people itself. In recent years it has become obvious that the same holds true of many other forms of 'consumption' — food, clothing, housing, recreation. Hence, the emphasis is put on 'productive' social policy. . . ." But this revolution implied another: "The tendency," Ohlin continued, "is in the direction of a 'nationalization of consumption,' as opposed to the nationalization of the 'means of production' of Marxian socialism."

The Keynesian turn soon led social democrats to develop a full-fledged ideology of the "welfare state." (Briggs, 1961) Social democrats defined their role as that of modifying the play of the market forces, in effect abandoning the project of nationalization altogether. The successful application of Keynesian instruments was seen as the demonstration that nationalization — full of problems and uncertainties that it proved to be — was not only impossible to achieve in a parliamentary way but was simply unnecessary. Keynes himself wrote that "It is not the ownership of the instruments of production which it is important for the state to assume. If the state is able to determine the aggregate amount of resources devoted to augmenting the instruments and the basic rate of reward to those who own them, it will have accomplished all that is necessary." (1964: 378) As Wigforss argued further (Lewin, 1975: 286), state ownership of particular industries would only result in the socialist government being forced to behave as a capitalist firm, subject to "the chaos of the market," while by indirect control the state could rationalize the economy as a whole and orient it toward the general welfare.

The theoretical underpinning of this new perspective was the distinction between the concept of property as the authority to manage and property as legal possession. Already Bernstein claimed that "the basic issue of socialization is that we place production, economic life, under the control of the public weal." (Cited by Korsch, 1975: 65) Instead of direct ownership, the state could achieve all the socialist goals by influencing private industry to behave in the general interest. "The essence of nationalization," wrote de Man in 1934 (Bergounioux and Manin, 1979: 114), "is less the transfer of property than the transfer of authority. . . ." If the state could regulate private industry when necessary and if it could mitigate the effects of the free play of market forces, then direct ownership would be unnecessary and inadvisable: this became the motto of social democracy in the aftermath of the Keynesian revolution.

In sum, unable as minority governments to pursue the socialist program, in the mid-thirties, social democracy found a distinct economic policy which justified its governmental role, which specified a number of intermediate reforms that could be successively accomplished within the confines of capitalism, and which provided in several countries a successful electoral platform. Caught in the twenties in an all-or-nothing position, social democrats discovered a new path to reform by abandoning the project of nationalization for that of general welfare. The new project did involve a fundamental compromise with those who were still being denounced as exploiters, but it was economically workable, socially beneficial, and, perhaps most importantly, politically feasible under democratic conditions.

The Abandonment of Reformism

The abandonment of programmatic nationalization of the means of production did not imply that the state would never become engaged in economic activities. In contemporary Western European countries between 5 and 20 percent of gross product is now being produced by enterprises of which the state is in some form a complete owner (*Le Monde*, 1977). The paths by which this "public sector" developed are too varied to recount here. In Italy and Spain the public sector constitutes mainly a fascist legacy; in Austria it consists predominantly of confiscated German properties; in Great Britain and France a wave of nationalizations followed World War II. Outright nationalizations – the transfer of existing private companies into state property – have been very rare, but in several countries the state has developed economic activities of its own. In most countries the public firms have the same legal status and operate with the same rationality as private companies; the state is simply a stockholder. In Italy, Great Britain, and France state firms have been used occasionally as instruments of economic policy. Yet in spite of these variations, the general philosophy of public ownership is widely shared: social democrats are committed to the free market whenever possible, public ownership when necessary.

Characteristically, state enterprises are limited to credit institutions, coal, iron and steel, energy production and distribution, transport, and communication. Outside these sectors only those companies which are threatened with bankruptcy and hence a reduction of employment pass into public hands. Instances in which the state would be engaged in producing and selling final-demand goods are extremely rare; they seem to be limited to the automobile industry. The state engages in those economic activities which are necessary for the economy as a whole and sells its products and services mainly to private firms. These private firms then sell to consumers. Hence, the state does not compete with private capital but rather provides the inputs necessary for the profitable functioning of the economy as a whole.

This division between the state and the market has been enshrined in the "public goods theory of the state." (Samuelson, 1966; Musgrave, 1971) This theory assumes that the capitalist market is a natural form of economic activity; the existence of the market and its laws are taken as given. The role of the state is supposed to be limited to the provision of so-called "public goods": those that are indivisible and which can be supplied to everyone if they are supplied to anyone. It is proper for the state to construct public roads or to train the labor force: rational private entrepreneurs will not provide such goods since they cannot prevent people from using roads or from selling their newly acquired skills to competitors. The role of the state is thus supposed to be limited to those activities that are unprofitable for private entrepreneurs yet needed for the economy as a whole. True, the state in several countries is also engaged in the production of goods that are private – such as coal and steel – but here again the transfer into the public sector occurred with few exceptions when and because these industries were unprofitable under the conditions of international competition. Indeed, these were the industries that could be most easily nationalized and maintained in the public sector since their owners had no reason to fight against nationalization of unprofitable industries.

Hence, the structure of capitalist systems built by social democrats turned out to be the following: (1) the state operates those activities which are unprofitable for private firms but necessary for the economy as a whole; (2) the state regulates, particularly by pursuing anti-cyclical policies, the operation of the private sector; and (3) the state mitigates, through welfare measures, the distributional effects of the operation of the market.

The regulatory activities of the state are based on the belief that private capitalists can be induced to allocate resources in a manner desired by citizens and expressed at the polls. The basic notion is that in a capitalistic democracy resources are allocated by two mechanisms: the "market," in which the weight of preferences of decision-makers is proportional to the resources they control, and the state, in which the weight of preferences is distributed equally to persons qua citizens. The essence of contemporary social democracy is the conviction that the market can be directed to those allocations of any good, public or private, that are preferred by citizens and that by gradually rationalizing the economy the state can turn capitalists into private functionaries of the public without altering the judicial status of private property.

The intervention of the state in the economy is to be guided by criteria of efficiency, which are sharply distinguished from a concern for justice. The notion of efficiency is independent of any distributional considerations. An efficient allocation of resources – in the light of the criterion shared across political lines and viewed as technical – is that in which no one can be better off without someone else being worse off. Under such an allocation some people can be much better off than others but the problem of distribution is, in this view, better managed when it is treated ex post. Hence the social policy of social democrats consists largely of mitigating the distributional effects of allocations of resources guided by criteria of efficiency. This policy is not designed to transform the economic system but only to correct the effects of its operation.

Having made the commitment to maintain private property of the means of production, to assure efficiency, and to mitigate distributional effects, social democracy ceased to be a reformist movement. (See particularly Brandt's views in Brandt, Kreisky, and Palme, 1976.) Reformism always meant a gradual progression toward structural transformations; reformism was traditionally justified by the belief that reforms are cumulative, that they constitute steps, that they lead in some direction. The current policy of social democrats by its very logic no longer permits the cumulation of reforms.

The abandonment of reformism is a direct consequence of those reforms that have been accomplished. Since the state is engaged almost exclusively in those activities which are unprofitable from the private point of view, it is deprived of financial resources needed to continue the process of nationalization. If the publicly owned industries had been those that are most profitable, then the profit could be used to purchase or develop other industries. But having gotten involved in deficitary sectors, social democrats undermined their very capacity to gradually extend the public realm. Moreover, the ideological effects cannot be neglected: the situation was created in which the public sector is notoriously inefficient by private capitalist criteria and the result has been a backlash against the growth of the state. That is, the firms that landed in the public sector were mostly those that were inefficient by capitalist criteria and now it seems that they are inefficient precisely because they are public. Hence the main preoccupation of all governments, socialist or not, becomes cost-cutting, which in turn means that the publicly owned industries cannot even be utilized as instruments of macro-economic policy, for example, by holding down prices of steel to reduce inflationary pressures.

At the same time, having strengthened the market, social democrats perpetuate the need to mitigate the distributional effect of its operation. Welfare reforms do not even have to be "undone" by bourgeois governments. It is sufficient that the operation of the market is left to itself for any length of time and inequalities increase, unemployment fluctuates, shifts of demand for labor leave new groups exposed to impoverishment, etc. As Martin put it with regard to Great Britain, "The 'basic structure of the full employment welfare state' did not prove as durable as Crosland's analysis would lead us to expect. However, this was not because Conservative governments between 1951 and 1964 proceeded to dismantle it. . . . All that was necessary to undermine the full employment welfare state was for the Conservative Governments simply to do nothing to counteract these processes." (1975: 28) Mitigation does not become transformation: indeed, without transformation the need to mitigate becomes eternal. Social democrats find themselves in the situation which Marx attributed to Louis Bonaparte: their policies seem contradictory since they are forced at the same time to strengthen the productive power of capital and to counteract its effects.

The final result of this orientation is that social democrats again find themselves without a distinct alternative of their own as they face a crisis of the international system. When in office they are forced to behave like any other party, relying on deflationary, cost-cutting measures to ensure private profitability and the capacity to invest. Measures oriented to increase democracy at the work-place – the recent rediscovery of social democrats (Brandt, Kreisky, and Palme, 1976) – not surprisingly echo the posture of the movement in the 1920s, another period when the Left lacked any macro-economic approach of its own. These measures will not resolve pressing economic problems. It remains to be seen what will happen if the current international crisis seriously undermines the electoral basis of social democratic support.

Economic Bases of Class Compromise

As soon as social democrats formed governments after World War I, they discovered that their concern with justice was not immediately compatible with the goal of increased productivity. In Wigforss' words, "Because Social Democracy works for a more equal and more just distribution of property and incomes, it must never forget that one must produce before one has something to distribute." (Tilton, 1979: 516) The concern for restoring and extending industrial productive capacity quickly came to dominate the first discussions of socialization of industry in Germany and Sweden (Maier, 1975: 194; Tingsten, 1973: 230). Certainly a just distribution of poverty was not the socialist promise, and to enhance general affluence social democrats had to focus their efforts on increasing productivity.

But without nationalization of the means of production, increases of productivity require profitability of private enterprise. As long as the process of accumulation is private, the entire society is dependent upon maintaining private profits and upon the actions of capitalists allocating these profits. Hence the efficacy of social democrats — as of any other party — in regulating the economy and mitigating the social effects depends upon the profitability of the private sector and the willingness of capitalists to cooperate. The very capacity of social democrats to regulate the economy depends upon the profits of capital. This is the structural barrier which cannot be broken: the limit of any policy is that investment and thus profits must be protected in the long run. Since profits are private, the decisions of individual capitalists concerning the volume and direction of investment condition the effectiveness of interventions by the state and must be anticipated. The state which intervenes in the economy depends upon actions of capitalists for its fiscal resources, for information, for the capacity to elaborate policies and to plan, for its capacity to provide social services, and so on. Moreover, the very electoral support for any particular government depends upon actions of capitalists. People do not vote exclusively for "public goods" when they vote for a party: they vote against the incumbent government when their personal income falls or unemployment increases (Kramer, 1971; Stigler, 1973). Hence any party is dependent upon private capital even for its electoral survival in office.

Any government in a capitalist society is dependent upon capital (Offe and Runge, 1975: 140). The nature of political forces which come to office does not affect this dependence, for it is structural: a characteristic of the system and not of occupants of governmental positions, the winners of elections. Being "in power" gives little power: social democrats are subject to the same structural dependence as any other party.

The basic compromise of social democrats with private capital is thus an expression of the very structure of capitalist society. Once private property of the means of production was left intact, it became in the interest of wage-earners that capitalists appropriate profits. Under capitalism the profits of today are the condition of investment and hence production, employment, and consumption in the future. As Chancellor Schmidt put it, "The profits of enterprises today are the investments of tomorrow, and the investments of tomorrow are the employment of the day after." (*Le Monde*, July 6, 1976) This expectation – that current profits would be transformed into future improvements of material conditions of wage-earners – became the foundation of the social democratic consent to capitalism. Social democrats consent to the right of capitalists to withhold a part of societal product because the profits appropriated by capital are expected to be saved, invested, transformed into productive capacity, and partly distributed as gains to other groups. Hence this consent rests on an economic basis: it is a reflection of material interests of wage-earners within the capitalist society.

Social democrats protect profits from demands of the masses because radical redistributive policies are not in the interest of wage-earners. No one drew the blueprint and yet the capitalist system is designed in such a way that if profits are not sufficient, then eventually wage rates or employment must fall. Crises of capitalism are in no one's material interest; they are a threat to wage-earners since capitalism is a system in which economic crises must inevitably fall on their shoulders.

This is why social democrats trade off the abolition of private property of the means of production for cooperation of capitalists in increasing productivity and distributing its gains. This is why social democrats not only attempt to reproduce capitalism but struggle to improve it even against the resistance of capitalists. Nationalization of the means of production has turned out to be electorally unfeasible; radical redistributive policies result in economic crises which are not in the interest of wage-earners; and general affluence can be increased if capitalists are made to cooperate and wage-earners are continually disciplined to wait.

Social Democracy and Socialism

Social democrats will not lead European societies into socialism. Even if workers would prefer to live under socialism, the process of transition must lead to a crisis before socialism could be organized. To reach higher peaks one must traverse a valley, and this descent will not be completed under democratic conditions.

Suppose that social democrats win elections and attempt to use their position for a democratic transition to socialism. Given the social structure of capitalist societies, such an electoral victory is possible only if support can be obtained from several groups: industrial workers, non-manual employees, petite bourgeoisie, farmers, housewives, retired people, and/or students. Hence pressures for a significant improvement of material conditions erupt from several groups. Wages, particularly the minimal or "vital" wages (*sueldo vital* in Chile, *SMIC* in France), must be increased. Unemployment must be reduced. Transfers, particularly family allowances, must be raised. Credit for small enterprises and farms must become cheaper and available at a higher risk. These demands can be financed by (1) a redistribution of personal incomes (through both direct taxation and a reduction of wage differentials), (2) increased utilization of latent capacity, (3) spending of foreign reserves or borrowing, and/ or (4) reduction of the rate of profit (Kolm, 1977). The sum of the first three sources will not be sufficient to satisfy the demands. Redistribution of top incomes does not have much of a quantitative effect, and it cannot reach too far down without threatening the electoral support of salaried employees. Suddenly activated latent capacity generates bottlenecks and is quickly exhausted. Foreign reserves must be spent carefully if the currency is not to be left at the mercy of foreign lenders and speculators. Moreover, even if the accounts balance in money terms, an economy organized to produce certain goods and services cannot be transformed overnight to satisfy the new demands for wage goods.

Forced to pay higher wages and to keep employment beyond the efficient level, capitalists can respond only by increasing the prices of wage goods. Inflation is also fueled by balance of payment difficulties resulting from the necessity to import wage goods and from speculatory pressures. Hence, either an inflationary dynamic sets into motion or, if prices are controlled, scarcities appear, a black market is organized, and so on. Eventually nominal wage increases become eroded, as they were in France in 1936 (Kalecki, 1936), in Chile and in Portugal.

Under normal circumstances it can be expected that the increase of aggregate demand should stimulate investment and employment. Redistributional measures, even if they include inorganic emission, are usually justified by appeals not only to justice but also to efficiency. As lower incomes increase, so does the demand for wage goods. The utilization of latent capacity and foreign reserves are seen as a cushion that would protect prices from increased demand during the short period before investment picks up and eventually when supply rises. It is expected that profits from a larger volume of sales will be reinvested and thus the economy will be stimulated to develop at a faster pace. This was, for example, the Vuskovic program in Chile – not at all unreasonable under normal circumstances.

Such a program cannot be successful, however, when economic demands grow spontaneously and when they are accompanied by structural transformations. Wage demands are likely to become confiscatory under such circumstances, and capitalists expect that these demands will be enforced or at least condoned by the government. As Bevin put it, "we will be in the position of having to listen to the appeal of our own people." (Lyman, 1957: 219) Increased government intervention means precisely that non-market rationality is imposed upon the process of accumulation, that is, that capitalists are forced to make allocations which are suboptimal with regard to profit. Measures of nationalization, distribution of land, and monopolization of credit and foreign exchange by the state threaten the very institution of private profit. Under such circumstances, rational private capitalists will not invest. No political organization and no conspiracy is even necessary; rational entrepreneurs do not invest if the return on investment is expected to be zero or negative and when the risk is high.

And yet production must continue: for in Kautsky's words, "If production does not continue, the entire society will perish, the proletariat included." "The victorious proletariat," Kautsky continued, "hence not only has all the reasons to facilitate the continuation of capitalist production in all the sectors where immediate socialization is not advisable, it should moreover prevent socialization from unleashing an economic crisis." (1925: 273) But capitalists whose means of production are saved from socialization for the time being will not invest if they fear that this moment would come. This is why Lange (1964: 125) thought that nationalization must be done "in one stroke":

A socialist government really intent upon socialism has to decide to carry its socialization program at one stroke, or give it up altogether. The very coming to power of such a government must cause a financial panic and economic collapse. Therefore the socialist government must either guarantee the immunity of private property and private enterprise in order to enable the capitalist economy to function normally, in doing which it gives up its socialist aims, or it must go through resolutely with its socialization program at maximum speed.

Yet even if the socialist government is resolute, even if it makes all necessary attempts to reassure small entrepreneurs and property holders as Lange recommended, transformation of relations of production must be accompanied by an economic crisis. The pressure toward immediate consumption still operates with regard to public as much as private enterprises. Even if these enterprises are self-managed, each is still better off charging high prices for its products. The rigidities which prevent a sudden shift to production of wage goods are physical, not merely organizational. Moreover, nationalization generates economic problems of its own. Whether or not it was a deliberate political strategy, as Bologna (1972) and Marglin (1974) contend, capitalist production became reorganized in the aftermath of the council movement in such a manner that the immediate producers as a class lost the capacity to run the system of production on their own. The working class as seen by Marx was characterized not only by its exploitation but at the same time by its capacity to organize, at the social scale, the socialist system of production. Yet if ever true, it is no longer possible for the immediate producers to instantaneously assume control over the process of societal production: perhaps any cook can be taught how to administer the socialist society but a long apprenticeship is necessary. Socialist transformation requires an organizational and administrative capacity that cannot be acquired overnight. There are no blueprints and the experience is limited. Learning by trial and error and the blunders it involves are inevitable.

A transition to socialism must therefore generate an economic crisis. Investment falls sharply, prices increase, nominal wage gains become eroded, and eventually output falls, demand slackens, unemployment reappears as a major problem. What is not possible is thus the program articulated by Allende when he said that "the political model toward socialism that my government is applying requires that the socio-economic revolution take place simultaneously with an uninterrupted economic expansion." (De Vylder, 1976: 53) What is not possible is the realization of Blum's belief "that a better distribution . . . would revive production at the same time that it would satisfy justice." (Weill-Raynal, 1956: 54) What is not possible is a transition to socialism that begins with "une augmentation substantielle des salaires et traitement. . . ." (Parti Socialiste Français, Parti Communiste Français, 1972: I.1.1.)

Faced with an economic crisis, threatened with loss of electoral support, concerned about the possibility of a fascist counter-revolution, social democrats abandon the project of transition or at least pause to wait for more auspicious times. They find the courage to explain to the working class that it is better to be exploited than to create a situation which contains the risk of turning against them. They refuse to stake their fortunes on a worsening of the crisis. They offer the compromise; they maintain and defend it. The question which remains is whether there exists a way to escape the alternative defined for the Left of Olof Palme: "either to return to Stalin and Lenin, or take the road that joins the tradition of social democracy." (Brandt, Kreisky, Palme, 1976: 120)

2. Proletariat into a Class: The Process of Class Formation

Introduction

The difficulties encountered by marxist theory in analyzing the class structure of concrete capitalist societies had already appeared at the time of the formation of the socialist movement. Their roots are to be found in the formulation by Marx of the problematic in which processes of class formation are seen as a necessary transition from a "class-in-itself" to a "class-for-itself," a formulation in which economic relations have the status of objective conditions and all other relations constitute realms of subjective actions.

In place of this formulation we must think along the lines, also suggested by Marx, in which economic, political, and ideological conditions jointly structure the realm of struggles that have as their effect the organization, disorganization, or reorganization of classes. Classes must thus be viewed as effects of struggles structured by objective conditions that are simultaneously economic, political, and ideological.

Class analysis is a form of analysis that links social development to struggles among concrete historical actors. Such actors, collectivities-in-struggle at a particular moment of history, are not determined uniquely by objective conditions, not even by the totality of economic, political, and ideological conditions. Precisely because class formation is an effect of struggles, outcomes of this process are at each moment of history to some extent indeterminate.

Class analysis cannot be limited to those people who occupy places within the system of production. It is a necessary consequence of capitalist development that some quantity of the socially available labor power does not find productive employment. This surplus labor power may become socially organized in a number of different forms. These forms are not determined by the process of accumulation but directly by class struggle.

Processes of formation of workers into a class are inextricably fused with the processes of organization of surplus labor. As a result, a number of alternative organizations of classes is possible at any moment of history.

Scientific Socialism as of 1890

Karl Kautsky's *The Class Struggle* is of interest for a number of reasons. It was a semiofficial document of the German Socialist Party: an extensive commentary on the program adopted by the party at its Erfurt Congress in 1891, a program largely designed by Kautsky himself. As such, it constituted the authoritative exposition of the socialist doctrine for the purposes of political activity by socialist militants. It represented the theory of scientific socialism in its politically operational form, as that theory was known to active socialists.[1] In addition to the *Communist Manifesto* and parts of Engels' *Anti-Duhring*, it was precisely Kautsky's "catechism of Social Democracy," as he himself described the book in the preface to the first German edition, that organized the thoughts and the efforts of socialists, not only in Germany but wherever socialist parties existed.[2] Kautsky, as editor of the party's theoretical journal, was at the time the official theoretician of the party, the "Pope of Socialism," as Joll calls him (1966: 91)[3]

Perhaps even more importantly, Kautsky's book represents "orthodox marxist thought," as this thought functioned not only within the context of the debates of the time, but in the form in which it has been perpetuated for nearly a century. Afraid of simplifying orthodoxy, Marx disclaimed being "a Marxist." Kautsky was a marxist, and his book is a codified summary of "marxism."[4]

[1] We must not forget, in the midst of the contemporary discussions of Marx's thought, that the *Grundrisse* and several other notes written by Marx after 1853 were not known to marxist theoreticians until recently, while his early manuscripts were first published in the 1920s and did not become generally known until the 1950s. Whatever is the thought that can be recognized today as that of Marx, this is not the thought that underlay the activity of socialists during the greater part of the history of working-class movements.

[2] According to Hans Kelsen, "the works of Kautsky not only systematized the thought of Marx and Engels and made them, in an exemplary fashion, fruitful in the current historical situation but also contributed to making this thought accessible to broad circles. Marxism spread around the world not so much in the form of original writings of Marx and Engels as through the work of Kautsky." (Waldenberg, 1967: 3) Similar statements concerning the impact of Kautsky were made by the Mensheviks of Nikolayevski and Abramovitsch concerning Russia, by Topolevic concerning Serbia, by Daszynski concerning Poland, and up to a certain moment by Lenin. *The Class Struggle* was translated into fifteen languages before 1914; in Russia eight editions appeared during this period.

[3] For the status of Kautsky as the successor to Marx see Droz (1966). Werner Sombart (1909) cites an anecdote that best illustrates Kautsky's position. At the Amsterdam Congress of the Second International, Jaures attacked the German comrades: "You hide your importance behind the verbiage of mere theoretic formulas, which your distinguished comrade Kautsky will supply you with until the end of his days." On the role of Kautsky at the Erfurt Congress, for which *The Class Struggle* was written, see Lichtheim, *Marxism* (1965: 259–78).

[4] Benedict Kautsky's assessment of the work of his father merits citing: "Kautsky was – as his master, Marx – simultaneously an economist, a sociologist, and an historian. Only because of this he could have created a consistent system, constituting only then marxism out of fragments left by Marx – fragments which Engels only began to build as a unified structure. In order to complete this task. Kautsky had to simultaneously strive towards two goals: he had to popularize Marx and to fill with his own investigations the numerous gaps left in Marx's legacy. In both tasks he was highly successful, and it is principally Kautsky's merit that marxism was not only a scientific doctrine but also a force exerting strong influence upon politics and social development." (Waldenberg, 1967: 3)

To understand the place of *The Class Struggle* in the history of marxist thought is to understand that 1890 was precisely the moment when marxism, socialist theory, and the socialist movement became fused within continental socialism. Earlier socialist thought was motivated by moral and thus ahistorical ideals, and this ethical foundation reappeared in an altered form in Bernstein's return to Kant. Socialism was originally an invention of a morally sensitive bourgeoisie. This socialism, which Marx and Engels described as utopian, was founded upon individual judgments of rights and wrongs of existing and future societies.

Marxism was the theory of scientific socialism. The existing society, identified as capitalist, was historical, doomed to extinction. A new, socialist society was inevitably present on the historical horizon not because capitalism was morally wrong or unjust, but because an inquiry into the laws of development of capitalist society was sufficient to persuade any impartial observer that it is a necessary consequence of the very organization of the capitalist society that this society would "burst asunder."[5]

Marx was thought to have discovered the laws of motion of capitalist society. These are laws in the sense that they operate with inevitability in some, even if not specified, long run. The developments they describe are necessary: neither the ingenuity of capitalists exercised in defense of capitalist relations, nor the passivity on the part of the workers can alter the long-term developments. But these developments can be retarded or accelerated by actions of organized classes. Moreover, this inevitability itself operates through human agency. It imposes a historical mission on the specific class that suffers most under capitalist relations and that is uniquely in the position to alter these relations, namely, the proletariat. Socialism, the inevitable consequence of capitalist development, and the working class, those who "having nothing to lose but their chains" and whose emancipation would bring a universal emancipation, are related as mission and agent. "When we speak of the irresistible and inevitable nature of the social revolution," Kautsky emphasized, "we presuppose that men are men and not puppets; that they are beings endowed with certain wants and impulses, with certain physical and mental powers which they will seek to use in their own interest. . . . We consider the breakdown of the present social system

---

[5] Thus the *Communist Manifesto* asserts that "the theoretical conclusions of the communists are in no way based on ideas or principles that have been invented, or discovered, by this or that would-be universal reformer. They merely express, in general terms, actual relations springing from an existing class struggle, from a historical movement going on under our very eyes." (1967: 150) In "Socialism: Utopian and Scientific" Engels described the status of the theory: "From that time forward socialism was no longer an accidental discovery of this or that ingenious brain, but the necessary outcome of the struggle between two historically developed classes – the proletariat and the bourgeoisie. Its task was no longer to manufacture a system of society as perfect as possible; but to examine the historico-economic succession of events from which these classes and their antagonism had of necessity sprung, and to discover in the economic conditions thus created the means of ending the conflict." (1959: 89)

to be unavoidable, because we know that the economic evolution inevitably brings on the conditions that will compel the exploited classes to rise against this system of private ownership." (1971: 90)

Thus socialism was but an enlightened expression of historical inevitability. To be a socialist was to be scientific, to have understood the necessary laws of social development. To be scientific was to be a socialist, to have rejected the bourgeois ideology of the eternal nature of any system of social relations.[6] Hence to be a socialist was to be a marxist.[7]

Kautsky's book thus constitutes an expression of a political movement at a crucial stage of its development, a source for the understanding of the doctrine carried by socialists into factories and parliaments, homes and lecture halls. Yet its importance is contemporary. It is not possible to understand contemporary controversies concerning the concept of class without identifying the root of these controversies. And this root, I shall argue, lies exactly in the doctrine of scientific socialism: in marxist theory in its political form as the guiding doctrine of the socialist movement. And here Kautsky's book is a key.

Kautsky's discussion of classes is separated into two main themes. He begins by specifying those aspects of the development of capitalism that affect the structure of capitalist relations of production. This is a theory of "empty places" – places within a social formation dominated by large capitalist production. At this level classes appear only as categories of persons occupying similar positions vis-à-vis the means and the process of production. Concrete persons appear only as "personifications" of such categories, as "carriers" or "supporters" of the places. This is the level of "class-in-itself," class identified in terms of objective characteristics. At this level the occupants of places are "sacks of potatoes": they share the same relation to the means of production and hence the same objective interests; yet they remain simply as categories, not as subjects.

Having identified the effects of capitalist development for the structure of places within the system of production, Kautsky systematically examines the

---

[6] Sombart, who was highly critical of Marx's theory, is perhaps the best contemporary observer to cite. In a book written originally in 1896, he summarized as follows "the historic significance of the Marxian doctrines for the Social Movement:" "Marx laid down the two foundations on which the movement was to rest, when he enunciated that its end in view was the socialization of the instruments of production, and the means to achieve that end class war. . . . By making the Social Movement the resultant of historic development, Marx showed what the real factors were which brought it about, showed how the movement was based on the economic conditions of a particular time at a particular place, and on the personal characteristics of the men and women living in those conditions. In other words, he proved that on economic and psychological grounds it was inevitable, and he thus became the founder of historical (as opposed to rationalistic) or realistic (as opposed to Utopian) Socialism. (1909: 63)

[7] When in 1911 a contributor to a Swedish socialist journal suggested that one can be a socialist without being a marxist, because of a moral rejection of inequality and injustice, his voice was regarded as heresy (Tingsten, 1973: 129).

relation of each of these categories to the socialist movement. Specifically, he analyzes those effects of capitalist development and of capitalist ideological relations that make the particular categories prone to supporting or opposing the socialist movement by virtue of their interests.

In Kautsky's view capitalist development distributes members of a society into economic categories. Members of these categories become organized into classes. The problem for political analysis is to identify those categories generated in the course of capitalist development whose interests make them vulnerable to class organization.

Is this a "historicist" formulation of the transformation of a class-in-itself into a class-for-itself? Are classes formed at the level of relations of production alone, to appear politically only as epiphenomena, as necessary "reflections" at the level of the superstructures of the relations of production? What are the "classes' that move history: those defined as places in the relations of production or those that appear as political forces? Finally, what is the function of socialist movements in the process of class formation?

These are questions that have only recently become explicitly problematic. They certainly have no part in Kautsky's thought. What happened in the history of marxist thought was that the problem of class became conceptualized in a particular way, based in one form or another on the distinction, introduced in the *Poverty of Philosophy*, between class-in-itself and class-for-itself. Class-in-itself was a category defined at the level of the "base" – a base that is simultaneously objective and economic. Class-for-itself became the group in the sociological meaning of this term, that is, class characterized by organization and consciousness of solidarity. Given these categories, the problem – both theoretical and practical – became formulated in terms of transformation of "objective," that is, economic, into "subjective," that is, political and ideological class relations.

This kind of formulation can generate only two answers, regardless of the specific form they assume in concrete historical situations. In the deterministic version, objective relations necessarily become transformed into subjective relations. Since objective relations define interests and since politics is a struggle about realization of interests, it becomes a matter of deduction that objective positions, the positions in the relations of production, become "reflected" in expressed interests and political actions. One way or another, sooner or later, objective class relations spontaneously "find expression" at the level of political activity and consciousness.[8]

---

[8] The limiting case of this solution are the views of Rosa Luxemburg, which certainly lend themselves to a number of interpretations. Her "spontaneism," if this is what it was, rested on the notion that classes are formed only in the course of class struggles, economic and at the same time political. As Nettl emphasized,

The second response is ultimately voluntaristic. In this view, objective conditions do not lead spontaneously, "of themselves," to political class organization; or they lead at most, as in one celebrated analysis, to the formation of a reformist, syndicalist, bourgeois consciousness of the proletariat. Classes become formed politically only as a result of an organized intervention of an external agent, namely, the party. The process of spontaneous organization stops short of assuming a political form. This political form can only be infused by parties under concrete historical conditions of crises.[9]

Where then did Kautsky stand in terms of this external *problématique* of marxist thought? He asserts that the function of the socialist movement is to "give to the class-struggle of the proletariat the most effective form." The duty of socialists is to "support the working-class in its constant struggle by encouraging its political and economic institutions." These definitions of the function of socialist parties appear in his discussion of the *Communist Manifesto*. The work of Marx and Engels raised "socialism beyond the utopian point of view" and "laid the scientific foundation of modern socialism." Marx and Engels gave to "the militant proletariat a clear conception of their historical function, and placed them in a position to proceed toward their great goal. . . ." Hence it seems that the proletariat is defined as a class at the level of economic relations, that it spontaneously acquires consciousness of its historical mission, and that the function of the party is but to assist, support, participate in the political struggle of that economically defined class (1971: 199).

Yet these explicit struggles seem to contradict the theoretical conception implicit in Kautsky's formulation of the problem of the class struggle. Indeed, Kautsky's problem is better defined in terms of the function assigned by Marx

the *existence* of the party was not enough; only repeated confrontations, particularly the mass strike, could lead to political organization of the working class. Yet at the same time, the transformation of objective into subjective class was *necessary* in her view: organization led to increased intensity of class conflicts, class conflicts generated increased organization and consciousness, and so on, dialectically history marched on (Nettl, 1969: 137). For a discussion of alternative interpretations of Luxemburg's views see Frölich (1972), and Magri (1970).

9 Lenin's conception is too well known to require a summary. But in the context of this discussion it is interesting to note that it was first presented in *What Is to Be Done* (1964: 38) through the words of Kautsky's commentary on the 1901 Programme of the Austrian Social Democratic Party, words that Lenin described as "profoundly true and important": "Many of our revisionist critics believe," Kautsky said, "that Marx asserted that economic development and the class struggle create, not only the conditions for socialist production, but also, and directly, the *consciousness* of its necessity. . . . But this is absolutely untrue. Of course, socialism, as a doctrine, has its roots in modern economic relationships just as the class struggle of the proletariat has, and, like the latter, emerges from the struggle against capitalist-created poverty and misery of the masses. But socialism and the class struggle arise side by side and not one out of the other; each arises under different conditions. Modern socialist consciousness can arise only on the basis of profound scientific knowledge. . . . The vehicle of science is not the proletariat, but the *bourgeois intelligentsia*: it was in the minds of individual members of this stratum that modern socialism originated, and it was they who communicated it to the more intellectually developed proletarians, who in their turn introduced it into the proletarian class struggle from without and not something that arose within it spontaneously."

and Engels to the communist movement in the *Manifesto*: the formation of the proletariat into a class (1967: 150). Marx had always insisted that the proletariat exists as a class only in active opposition to the bourgeoisie, that it becomes organized as a class only in the course of struggles, that it is a class only when it becomes organized as a political party. It is not exactly clear how Marx saw the transformation of economic categories into politically organized classes taking place – what role he assigned to spontaneous self-organization[10] or what role he attributed to parties and other agents of class formation.[11] Yet he did think of classes as being formed in the course of class struggles, and, particularly in his historical analyses, he emphasized the independent impact of ideological and political relations upon the process of class formation.

Kautsky's analysis is based on the assumption of the active role of parties and other political forces in the process of class formation. Some of this process *is* spontaneous. Workers are in his view, for example, spontaneously distrustful of socialist ideology as something introduced from the outside. Yet socialist parties, trade-unions, and ostensibly nonpolitical organizations all play an active role in the process of class formation. Indeed the very problem of the class struggle concerns the conditions of the organization of workers by socialist parties.

Why then this apparent inconsistency between the construction of the problematic and the explicit statements concerning the function of socialist movements? The reason is, I believe, fundamental for the understanding of the long-standing difficulties concerning the organization of workers as a class. It seems that Kautsky believed that by 1890 the formation of the proletariat into a class was a *fait accompli*; it was already formed as a class and would remain so in the future. The organized proletariat had nothing left to do but to pursue its historical mission, and the party could only participate in its realization.

When Marx and Engels wrote the *Communist Manifesto*, socialism was an idea that was available to workers only "from above." Kautsky himself observed that "socialism is older than the class struggle of the proletariat. . . . The first root of socialism was the sympathy of upper-class philanthropists for the poor and

[10] "Organize *itself* as a class." (Marx and Engels, 1967: 162)
[11] According to Magri, Marx himself was not aware of the problems generated by this formulation. In Magri's words these problems are the following: "Confined to the immediacy of prevailing conditions, the proletariat cannot achieve a complete vision of the social system as a whole, nor promote its overthrow. Its practice as a class can only develop by transcending this immediacy via the mediation of revolutionary consciousness. What then is the process, the mechanism by which this consciousness is produced? Or, to pose the question more precisely, can this class consciousness develop within the proletariat spontaneously, by virtue of an intrinsic necessity, based on the elements that are already present in its social objectivity and which gradually come to dominate over the other elements that originally condemned it to a subordinate and fragmented condition? Or must revolutionary consciousness represent a transcendence of the immediacy of the proletariat, produced by a qualitative dialectical leap, a complex interaction between external forces and the spontaneous action of class itself? Marx did not confront this problem." (1970: 101)

miserable. . . . Socialism was the deepest and most splendid expression of bourgeois philanthropy." (1971: 192) As such it was an idea that was infused into the working class from the outside. Yet whether the exact place was Peterloo, Lyon, or Paris, at some time during the first half of the nineteenth century the proletariat appeared on the historical horizon as a political force, distinct from the amorphous masses of the "lower classes." This was exactly the point of Marx's analysis of the June insurrection – the insurrection that in his view marked the appearance of the class struggle characteristic of capitalism, namely, the political struggle between the bourgeoisie and the proletariat.[12]

By 1848 the problem was to organize this emerging proletariat into a class, to separate it from the masses of *le peuple*, to imbue it with consciousness of its position and its mission, and to organize it as a party. In comparison, by 1890 the proletariat indeed seemed already organized as a class. Workers were militant; they were organized into parties, unions, cooperatives, clubs, associations. They voted in elections, participated in strikes, appeared at demonstrations. In 1890 there were mass political organizations clearly identified as those of the proletariat. And although, as Bernstein pointed out (1961: 105), it was perhaps true that the proletariat was not organized in its entirety as a mass political party, Kautsky's perception of the role of the party seems only natural.[13]

The leading socialist theoreticians of the period, men like Kautsky, attempted to unite only those views which were actually present among the workers with the general doctrines of Marxism. It would be completely false and unhistorical, however, to maintain that Kautsky and his friends invented the principles of the Second International. On the contrary, the socialist labour movement during the period of the Second International from 1889 to 1914 is the historical product resulting from the evolution of the European proletariat. This type of labour movement necessarily resulted from the conditions which had developed up to 1889. (Rosenberg, 1965: 291).

Thus it seems that Kautsky thought that the task set by the *Manifesto* – the formation of the proletariat into a class – had already been accomplished. The proletariat was already organized as a class, and the socialist party was nothing but "a part of the militant proletariat." (1971: 183) As the process of

[12] Hobsbawm dates this political emergence of the proletariat to 1830: "The second result [of the revolution of 1830] was that, with the progress of capitalism, 'the people' and 'the labouring poor,' i.e., the men who built barricades, could be increasingly identified with the new industrial proletariat as 'the working class.' A proletarian socialist revolutionary movement came into existence." (1962: 146) By 1848 political reactions of the *classes inférieures* ceased assuming the form of sporadic riots against prices or taxes, as the proletariat broke away from *le peuple* and for the first time became organized. In particular, the introduction of universal suffrage provided the working class with a form of organization and separated it from other classes (Furet, 1963: 473).

[13] But in Rosa Luxemburg's view as of 1899: "The great socialist importance of the trade-union and political struggle consists in socializing the knowledge, the consciousness of the proletariat, *in organizing it as a class.*" (Nettl, 1969: 411; italics supplied.)

proletarianization of other classes proceeded, various groups would join the ranks of the proletariat and become members of the working class, which was then becoming the "immense majority." Now the function of the party was simply to support the struggle of the proletariat, already formed as a class.

Who Are the "Proletarians"?

But who were these "proletarians" of whom a class was formed, of whom the socialist party was nothing but a part? Three years before writing *The Class Struggle*, Kautsky published an article in which he distinguished between the concepts of "the proletariat" and "the people." In this article, he maintained that although in the future "the people" would become proletarianized, and the socialist movement will become the movement, in Marx's words, "of the immense majority for the immense majority," at the moment the proletariat was not a majority in any country (Tingsten, 1973: 135). In the book he maintains that the proletariat already is the largest class in "all civilized countries." He constantly moves back and forth between a narrow and broad definition; the narrow one in which proletarians are the manual wage-earners in industry, transport, and agriculture, and the broad one in which proletarians include all those who do not own means of production and must, therefore, sell their labor power if they are to survive. Actually, at one point he even includes in the proletariat "the majority of farmers, small producers, and traders [since] the little property they still possess today is but a thin veil, calculated rather to conceal than to prevent their dependence and exploitation." (1971: 43)

Hence the concept of proletariat has the consistency of rings of water: the core of it consists of manual, principally industrial workers; around it float various categories of people who have been separated from the means of production; and on the periphery there are those who still hold on to the property of means of production but whose life situation, conceived in quite Weberian terms, distinguishes them from the proletarians only by their "pretensions."[14]

In order to understand the source of Kautsky's ambivalence it is necessary to note that the concept of the proletariat seems to have been self-evident for the founders of scientific socialism. Proletarians were the poor and miserable people who were thrown off the land and forced to sell themselves, piecemeal, as a commodity, "like every other article of commerce," to a capitalist. They were

---

[14] French linguistic tradition includes a term for each of these rings. *Les classes inférieures* traditionally included all those who were not distinguished by virtue of birth or status. *Les classes laborieuses* comprised all who worked. The newcomer, *la classe ouvrière*, eventually became Marx's "proletariat." The corresponding English terms – lower classes, laboring classes, and the working class – do not seem to have such a standardized meaning.

"an appendage of the machine," of whom "only the most simple, most monotonous, and most easily acquired knack" was required (Marx, 1967: 141). The proletariat, Engels wrote, was called into existence through the introduction of machinery, and the first proletarians belonged to manufacture and were begotten directly through it (Marcus, 1975: 142).[15] They were the people who toiled day and night, next to a machine, in noise and dirt, producing they knew not what just to survive until the following day so that they could sell themselves again.

At the same time, proletarians were important as those who put into motion the modern, that is, socialized, means of production. Although farmers and independent small producers also "worked," socialization of production was the necessary course of future capitalist development. Hence proletarians occupied a unique position in the capitalist society: they were the ones who actually applied the modern means of production to produce all that which was made. They were the only people who were necessary to make all that the society required, and they could make it on their own, without those who did nothing but live off their labor and appropriate its fruit.[16] As Mandel emphasized, Marx and Engels "assigned the proletariat the key role in the coming of socialism not so much because of the misery it suffers as because of the place it occupies in the production process." (1971: 23)

In 1848 one simply knew who were the proletarians. One knew because all the criteria – the relation to the means of production, manual character of labor, productive employment, poverty, and degradation – all coincided to provide a consistent image. "If a working man doesn't smell of filth and sweat two miles off, he isn't much of a fellow": this remark of a Norwegian capitalist best tells the story (Bull, 1955: 67).[17] "Class position" and "class situation" were synony-

---

[15] For a general discussion of the impact of the introduction of machines upon the formation of an industrial proletariat see Kuczynski (1967: chap. 2). Bergier formulates this relationship succinctly: "the introduction of a new power source superseding that of man, wind, or running water soon wrought a clear distinction between the industrialist, who owned this comparatively expensive machine and the looms it drove, and the worker, who was paid to run it." (1973: 397)

[16] Marx in *Capital* (1967) and Engels in *Anti-Duhring* (1959) both emphasized the technical role of capitalists as organizers of the process of production. Yet the development of public companies was sufficient to demonstrate that the function of the organization of production is independent technically of the property of the means of production, and workers can organize the process of production on their own. See below for a more detailed discussion of the concept of "productive labor."

[17] National differences in the timing and the form of development of industrial proletariat were profound. Moreover, there are significant historiographical controversies concerning both the origins of factory workers and their standard of living, as compared with artisans and peasants of the last generation before the industrial revolution. Nevertheless, there is a sufficient agreement to a number of generalizations supporting the thesis of the coincidence of various criteria of the status of workers: (1) workers became concentrated in factories and mines, primarily in textiles, metallurgy, and mining; (2) they operated machines; (3) they lived in abominable conditions; (4) they worked in exactly the same conditions. Workers were distinct from artisans because they owned none of the tools that they used and worked where the

mous. And, as Rosenberg observed: "The class-consciousness with which the industrial workers of Europe were imbued led them to lay great emphasis on their specific position and on those factors which differentiated them from all other economic groups." (1965: 291)

To restate the point more abstractly: *in the middle of the nineteenth century the theoretical connotation of the concept of proletariat, defined in terms of separation from the means of production, corresponded closely to the intuitive concept of proletariat conceived in terms of manual, principally industrial, laborers.* No ambiguity had yet arisen because material conditions closely corresponded to their theoretical description.

It is, therefore, perhaps indicative that Engels felt it necessary to introduce a definition of the proletariat as a footnote to the 1888 English edition of the *Communist Manifesto*. According to this definition, "by proletariat [is meant] the class of modern wage labourers who, having no means of production of their own, are reduced to selling their labour power in order to live." (1967: 131) Kautsky echoed this definition: "proletarians, that is to say . . . workers who are divorced from their instruments of production so that they produce nothing by their own efforts and, therefore, are compelled to sell the only commodity they possess – their labour power." And in a summary of an international discussion conducted in 1958 by communist journals and research institutes, the Soviet commentators defined the proletariat as "the class of people separated from the means of production, having therefore to live from the sale of their labour power to the owners of capital and exploited in the process of capitalist production." (*Przemiany*, 1963: 43)

But by 1958 this definition includes secretaries and executives, nurses and corporate lawyers, teachers and policemen, computer operators and executive directors. They are all proletarians, they are all separated from the means of production and compelled to sell their labor power for a wage. Yet a feeling of uneasiness, already visible in Kautsky, continues to be pronounced. For whatever reasons, some of the proletarians neither act as proletarians nor think like proletarians. In the 1958 discussion, voice after voice repeats the same message: salaried employees are proletarians, but they do not yet know that they are. The German Economic Institute participated in the discussion with the argument that the majority of salaried employees "like workers do not own means of production and are compelled to sell their labor. The price which they

tools were. They were distinct from beggars, and so on, because they worked. They were distinct from serfs and slaves because they were free.

For summaries of literature concerning early industrial workers see Kuczynski (1967) and Bergier (1973). Elster (1975) contains a superb clarification of the issues involved. Marcus, *Engels, Manchester, and the Working Class* (1975), is clearly worth reading, but perhaps most important for the understanding of Marx's and Engels' vision of workers in the latter's *The Condition of the Working Class in England in 1844* (1958).

obtain for this commodity – their salary – is in most cases not higher than that of workers. In spite of it a large part of salaried employees does not include itself, as it is known, into the working class and is predisposed to bourgeois ideology. The cause of this fact should be sought first of all in that their work differs from the work of workers." The American Institute of the Problems of Work as well as the British journal *Marxism Today* dispute the diagnosis of their German comrades but agree with the factual assertions. "If there ever existed any objective conditions allowing us to consider white-collar workers as representatives of the middle class," says the American Institute, "now these conditions have disappeared. Only their subjective evaluation of their situation has not yet changed. . . ." The editors of the British journal repeat that "in terms of conditions of work and size of revenues white-collar workers are becoming increasingly similar to workers, although most of them do not yet realize it." And the Soviet summary reflects the discussion: salaried employees are workers but they do not yet realize it, so that the unification of the working class is yet to be achieved (*Przemiany*, 1963: 78, 88, 96, 54).

This line of argumentation is so widespread that it may seem peculiar to have singled out this discussion as a subject of particular attention.[18] But what is striking about these analyses is the repeated emphasis on the "not yet" status of consciousness and organization of salaried employees. Already in the *Manifesto*, Marx and Engels observed that capitalism "has converted the physician, the lawyer, the priest, the poet, the man of science, into wage labourers." (1967: 135) And Kautsky echoed Marx again, at the time anticipating by sixty-five years that "not yet": "a third category of proletarians . . . has gone far on the road to its complete development – the education proletarians. . . . The time is near when the bulk of these proletarians will be distinguished from the others only by their pretensions. Most of them imagine that they are something better than proletarians. They fancy they belong to the bourgeoisie, just as the lackey identifies himself with the class of his master." (1971: 36, 40)

By 1890 the term *proletariat* seems to have already lost that immediate intuitive sense that is conveyed at the time of the *Manifesto*. It is again instructive to listen to a contemporary observer. Writing in 1896, Sombart analyzed the meaning of the term:

In order to get a true conception of this class we must free ourselves from the picture of a ragged crowd which the term brought to mind before we read Karl Marx. The term

---

[18] I cannot resist one more illustration: "salaried workers . . . find themselves carefully *separated* from the rest of the proletariat by the artifice of the bourgeoisie, not by scientific analysis. The fact that they wear a white shirt and are paid at the end of the month is hardly sufficient to place in question their objective membership in the working class, even if their subjective consciousness remains confused." (Ajam-Bouvier and Mury, 1963: 63)

"proletariat" is now used in a technical sense to describe that portion of the population which is in the service of capitalist undertakers in return for wages and elements akin to them. The word in this meaning is taken from French writers, and was introduced into Germany by Lorenz von Stein in 1842.

And again, the same problem appears. The bulk of this class is according to Sombart formed by "the free wage-earners." They are a minority, about one-third of the German population. "But the picture becomes entirely different," Sombart continued, "when to the true proletariat, to the full bloods, are added the innumerable half-bloods — the poorest class of the population, *il popolino* — and also those amongst small farmers and mechanics who live the life of the proletariat, as well as the lowest grade among officials, such as those in the Post Office." (1909: 6) The problem is even further compounded by the fact that wage-earners are not always the poorest people around. They are not only better off than the Russian peasant or the Chinese coolie; some wage-earners earn more than university teachers, and "in America the average income of this class falls not much below the maximum salary of an extraordinary professor in Prussia." (Ibid.) No wonder Max Weber felt it necessary to distinguish between "class situation" and "status situation" (see Goldthorpe and Lockwood, 1963).

When applied in the 1890s, the abstract definition of proletariat includes "full-bloods" and "half-bloods," wage-earners and others who live like them, those who are ragged and those who wear the uniforms of the Prussian officialdom. And in 1958, while the Soviet theoreticians did not tire in pointing out that only those who are incapable of thinking in dialectical terms could commit the error of not understanding that salaried employees are simply proletarians, they argued in the same breath that the role of different fractions of the proletariat is not the same, that industrial manual workers play the leading role in class struggle; more, the program of the Communist Party of the Soviet Union insisted on "the alliance between the working class and the broad strata of salaried employees and a large part of the intelligentsia." (*Przemiany*, 1963: 54) Full-bloods and half-bloods, blue-collar and white-collar, proletarians and "the people," workers and "masses of the exploited and oppressed": all these terms are symptomatic of an obvious theoretical difficulty, of a problem that seems no nearer a solution today than in the 1890s.

Proletarianization and Class Structure

Kautsky was wrong. Neither he nor Marx drew from Marx's theory of capitalist development the consequences for the evolution of class structure. The source of the ambiguity of the concept of the proletariat lies in the dynamic of capitalist development itself.

I will argue below that the proletariat could not have been formed as a class once and for all by the end of the nineteenth century because capitalist development continually transforms the structure of places in the system of production and realization of capital as well as in the other manners of production that become dominated by capitalism. More precisely, the penetration of the capitalist manner of producing into all areas of economic activity results in the separation of various groups from the ownership of the means of production or from the effective capacity to transform nature into useful products. At the same time, the increasing productivity of labor decreases in relative terms the capitalist utilization of labor power. As a result, the process of proletarianization in the sense of separation from the means of production diverges from the process of proletarianization in the sense of creation of places of productive workers. This divergence generates social relations that are indeterminate in the class terms of the capitalist mode of production, since it leads exactly to the separation of people from any socially organized process of production.

Let us examine this argument and its implications in some detail. Kautsky's own description of capitalist development and of its effects upon class structure was based on the first section of the Erfurt Programme, which asserted that:

production on a small scale is based on the ownership of the means of production by the laborer. The economic development of bourgeois society leads necessarily to the overthrow of this form of production. It separates the worker from his tools and changes him into a propertyless proletarian. The means of production become more and more the monopoly of a comparatively small number of capitalists and landowners. (1971: 7)

Kautsky examines carefully the categories of places being destroyed in the course of capitalist development. Thus he first talks about the "disappearing middle classes – small business and farmers." As capitalism permeates all forms of production, small property of various kinds is destroyed, particularly when capital becomes concentrated in periodic crises. Only small stores are surviving, but they are becoming "debased," becoming increasingly dependent upon the rhythm of capitalist accumulation. Another mechanism of proletarianization is the capitalist organization of service and productive activities traditionally performed in the household such as weaving, sewing, knitting, and baking. The externalization of production and services from the household does constitute a form of separation from the means of production, since those who have previously performed these activities, particularly women, are forced to seek employment outside the household because of increasing poverty and are obliged to purchase the products and services previously generated internally.[19]

---

[19] The notion of "separation from the means of production" requires more elaboration than it has received thus far. In Marx's analysis of primitive accumulation, this separation consisted of the legally forced

What are the places simultaneously being created as smallholders, craftsmen, artisans, and women become proletarianized? Are they separated from the means of production or from the capacity to produce on their own? Some are the places of industrial proletarians. While this process is nowhere described systematically, Kautsky seems to think that capitalist development constantly increases the number of factory workers.[20] Moreover, this industrial proletariat is supposedly becoming increasingly homogeneous. While Kautsky observes with an unusual degree of bitterness what he considers to be the remnants of internal divisions among workers – divisions based on skill – he is persuaded that the introduction of machinery which eliminates the need for skill, and the growth of surplus labor, which pushes wages down, are removing the internal differentiation of the proletariat and increasing internal homogeneity.

But the process of proletarianization spreads to areas of economic activity other than industrial production. "It is not only through the extension of large production," Kautsky argues, "that the capitalist system causes the condition of the proletariat to become more and more that of the whole population. It brings this about also through the fact that the condition of the wage-earner engaged in large production strikes the keynote for the condition of the wage earners in all other branches." Thus, for example, in the large stores "there is constant increase in the number of employees – genuine proletarians without prospect of ever becoming independent." (1971: 35–6)

Yet, most importantly, the rate at which capitalism destroys small production is greater than the rate at which it generates places of productive capitalist employment. The process of proletarianization – separation from the means of production – creates "the army of superfluous laborers." "Enforced idleness," Kautsky asserts, "is a permanent phenomenon under the capitalist system of production, and is inseparable from it." (Ibid.: 85)

"Proletarianization" is thus a concept with a double meaning. In terms of the destruction of places in pre- and early-capitalist organization of production it means separation from the ownership of the means of production and from the

separation of cultivators from the land. In the theory of concentration of capital, the notion is that small producers will not be able to compete economically with large capitalist firms. But this separation can assume more subtle forms, for example, when services traditionally performed within the household become externalized into capitalistically organized activities. (See below for Kautsky's analysis of this phenomenon.) Furthermore, should not compulsory retirement and compulsory education be treated as such a separation? The question also arises whether separation from the means of *production* is sufficiently broad as a description of the process by which various groups are hurled into the capitalist labor market. Beggars, for example, of whom in France in 1800 there were probably as many as workers, lost their means of subsistence legitimized by Catholic ideology when the "economic whip" replaced the concept of communal responsibility for the poor.

[20] Bernstein (1961) felt that there is an inconsistency in the argument according to which accumulation of capital is supposed to reduce need for labor yet numbers of workers are said to increase with the growth of the mass of capital. Clearly the issue concerns the relative rates of the growth of capital and of the productivity of labor. This is not a simple issue, as the controversies concerning the concept of capital manifest.

capacity to transform nature independently. But in terms of creation of new places within the structure of advancing capitalism it does not necessarily denote creation of new places of productive, manual labor. Craftsmen, small merchants, and peasants do not become transformed into productive manual workers. They are transformed into a variety of groups the status of which is theoretically ambiguous. And contemporary debates make it abundantly clear that this gap has widened in the course of the past eighty years. The problems in the conceptualization of class structure arise principally, although not exclusively, from the appearance of people variously termed salaried employees, white-collar workers, nonmanual workers, *ouvriers intellectuels*, service workers, technicians, "the new middle classes."

Again Kautsky's book provides some interesting clues concerning the origin of this difficulty. "Idle labor" includes the unemployed, the "slums," personal servants, the military, and numerous people who somehow find pursuits that provide them with subsistence. Thus "idle labor" should not be understood to mean labor that is not expended in any manner but merely as labor that is not applied to produce any of the things that a society needs. But what are the mechanisms by which this idle labor becomes structured in these particular social forms?

While the destruction of small property and the generation of "enforced idleness" are discussed in structural terms as necessary consequences of capitalist development, the creation of particular forms assumed by this labor seems to result from individual entrepreneurship. Most revealing is Kautsky's discussion of the group he calls the "educated proletarians." How is this category generated in the process of capitalist development?

Having listed the emergence of proletarians in large industrial production and in commerce, Kautsky announces the "there is still a third category of proletarians far on the road to its complete development – the educated proletarians." (Ibid.: 36) At this moment the discussion suddenly focuses on the household. We are told that the petit bourgeois knows that the only way in which he can prevent his son from becoming a proletarian is to send him to college. But he must be concerned not only about his sons, but also about his daughters. Division of labor results in externalization from the household into industries of several activities such as weaving, sewing, knitting, and baking. It thus becomes a luxury to maintain a household in which the wife is only a housekeeper, a luxury that small property holders can less and less afford. "Accordingly," Kautsky maintains, "the number of women wage-earners increases, not only in large and small production and commerce, but in government offices, in the telegraph and telephone service, in railroads and banks, in the arts and sciences." (Ibid.: 38–9) Nothing is said about those laws of capitalist development that would describe the growing need for government positions, telegraph and telephone services, railroads and banks, and so on. People, particularly middle-class women, are forced to seek education. Hence they become educated; hence they are employed in all these offices. But where do the offices come from? The entire argument is limited to the supply side. It is a "human capital" argument.

Does Kautsky at all anticipate the growth of the new middle class? He mentions the office workers in the context of evolution of households. Later he anticipates the appearance of some personal service occupations in their proletarianized rather than personal form, namely, barbers, waiters, cab drivers, and so on (Ibid.: 167). But the group that Kautsky sees as ever-increasing is that "crew of social parasites who, having all avenues of productive work closed to them, try to eke out a miserable existence through a variety of occupations, most of which are wholly superfluous and not a few injurious to society — such as middlemen, saloonkeepers, agents, intermediaries, etc." (Ibid.: 85) Here are the very nerves of the modern capitalist society: the superfluous parasites. In all these cases — office workers, barbers, and middlemen — Kautsky feels that these are occupations that people pursue only because they are separated from the means of production and yet cannot find productive employment. Hence they resort to such superfluous pursuits in order to survive.

This is all that Kautsky had to say in *The Class Struggle*[21] about those places in the system of production that nowadays constitute perhaps more than a half of the labor force.[22] He saw nothing structural about the appearance of the "new middle classes," viewing all the middle-class pursuits as ephemeral, marginal forms in which people pushed out of the process of production attempt to escape the fate to which they are exposed by capitalist development. Is this just an individual limitation, an accidental error of a distinguished yet fallible marxist theoretician?

And Where to Fit the "Middle Class"?

Ever since the 1890s when the concept of proletariat first became problematic, time after time, conjuncture after conjuncture, this issue appears with renewed theoretical and political urgency. Who are all those people whom capitalism

[21] This is not to say that elsewhere, particularly in the polemic against Bukharin, he did not see "foremen, engineers, technicians, agronomers, managers, administrators, and directors" as necessary functions in the capitalist organization of production. For a summary of this polemic and its attendant issue see Wiatr (1965: 200ff.)

[22] One should note that in industry (including mining and construction) — which was supposed to represent the future of the capitalist society — class structure *was* nearly dichotomous. According to the 1882 German census, there were about 1,500,000 employers, about 3,500,000 workers, and only 90,000 clerical and technical personnel in this sector. The respective figures for Sweden in 1900 are 125,000 employers, 442,000 workers, and 22,000 office and technical personnel. In France in 1881 there were 1,169,000 employers, about 3,000,000 workers, and 236,000 office employees. The data for Germany and Sweden are from the respective censuses. French information is based on Toutain (1963, Tables 75–7).

generates at an ever accelerating pace, who are separated from the means of production, who are forced to sell their labor power for a wage, and yet who do not quite work, live, think, and act like the proletarians? Are they workers, proletarians? Or are they "middle class"? Or perhaps simply "non-manuals," as in the practice of survey researchers? Or "la nouvelle petite bourgeoisie"? Or agents of capitalist reproduction and hence simply the bourgeoisie?

The problem could not be resolved by fiat. What was needed was some model of a "developed class structure," some way to abandon the fiction of a dichotomous class division of capitalist social formations, some way of analyzing class positions that would go beyond the notion of two classes being associated with each mode of production, plus the eternal petite bourgeoisie. Kautsky's method was to think of all classes other than the proletariat and the bourgeoisie as ascending or descending to these basic "poles" in the course of history of capitalism; hence, to classify them by direction of their motion. This method reappeared in a little known but most interesting analysis by Courtheoux of the 1962 French census. But the critical influence was Weber's.

Weber's critique of Marx's concept of class provided the theoretical foundations for the analysis of social differentiation (stratification) within the bourgeois sociology. This critique asserted that the position within the relations of production (property of the means of production) is not sufficient to determine class situation, since the positions in the relations of distribution (market, life-style, and attendant status) and in the relations of authority (power) do not reflect only the relations of property. Moreover, status and power are not dichotomous. The system of stratification distributes people along continuous strata, bulging in the middle to generate the "middle class." The resulting consequences are well known: empirical descriptions of "socioeconomic standings" became independent of any historical understanding; the vision of classes as historical actors became replaced by statistical analyses of distributions of income, education, and prestige; the analysis of social differentiation became separated from the analysis of conflict. Attention has focused on "status incongruence," and the foreman became a typical victim of this disease.

Returning to Geiger's analysis of 1925, Dahrendorf (1959) examined systematically the consequences of the Weberian orientation for Marx's theory of class without rejecting it *tout court*. The result of his analysis was an "objective pluralism." Modern capitalist societies, Dahrendorf argued, consist of a multitude of groups, but these groups are not formed arbitrarily. They are generated by objective relations: relations of property and relations of authority, mutually independent from each other. He did eventually reject the very foundation of Marx's analysis, arguing that property relations are defined by the authority to dispose of the means of production and the product. Hence property is only a special case of authority; society is built upon authority, not exploitation, and so on.

Wright's *New Left Review* article (1976) recuperates the problematic of the objective determination of class. Since even the economically active population in the United States cannot be easily "pigeon-holed" into the boxes of workers and capitalists, Wright proceeds to generate additional dimensions. "Substantive social processes comprising class relations" are thought to distribute individuals into classes independently of the "juridical categories of class relations," and a gradation is introduced to distinguish "full," "partial," "minimal," and "no" control over resources, means of production, labor power, and the degrees of legal ownership (1976: 33). The result is "contradictory locations": all kinds of places where these degrees do not exactly coincide. The foreman reappears as "the contradictory location closest to the working class." Numbers of people falling into each category are then counted on the basis of 1969 United States data, and the conclusion is that "somewhere between a quarter and a third of the American labour force falls into these locations near the boundary of the proletariat." Added to the 40–50 percent of the noncontradictory working class, these numbers constitute a great majority having "a real interest in socialism." (1976: 41) We are then told that:

class struggle will determine the extent to which people in these contradictory locations join forces with the working class in a socialist movement. . . . And the possibilities of a viable socialist movement in advanced capitalist societies depend in part on the capacity of working-class organizations to forge the political and ideological conditions which will draw these contradictory locations into closer alliance with the working class. (1976: 44)

Or as Kautsky prophesied, "the more unbearable the existing system of production, the more evidently it is discredited . . . the greater will be the numbers of those who stream from the non-proletarian classes into the Socialist Party and, hand in hand with the irresistibly advancing proletariat, follow its banner to victory and triumph." (1971: 217)

The problem of the relation between objectively defined classes and classes qua historical actors will not be resolved by any classification, whether with two or many objective classes, with or without contradictory locations. The problem persists because such classifications, whether made in party headquarters or within the walls of academia, are constantly tested by life, or more precisely, by political practice. Wright's "contradictory locations" are contradictory only in the sense that his assertions about the "real interest in socialism" are not borne out by the consciousness and the organization of those who are supposed to have this interest. On paper one can put people in any boxes one wishes, but in political practice one encounters real people, with their interests and a consciousness of these interests. And these interests, whether or not they are "real," are not arbitrary; their consciousness is not arbitrary; and the very political practice that forges these interests is not arbitrary.

The problematic of class-in-itself places the problem of classification at the center of analysis because classes as historical actors, the classes that struggle and whose struggle is the motor of history, are thought to be determined in a unique manner by objective positions. Underlying this problematic is the assertion of the objective conflict of short-term material interests of workers (wage-earners) and capitalists (surplus-takers). Capitalism is supposed to be characterized by the objective conflict of short-term material interests imputed to individuals in their status as carriers or personifications of objective places. Class-in-itself is viewed as a category of individuals who have common interests by virtue of the positions they occupy. At the same time, the defense of short-term objective interests is supposed to constitute the mechanism by which class organization is set into motion, leading eventually to the realization of a long-term and equally objective interest in socialism. Hence, a classification of objective positions (locations, places, classes) seems sufficient to identify the interests that determine those classes that can emerge to struggle with each other. Once objective positions are identified, the potential classes-for-themselves are uniquely determined. "Class" denotes here a class of occupants of places; and the problem to be analyzed within this problematic is only how does a collection of individual-occupants-of-places become a collectivity-in-struggle for the realization of its objective interests.

This formulation of the problematic of class is exactly what makes so thorny the appearance of nonmanual employees. The only way in which their presence in a capitalist society can be accommodated within this problematic is by a redefinition of the relations that determine the objective bases of class formation. Hence a new classification of objective positions is required, and at the same time such a classification appears sufficient to resolve the problem.

In the remaining parts of this chapter I will argue that the question of class identity of nonmanual employees forces us to rethink the entire problematic of class formation. Classes as historical actors are not given uniquely by any objective positions, not even those of workers and capitalists. I will show that the very relation between classes as historical actors (classes-in-struggle) and places within the relations of production must become problematic. *Classes are not given uniquely by any objective positions because they constitute effects of struggles, and these struggles are not determined uniquely by the relations of production.* The traditional formulation does not allow us to think theoretically about class struggles, since it either reduces them to an epiphenomenon or enjoins them with freedom from objective determination. Class struggles are neither epiphenomenal, nor free from determination. They are structured by the totality of economic, political, and ideological relations; and they have an autonomous effect upon the process of class formation. But if struggles do have an autonomous effect upon class formation, then the places in the relations of production, whatever they are, can no longer be viewed as objective in the sense of the problematic of "class-in-itself," that is, in the sense of determining uniquely what classes will emerge as classes-in-struggle. What this implies is that classifications of positions must be viewed as immanent to the practices that (may) result in class formation. The very theory of classes must be viewed as internal to particular political projects. Positions within the relations of production, or any other relations for that matter, are thus no longer viewed as objective in the sense of being prior to class struggles. They are objective only to the extent to which they validate or invalidate the practices of class formation, to the extent to which they make the particular projects historically realizable or not. And here the mechanism of determination is not unique: several projects may be feasible at a particular conjuncture. Hence positions within social relations constitute limits upon the success of political practice, but within these historically concrete limits the formation of classes-in-struggle is determined by struggles that have class formation as their effect.

Classes are an effect of struggles that take place at a particular stage of capitalist development. We must understand the struggles and the development in their concrete historical articulation, as a process.

The Process of Class Formation

The great contribution of Gramsci (1971), a contribution developed by Poulantzas (1973), was to recognize that ideological and political relations are objective with regard to class struggles. At least two kinds of determination thus became distinguished: the determination, by the relations of production, of the organization of ideological and political relations and the determination, by the totality of these objective relations, of the relations among the concrete men and women who are their carriers, including the relations of class struggles. Economic, ideological, and political relations as a totality impose a structure upon class struggles, but they become transformed as effects of class struggles. Poulantzas' notion of "double articulation" is a novel and an important one in this context. The form of a class struggle is determined by the totality of economic, ideological, and political relations characterizing a particular historical situation, but it is determined only up to the limits of the possible effects of class struggles upon these relations. To simplify: given a particular conjuncture, a number of practices can be developed, but the range of effective practices, that is, of practices that can have the effect of transforming objective conditions, is determined by these very conditions. This view, which attributes to ideological and political relations the status of objective conditions of class struggles, breaks away from the economistic and historicist elements inherent in the formulation of the "class-in-itself."

Poulantzas rejects the view, which he terms "historicist," according to which classes as historical actors spontaneously appear in one way or another out of the relations of production. He emphasizes the independent role of ideology and political organization in the process of class formation. Yet in the heat of the polemic against historicism, history seems to be scorched with the same flame. It becomes a history that proceeds from relations to effects without any human agency (Cardoso, 1973).

Poulantzas thinks of classes in terms of "pertinent effects" in the political realm of the structure of social relations, which in turn are determined by the totality of forms in which the economic, ideological, and political relations are organized in a given socioeconomic formation. The differentiation of "levels" between economic, ideological, and political leads him to develop a large number of taxonomic categories by which political effects of classes can be identified without examining their organization. He thus develops an elaborate terminology to distinguish places of different classes and fractions in the "block in power": ruling, hegemonic, governing, supporting, and so forth. Yet these classes remain suspended in the air. They never acquire bodily representation; they are never more than "effects" that in turn affect something else, since Poulantzas never inquires into the manner in which classes emerge in a particular form from within the relations of production. Strictly speaking, there is nothing in Poulantzas' language that would allow him to speak of the "working class," "the bourgeoisie," and so forth. Classes appear as such at the level of "social relations," but we are not told how they happen to appear in any particular form.

This difficulty is not new. While Dahrendorf (1964: 252) represents perhaps a universally shared view when he asserts that "class involves a certain amount of class consciousness and political solidarity, if the term is to make any sense at all," already in 1909 Sombart felt that "the greatest impediment to clear comprehension of the term 'social class' is that it is confounded with 'political party'." (1909: 3) So did Plekhanov (Carr, 1966: 29).

The general problem is the following: If classes are thought to exist objectively at the level of the relations of production, then during many historical periods the concept of class may be irrelevant for the understanding of history, such as when these classes do not develop solidarity and consciousness or when they have no political effects. On the other hand, if classes are identified at the level at which they appear as organized or at least "pertinent" political forces, then the problem appears how to trace back these classes to places in the social organization of production. The distribution of the carriers of the relations of production does not become simply "reflected" at the level of politics and ideology; yet the emergence of political forces is nonarbitrary with regard to the distribution of carriers of these relations. Or, to put it bluntly, if everyone who is a manual worker in industry is expected to behave politically qua worker, then the theory is simply false; if everyone who is a potential socialist is considered a worker, then the theory is meaningless in the positivist sense of the word. The first interpretation of marxism is prevalent among many students of political behavior, who then discover a large "residuum" of cleavages other than class, sometimes larger than class cleavage. The second interpretation underlies the kind of voluntaristic thinking in which public service workers were thought not to belong to the working class when the prospects of their unionization seemed dim, yet today they are an integral part of the "working-class majority."

In order to resolve this difficulty it is necessary to realize that classes are formed in the course of struggles, that these struggles are structured by economic, political, and ideological conditions under which they take place, and that these objective conditions – simultaneously economic, political, and ideological – mold the practice of movements that seek to organize workers into a class. I will now examine these assertions.

Perhaps it is most important that the problem is simultaneously theoretical and political. Classes are not a datum prior to the history of concrete struggles. Social reality is not given directly through our senses. As Marx said, and as Gramsci was fond of repeating, it is in the realm of ideology that people become conscious of social relations. What people come to believe and what they happen to do is an effect of a long-term process of persuasion and organization by political and ideological forces engaged in numerous struggles for the realization of their goals (Gramsci, 1971: 192). Social cleavages, the experience of social differentiation, are never given directly to our consciousness. Social differences acquire the status of cleavages as an outcome of ideological and political struggles.[23]

---

[23] E. P. Thompson's succinct clarification of this point is useful: "The class experience is largely determined by the productive relations into which men are born – or enter involuntarily. Class-consciousness is the way in which these experiences are handled in cultural terms: embodied in traditions, value systems, ideas, and institutional forms. If the experience appears as determined, class-consciousness does not." (1963: 9–10)

In turn, Sartre's 1952 discussion is more problematic, in terms of both its place in Sartre's thought and its Leninist overtones. In that text Sartre argued that "the simple objective condition of producer defines the concrete man – his needs, his vital problems, the orientation of his thought, the nature of his relationships with others: it does not determine his belonging to a class." (1968: 96) He continued to argue that "classes do not naturally exist, but they are made," that classes are effects of struggles in which parties (or unions or whatever) are the conditions of effective identity, i.e. the identity of classes as subjects. These assertions express the theses of this chapter, but Sartre's own emphasis on the preideological, prepolitical "simple objective condition of producer" led him at that time to an external, voluntaristic view of the party, namely Leninism.

Classes are not prior to political and ideological practice. Any definition of people as workers – or individuals, Catholics, French-speakers, Southerners, and the like – is necessarily immanent to the practice of political forces engaged in struggles to maintain or in various ways alter the existing social relations. Classes are organized and disorganized as outcomes of continuous struggles. Parties defining themselves as representing interests of various classes and parties purporting to represent the general interest, unions, newspapers, schools, public bureaucracies, civic and cultural associations, factories, armies, and churches – all participate in the process of class formation in the course of struggles that fundamentally concern the very vision of society. Is the society composed of classes or of individuals with harmonious interests? Are classes the fundamental source of social cleavage or are they to be placed alongside any other social distinction? Are interests of classes antagonistic or do they encourage cooperation? What are the classes? Which class represents interests more general than its own? Which constitute a majority? Which are capable of leading the entire society? These are the fundamental issues of ideological struggle. The ideological struggle is a struggle *about* class before it is a struggle *among* classes.

The process of class formation is not limited, however, to the realm of ideology. Political struggles, organized in a particular manner, also have as their effect the very form of the organization of class struggles. Kautsky understood this link clearly. "The economic struggle," he argued, "demands political rights and these will not fall from heaven. To secure and maintain them, the most vigorous political action is necessary." (1971: 186) Political struggles concern the form of the state – of capitalist political relations – because the form of the state structures the form of class struggles (Poulantzas, 1973). In Marx's view, universal suffrage "unchains" class struggles by allowing the dominated classes to openly organize in pursuit of their interests and by providing social mechanisms by which these interests can be pursued within limits. Bonapartism, in turn, is a form of state that forcibly represses class struggle on the part of the workers as well as of the bourgeoisie.

Under capitalist relations of production the carriers of the relations of production do not appear as such at the level of political institutions. Capitalist ideological and legal relations individualize the relations between these carriers as they appear in politics. Within capitalist political institutions they become individuals, "citizens," rather than capitalists, workers, and so on.[24] But this

---

[24] Since Poulantzas' argument to this effect in *Political Power and Social Classes* (1973) is well known, we should perhaps cite an earlier view: "Every minority rule is therefore socially organized both to concentrate the ruling class, equipping it for united and cohesive action, and simultaneously to split and disorganize the oppressed classes. . . . With a more or less conscious division of labor, all these [ideological apparatuses]

clearly does not signify that collective political actors do not constitute class organizations. To the contrary, what it means is precisely that *if* classes are to appear in politics they must be organized as political actors. Again, political class struggle is a struggle about class before it is a struggle among classes.

Neither does economic class struggle emerge mechanically from places within the system of production. Within the context of the problematic of the class-in-itself, it seems as if the relations of production determine *at least* the classes qua historical actors at the level of economic struggles — classes-in-economic-struggle. Lenin, as we know, thought for some time that such classes in economic struggle are determined by the relations of production, but they are all that is determined. If economic struggles could indeed be separated from politics and ideology, or at least if classes were indeed first formed at the level of economic relations and only then became organized politically and ideologically, one could have thought that classes are objectively determined at the level of the empty places within the system of production. Economic struggles, however, always appear historically in their concrete articulation within the totality of struggles, always in a form molded by political and ideological relations. The very right to organize is an effect of struggles that in turn shapes the form of class organization. Hence, the organization of economic struggles is not determined uniquely by the structure of the system of production.

Let us then record some conclusions to which we shall return: (1) classes are formed as an effect of struggles; (2) the process of class formation is a perpetual one: classes are continually organized, disorganized, and reorganized; (3) class formation is an effect of the totality of struggles in which multiple historical actors attempt to organize the same people as class members, as members of collectivities defined in other terms, sometimes simply as members of "the society."[25]

E. P. Thompson once said that "class is defined by men as they live their own history, and, in the end, this is its only definition." (1963: 11) "In the end" this statement is correct, but we must understand more precisely what it means. It does not mean that classes organize themselves spontaneously, once and for all, or in a unique manner. What it does mean is that classes are the continual effects of the totality of struggles, struggles that assume particular forms given the organization of economic, ideological, and political relations.

further the aim of preventing the formation of an independent ideology among the oppressed classes of the population which would correspond to their own class interests; of binding the individual members of these classes as single individuals, mere 'citizens,' to an abstract state reigning over and above all classes; *of disorganizing these classes as classes. . . .*" (Lukacs, 1971: 65–6)

[25] Thus Gramsci says: "The history of a party . . . can only be the history of a particular social group. But this group is not isolated; it has friends, kindred groups, opponents, enemies. The history of any given party can only emerge from the complex portrayal of the totality of society and State. . . ." (1971: 151)

Struggles that take place at any particular moment of history are structured by the form of organization of economic, political, and ideological relations. Politics and ideology have an autonomous effect upon the processes of class formation because they condition the struggles in the course of which classes become organized, disorganized and reorganized.

Luxemburg's view of capitalist democracy emphasizing "the division between political struggle and economic struggle and their separation" is perhaps illuminating here. "On the one hand," Luxemburg wrote,

in the peaceful development, "normal" for the bourgeois society, the economic struggle is fractionalized, disaggregated into a multitude of partial struggles limited to each firm, to each branch of production. On the other hand, the political struggle is conducted not by the masses through a direct action, but, in conformity with the structure of bourgeois state, in the representative fashion, by the pressure upon the legislative body. (1970a: 202)

"The structure of bourgeois state" has at least two effects: it separates the economic from the political struggles and it imposes a particular form upon the organization of classes in each of these struggles. Trade unions become organizations separate from political parties, and the organization of classes assumes a representative form. It is important to have in mind the counterfactual, even if so brilliantly advocated, alternative: the mass strike, which is simultaneously economic and political and in which the entire class directly engages in struggle. The mass strike is viewed as the act of superseding precisely those determinants that are imposed upon the process of class formation by the structure of bourgeois state. Yet in the "parliamentary period," "normal for the bourgeois society," workers become organized to some extent independently by unions and parties, and the masses do not act directly. They act through their leaders who at this moment become "representatives," representatives in the bourgeois state.

The methodological tenets of this analysis are worth repeating. In Luxemburg's view a class becomes formed as more than one collectivity-in-struggle, in this case as unions and electoral parties, but conceivably as cooperatives, clubs, intellectual circles, neighborhood associations, and so on. These collectivities-in-struggle constitute forms of insertion of occupants of places within the system of production in the "bourgeois state," that is, in a particular system of political and ideological relations. The manner in which these multiple collectivities-in-struggle are formed is molded by the structure of the bourgeois state, that is, precisely by the manner in which political and ideological relations are organized in a capitalist society.

Democratic Capitalism and the Organization of Workers as a Class

The assertion that social relations structure class struggles must not be interpreted in a mechanical fashion. Social relations — economic, political, or ideological — are not something that people "act out" in ways reflecting the places that they occupy, but are a structure of choices given at a particular moment of history. Social relations are given to a historical subject, individual or collective, as realms of possibilities, as structures of choice. Society is not a play without a director in which carriers of social relations act out their parts, but rather it is a set of conditions that determine what courses of action have what consequences for social transformations. Classes do not emanate from social relations, whether economic relations alone or in combination with all other relations. They constitute effects of practices, the object of which is precisely class organization, disorganization, or reorganization. Social relations are objective with regard to the processes of class formation only in the sense that they structure the struggles that have the formation of classes as their potential effect.

It is necessary, therefore, to examine the manner in which the organization of a society as a capitalist democracy appears as a structure of choices to those movements seeking to form workers into a class. In particular, I will attempt to demonstrate that the practice of socialist movements is not arbitrary but rather is structured by the economic, political, and ideological relations of capitalist democracy in such a manner as to generate a particular pattern of class formation.

Socialist movements are an outgrowth of historical conditions, and as such they are subject to multiple determinations. Socialist theory itself is nonarbitrary since it constitutes a particular form of consciousness of historical reality. It contains a *telos*, and it is not free of interest, but it also interprets a concrete historical reality. Political predictions are always relative to a purpose, yet they are nonarbitrary in the anticipation of effects of political practices. "Measures of the sort proposed by the Socialist Party," says Kautsky at one point, with a full understanding of this determination, "are calculated to improve the position of the small producers so far as it is possible to improve it under existing conditions. To assist them as *producers* by fortifying them in the retention of their outlived method of production is impossible, for it is opposed to the course of economic development." (1971: 214)

To assert this kind of determination is not to argue, however, that political forces are always compelled by historical circumstances to correctly understand the historical processes in which they participate.[26] Yet unless one adopts the

[26] This seems to be the implication of Lukacs' view (1971) in which the party becomes the organizational

vision in which science develops in the laboratory, one must understand that political practice is a process of theory testing. "We *are* eating the pudding," as Althusser puts it.

This point bears some emphasis. That political forces interpret and mold social reality must not lead us to the conclusion that this process is therefore voluntaristic; that somehow objective constraints exist at the level of social reality qua object of knowledge and yet not at the level of the subject embedded in the very same relations the knowledge of which he produces. If social reality is lawful, so must be the social process that produces the knowledge of this reality.

Socialist forces enter into the process of class formation with a theory of capitalist development and class structure. They become organized on a terrain of particular institutions. Their mode of appeal and of organization is determined both by the theory and by the immediate goals compatible with the theoretical understanding of the concrete conjuncture. In the course of practical activities they discover that some aspects of the theory are not politically operational, that practice guided by the theory is politically or ideologically ineffective. They are compelled, by the very practice, to re-examine the theory in order to identify those elements of it that constitute barriers to effective practice.

What then are these barriers? I have argued that objective conditions appear to the historical actors as structures of choices, as realms of possibility and impossibility. What then are these choices?

The first choice faced by any movement attempting to form workers into a class is whether to participate in the bourgeois political institutions, more specifically, in the electoral institutions. This issue has continued to divide working-class movements, from the split within the First International in 1870 through the debates within the Second International about participation in bourgeois governments until today. Yet precisely because workers are exploited as immediate producers and precisely because elections are within limits instrumental toward the satisfaction of their short-term material interests, all socialist parties either enter into electoral struggles or lose their supporters.

This necessity of organizing workers on the terrain of electoral institutions has profound consequences for the political practice of socialist parties. They become the electoral parties of the working class. And practical consequences

mediation between the "potential" and the "actual" consciousness, where the former constitutes the closest approximation to objective "universal" truth that is possible at a given moment of historical development. See also Colletti (1972: 91) ; and Piccone's apt characterization of Hegelian marxism, in which "the historical validity of the proletarian perspective is *solely a result of its objective goal* of genuine universality through the abolition of classes altogether and, consequently, the realization of a society of subjects." (1975: 156; italics supplied) are sufficiently direct: elections are contests of numbers, electoral success requires recruiting the maximal number of supporters, whoever they may be.[27]

Thus electoral parties of workers face the choice whether to act as a class organization or to seek electoral success. Electoral success requires that class structure be conceptualized in terms of propensity of mobilization and support; it requires socialist parties to adhere to the broadest conceivable concept of the proletariat and even to go beyond this broad concept by emphasizing similar life situations and "parallel interests." In search for electoral support socialist parties appeal to members of other classes as they organize workers into a class.[28]

It may be instructive at this point to return to Kautsky. His analysis of the relations between the occupants of places within the system of production and the socialist movement is formulated in terms of an electoral strategy and its corollary search for support. Kautsky understands that socialist parties are not the only organizations of workers. Socialist parties must cope with the fact that workers are distrustful of socialism, that they still perceive socialism as an idea of the enlightened bourgeoisie. Moreover, differences in skill create an internal division among workers. But this distrust and these differences are being overcome in the form of the "movement of labor, or the labor movement." The proletariat is becoming homogenized: at the expense both of the labor aristocracy and of the disorganized mob. What emerges is a wage-earning industrial proletariat, and this proletariat increasingly comes to dominate all other proletarians. And, "it is precisely this militant proletariat which is the most fruitful recruiting ground for socialism. The socialist movement is nothing more than that part of this militant proletariat which has become conscious of its goal." (1971: 183)

However, the socialist party represents the interests not only of the narrowly defined proletariat, but of all people who are "oppressed and exploited" by capitalism. "The Socialist Party," the Erfurt Programme states, "struggles not for any class privileges, but for the abolition of classes and class-rule, for equal rights and equal duties for all, without distinction of sex and race." (Ibid.: 159) Most important for our discussion, the party represents not only the future universal interest. It promotes interests of people other than workers in its current activity, "it is the champion of all the exploited and oppressed." (Ibid.: 211) It is becoming a *national* party; "It tends to become the representative, not only of

[27] Already in 1886, Engels wrote to an American friend that "one or two million votes . . . in favor of a workers' party acting in good faith, are actually infinitely more valuable than a hundred thousand votes obtained by a platform representing a perfect doctrine." Letter from Engels to Vishnevetsky, December 28, 1886.
[28] Thus elections, contrary to MacIver's or Lipset's views, are not simply a peaceful *expression* of class struggles. They are a form of organization of class struggles. Classes do not simply become organized; they become organized in a particular way. See MacIver (1974) and Lipset (1960).

the industrial wage-earners, but of all laboring and exploited classes, or in other words, of the great majority of the population." (Ibid.: 210) The Socialist Party, the Erfurt Programme asserts, "opposes in present-day society, not only the exploitation and oppression of wage workers, but also every form of exploitation and oppression, be it directed against a class, a party, a sex, or a race." (Ibid.: 160)

But how do socialists appeal to workers, to carriers of capitalist relations of production? Exploitation is not immediately apparent to those whose surplus is being appropriated. The spontaneous experience is one of economic deprivation and one of opportunities for individual advancement. Capitalist relations must be demystified, must be criticized, if the exploitation and the possibility of emancipation are to become visible to the immediate producers. But if any ideology is to be effective in instituting an image of social relations, if it is to achieve the effect of generating a collective project of social transformation, then it must correspond to the manner in which people experience their everyday life. Hence, the effectiveness of socialist ideology with regard to workers depends upon characteristics of their life situation that are secondary from the point of view of class membership, namely, size of revenue, life-style, position within the relations of authority, work conditions, character of work – "misery," "poverty," "oppression." Socialist ideology becomes structured in terms of absolute or relative poverty ("equality"), in terms of work conditions, in terms of life conditions, in terms of all these Weberian characteristics. These characteristics are objective, in the same manner as height, weight, or eye color. Yet they become "real," they come to validate and invalidate the practices of class formation because socialist movements are forced to appeal to these characteristics by virtue of the immediate knowledge generated by the capitalist relations of production.

But these characteristics do not always, and did not since the middle of the nineteenth century, coincide with the theoretical denotandum of the working class.[29] Those separated from the means of production, forced to sell their labor power for a wage, and exploited in the course of capitalist production need not be poor in terms of historically relative criteria. Poverty, oppression, misery, boredom, fatigue, even alienation, do not distinguish workers denoted by the concept of exploitation from all kinds of people who happen to be poor, oppressed, or deprived. Moreover, these secondary characteristics internally differentiate the theoretically defined workers.

---

[29] This is one source of difficulties involved in Lenin's definition of class. According to this definition, "classes are large groups of people distinguished from one another by their positions in a given historical system of social production by their relations to the means of production (usually sanctioned and regulated by law), by their role in social organization of production and, what follows, by the manner of acquiring and the magnitude of the share of social wealth which they dispose. Classes are such groups of people of which one

In conclusion, the political practice of socialist movements has its determinants in the structure of capitalist economic, ideological, and political relations. Inserted into electoral competition, socialist movements view class structure in terms of the interest-determined likelihood of collective identification with the "working class." Given the rules of electoral competition, these movements become concerned about the numbers as they attempt to maximize politically expressed support. At the same time, they are forced to emphasize those characteristics of the narrowly defined proletariat that do not distinguish it from many other groups in capitalist societies.

Political and ideological relations of bourgeois democracy lead to the organization of the working class in the form of mass electoral parties. As a result, the process or organization of workers as a class becomes fused with the process of mobilization of popular political support. These parties at the same time organize workers and seek electoral support of the "masses." They continually seek support among the old petite bourgeoisie and, as capitalist development proceeds, they increasingly focus their organizing efforts on the various categories of people who do not participate directly in the capitalist process of production, in particular the "new middle class."[30]

This fusion of the process of formation of the working class with supraclass political mobilization has consequences that extend beyond a search for electoral allies. It has effects not only upon the manner of class organization of the nonmanual wage-earner, but also upon the general dynamic of ideology in capitalist societies and in turn upon the manner of organization of workers. As socialist movements appeal to people other than workers, they dissolve that privileged nexus, that unique relationship between the proletariat and "its party." They cease to be that "organic" expression of the historical mission of

can appropriate the labor of another because of their different positions in a given economic system." (1949–52, 29: 377)

The problem is that several characteristics that Lenin treats as synonymous do not remain in a constant relation to developmental stages of particular capitalist socioeconomic formations. Size of income need not follow closely the relation to the means of production: in contemporary Sweden incomes from employment slightly exceed those derived from property, although the latter do not include undistributed corporate profits. The role of the owners of the means of production in the social organization of production also becomes altered when the state assumes several functions of private firms.

[30] This elementary formulation of the problem of class formation has direct implications for arguments around the issue of "deradicalization" of the working class in the course of capitalist development. The debate about deradicalization is addressed to an incorrectly formulated problem. What it presupposes, as Bottomore (1966) observed, is that there was some glorious past in which the working class was militant. The working class was simply not organized as a class, and this absence of organization, coupled with a trigger-happy posture on the part of the bourgeoisie, led to instances in which workers were forced to revert to acts of heroism in desperate defense of their subsistence. In the course of history the working class became organized, largely in the form of unions and parties. Collective bargaining and competitive elections make such acts of sacrifice no longer necessary. Organized workers do not have to climb barricades every time capitalism experiences an economic crisis, but this implies little about their "militancy."

the proletariat, distinct from and opposed to all other parties. But the dissociation of the nexus between workers and the socialist movement has the general effect of reinforcing a classless image of society. It decreases the salience of class as the basis for collective identification. It leads, therefore, to the resurgence of other bases of collective identification, whether these are based on the size of revenue, character of work, religion, language, region, sex, or race. In this sense, the process of organization of the masses disorganizes the workers.

Conflicts About Class

Throughout the history of marxist thought the same problem has repeatedly appeared under various guises with regard to class analysis. This problem can be defined as a dilemma in terms of which classes are thought either to emanate spontaneously and uniquely from relations of production or to require a voluntaristic, external agent in the form of a vanguard party if they are to be formed as collective actors. This dilemma leads to practical controversies that focus on the form of party organization (mass versus vanguard), on the strategy of coalitions (tactical versus fronts versus blocks) and on the strategy of revolution (from above versus insurrectionary).

At the same time, this dilemma generates theoretical difficulties, for it makes it impossible to formulate the question of why carriers of economic relations do not act politically as class members, at least in terms other than "not yet." If the places occupied in the relations of production are thought to be the only determinant of collective organization, then, indeed, once the working class is formed as a "class-in-itself," it should progressively become a political actor. Thus, to the extent that workers do not act politically qua workers, marxist theory turns out to be at least "incomplete," and "residual" explanations must be found as to why, for example, French working-class Catholic widows are virtually certain to vote for the Right (Dogan, 1967).

These difficulties arise out of two assumptions that are traditionally found in marxist class analysis: (1) that only the relations of production constitute objective determinants of class relations, and (2) that classes are continuous historical subjects, that is, once they are formed, they only continue to develop as political actors.

An alternative formulation of the problematic of class analysis emerges when some consequences are drawn from Marx's theory of capitalist development and, in particular, when these consequences are placed within the perspective in which (1) ideological and political relations are seen as structuring the processes of class formation in concrete historical conjunctures, and (2) these relations are themselves viewed as being socially produced in the course of class struggles.

Classes then become viewed as continual effects of struggles enclosed within the structure of economic, ideological, and political relations upon the organization and consciousness of the carriers of the relations of production.

By recognizing the objective nature of ideological and political relations, this formulation permits us to analyze the effects of these relations upon the processes in the course of which classes are continually organized, disorganized, and reorganized. Hence, while organized movements are viewed within this perspective as active agents of class formation, their practices are neither "external" to anything nor free from determination. To the contrary, this formulation directs us to analyze the objective determinants of the practices of concrete historical actors with regard to the process of class formation. We have indicated possible directions for such an analysis by showing that, during "normal" times of capitalist democracy, working-class movements must become organized as mass electoral parties that do not distinguish workers from members of other classes.

This formulation leads at the same time to an emphasis on the discontinuity of class organization. Classes are no longer viewed as continuous historical subjects. Class struggles, by which we mean struggles *about* class formation as well as struggles *among* organized class forces, always take place in specific conjunctures. Their form becomes altered with the change of conjunctures, for example, with the introduction of universal suffrage or of legally enforced collective bargaining, with the decay of the legitimizing effects of the market, and, particularly, with changes in the form of capitalist state.

Thus class struggles cannot be reduced to struggles between or among classes. Or, to put it differently, classes-in-struggle are an effect of struggles about class. But who are those who are struggling if struggles about class are prior to classes? In what sense are they prior? Are all struggles class struggles? How can we recognize class struggles?

Who struggles about class formation if struggles about class are prior to classes-in-struggle? In each successive historical conjuncture some carriers of the relations of production are organized as such, some are not organized in any manner, and some appear in struggles about class organization in forms that do not correspond in a one-to-one manner to places occupied in even a broadly conceived system of production, such as "members of the society," "the poor," Catholics, Bavarians, and so on. Perhaps it is better to formulate the point in a converse form: students, women, Protestants, consumers are not classes and to the extent to which they appear as collective actors in struggles, these conflicts are not between or among classes. The concrete actors who appear at the phenomenal level, "in struggle" in a particular historical situation, need not corrrespond to places in broadly conceived relations of production, precisely because they are an effect of struggles. Indeed, the bourgeoisie is successful in the struggles about class when social cleavages appear at the phenomenal level in forms that do not correspond to positions within the relations of production. Thus, in each concrete conjuncture struggles to organize, disorganize, or reorganize classes are not limited to struggles between or among classes.

Does this view imply that Marx's statements concerning class struggle as the universal feature and the motor of history are tautological, since any struggle that might have led to class formation is a class struggle? To put it differently: can there be a historical period in which means of production are privately owned, yet in which no class struggles occur, or is it true by definition that there are always class struggles, whether or not the participants are classes? It seems to me that if class struggle is understood as one between or among classes, then these statements are empirical and false: there have been periods within different modes of production in which conflicts between classes did not occur. If class struggle is understood as any struggle that has the effect of class organization or disorganization, then these statements are tautological. This is how I think they *should* be interpreted. What they assert is that all conflicts that occur at any moment of history can be understood in historical terms if and only if they are viewed as effects of and in turn having an effect upon class formation. These statements play the role of a methodological postulate.

This postulate directs us to analyze the connections between conflicts at concrete moments of time and development over long periods of time. Here lies the uniqueness of marxist theory in general and of the marxist concept of class in particular. As Marx himself realized, the unique status of this theory rests neither upon the observation that societies are divided into classes, nor upon the assertion that societies undergo lawful transformations in the course of their histories; it rests instead upon the postulate according to which class struggle is the motor of history, that is, the concrete conflicts and the long-term developments *systematically* affect each other. Moreover, they do so in a particular manner: conditions inherited from the past determine the realm of possible transformations of these conditions at a particular moment. Under the conditions that are objective in the sense that they are inherited and are thus given at any moment, concrete actors enter into conflicts to preserve or to transform in a particular manner these conditions.

But why should the analysis of this connection between conflicts at a moment and development over time be a *class* analysis, why should it be formulated in terms of the relation between concrete collective actors and places within a system of production and exchange? Why should we ask questions concerning the composition of the concrete collectivities-in-struggle in terms of the locations of their members within the system of production? Why should we ask questions concerning the relations between the historical projects of such collectivities-in-struggle and the interests of people identified again by their location within the system of production? Conversely, why should we analyze outcomes of concrete struggles in terms of their consequences for the preservation or transformation of the relations of production?

It is obvious that concrete struggles can be analyzed in terms other than those of class: they can be analyzed as struggles among groups with different levels of income or different degrees of authority, as struggles between sexes, races, religious groups, regions, ethnic groups, and so on. Should then a conflict over local control of schools, the rift between Catholics and Protestants, or the division between Anglophones and Francophones be analyzed in class terms, and if so, why? Should the feminist movement? Should the black one?

I can only suggest an answer, incomplete and rudimentary. In analyzing any struggle, the questions to be considered are these: What brings the particular conflict about? What led the participants to be organized in the particular form? What are the potential outcomes? What are the consequences of these outcomes for future development? All of these questions concern objective conditions; the conditions that made the emergence of a particular conflict possible, the conditions that made the particular organization, ideology, relations and forces possible, the conditions that make particular outcomes plausible or implausible; and finally, but importantly, the conditions that may be created as the result of a particular conflict. The feminist movement could have become a mass movement only when economic conditions permitted a new division of labor: racial problems in the United States cannot be resolved without a major economic transformation, and so on. This is not to argue that economic, political, or ideological conditions uniquely determine the dynamics of such movements and that the analysis of struggles can therefore be reduced to an analysis of objective conditions. Objective conditions determine realms of possibility, but only of possibility: their analysis is thus necessary but not sufficient for the understanding of concrete struggles.

The theoretical function of class analysis is thus to identify the objective conditions and the objective consequences of concrete struggles. "Class" then is a name of a relation, not of a collection of individuals. Individuals occupy places within the system of production; collective actors appear in struggles at concrete moments of history. Neither of these — occupants of places or participants in collective actions — are classes. Class is the relation between them, and in this sense class struggles concern the social organization of such relations.

Surplus Labor and the "Middle Class"

None of these conclusions should be treated as anything but possible directions into which marxist class analysis might move or perhaps is moving. Several arguments certainly require clarification; several hypotheses call for a historical validation. Nevertheless, it might be useful to examine the implications of this perspective for the specific problem that served as the leitmotif throughout this chapter, namely, the class character of the "middle class."

It has been suggested recently that the theory of the growing polarization between the bourgeoisie and the proletariat was not the only theory developed by Marx, or at least not the only theory consistent with the main core of his economic thought. Nicolaus, in particular, has argued that the polarization thesis dates back to the *Communist Manifesto*, a text written "before Marx had more than the vaguest notions of the political economy of capitalism." But as Marx freed himself from the "Hegelian choreography," he developed a theory that fully anticipated the necessity of the growth of new intermediate classes in the course of capitalist development. The textual evidence cited by the proponents of this thesis consists principally of one quote from the *Theories of Surplus Value*, in which Marx criticizes Ricardo, who "forgot to emphasize . . . the constant increase of the middle classes, who stand in the middle between the workers on the one side and the capitalists and landed proprietors on the other side, who are for the most part supported directly by revenue, who rest as a burden on the laboring foundation, and who increase the social security and the power of the upper ten thousand." (Nicolaus, 1967: 45; Urry, 1973: 176; Gough, 1972: 70)

But the issue does not concern the text. The problem is whether "the law of the surplus class," as Nicolaus terms this thesis, follows from Marx's economic theory or at least is logically consistent with it. Nicolaus, in particular, argues that the emergence of middle classes is a necessary logical consequence of Marx's theory. His argument rests completely on an underconsumptionist reading of Marx. Since workers consume less than they produce, Nicolaus argues, someone must consume more than they produce, ergo, there must emerge a "surplus class." A few quotes from Marx concerning Malthus are then adduced in support of this interpretation.

It is true that production of surplus beyond workers' subsistence is in any society a necessary condition for physical survival of persons who are not directly engaged in the production of those commodities satisfying basic material needs. If there is no surplus, no one but workers can survive. But the converse of this argument − that surplus is a *sufficient* condition for the emergence of the middle class − is both unpersuasive and incomplete.[31]

---

[31] The concept of the "middle class" carries distributional connotations. It has indeed happened in most

The problem of places other than capitalists and workers appears in Marx not because there is surplus product that cannot find consumers but because there is surplus *labor power* that cannot find productive employment. Rejecting the regulatory character of Malthusian population dynamic, Marx argued that, regardless of the dynamic of population, capitalism will in the course of its development reduce the relative number of people who are necessary to produce, thereby generating the "relative surplus population." This is indeed a fundamental law of capitalist accumulation: the production of "relative surplus population" that, as Marx said, "exists in every possible form. Every labourer belongs to it during the time when he is only partially employed or wholly unemployed." (1967, I: 640–4)

The starting point of the analysis of the middle class must be the dynamic of capitalist accumulation. This accumulation has one structural effect of basic importance from our point of view, namely, that it generates surplus labor as a long-term tendency as it generates surplus product repeatedly in single cycles of production. Marx's model, faithfully followed by Kautsky, is the following. Accumulation of capital is a necessary condition of capitalist production. As capital becomes accumulated, capitalist relations of production expand to all areas of economic activity. Subjected to capitalist competition, small producers of all kinds are pushed out of the process of production. They become available for purchase as sellers of labor power, the only commodity they can sell if they are to survive. Yet at the same time, under the pressure of competition, capitalists are compelled constantly to develop and introduce labor-saving innovations, to revolutionize methods of production by increasing the mass and the value of capital in its objectified form and thereby by making production independent of living labor. The result is a growing hiatus between the quantity of available labor power and labor necessary for capitalist production. In a rational society, labor would be distributed in such a way as to provide some free time for everyone.[32] But under capitalism some people are simply excluded from productive exercise of their labor power.

developed capitalist societies that some salaried employees and petits bourgeois obtain incomes larger than most workers and smaller than most capitalists. These patterns of income distribution are important for they construct the immediate experience of social relations and thus serve to validate competing ideologies. But they do not explain, they must be explained. That some people obtain incomes larger than some yet smaller than others does not account for their role as a historical subject in the process of transformation or preservation of social relations. The question is precisely why did class struggles result in the situation in which particular categories of places in the capitalist system obtain particular shares of surplus as revenue. To treat the distributionally defined "middle class" as an actor in the struggles by which shares of surplus product become allocated to particular categories would be clearly tautological, for it would assume exactly that which must be explained. The question is why certain sectors of the petite bourgeoisie and of salaried employees are located in the middle of income distribution; the answer cannot be that it is because they are the "middle class."

[32] There is nothing utopian about fishing in the afternoons.

Surplus labor power is thus generated when capitalist development simultaneously destroys other forms of organization of production and reduces the relative need for labor within the capitalist system of production. The rates of the process by which surplus labor power is generated depend upon (1) the marginal rate of growth of labor productivity with regard to the growth of capital (measurement problems are obvious), (2) the marginal rate at which noncapitalist places of production are destroyed when the productivity of capitalist labor expands, (3) the rate of growth of capital with regard to time, and (4) the rate of growth of population. These indications are probably sufficient to abandon the façade we have maintained above: that this is a simple process, proceeding smoothly and steadily. Clearly, one is directed right back to a theory of capitalist development, and it is at least uncertain whether any such theory can today answer the questions posed by this formulation.

Nevertheless, whatever the exact dynamic of this process, in order to develop a theory of class structure in capitalist formations it is necessary to understand the forms of class organization assumed by this surplus labor power. The problem for Nicolaus is to explain how the "surplus class" assumes the particular form of a "middle class" (Urry, 1973). It is conceivable that all surplus product would accrue to capitalists and surplus labor would starve; it is conceivable that it would be consumed by a "welfare class," composed of those permanently excluded from economic activities; that it would be distributed over the life-spans of different individuals, and so on. In none of these cases would there be a middle class standing "between" workers and capitalists.

Faced with this problem, both Nicolaus and Urry argue that capitalist development makes it technically necessary that a middle class would emerge. "The rise in productivity," Nicolaus asserts, "requires such a class of unproductive workers to fulfill the functions of distributing, marketing, researching, financing, managing, keeping track of and glorifying the swelling surplus product. This class of unproductive workers, service workers, or servants for short, is the middle class." (1967: 46)

It is within this context that we must view the role played by the concept of "productive labor" within the recent controversies about class (Gough, 1972; Poulantzas 1974b; Terray, 1972; Vaisov, 1971). If we accept Mandel's succinct summary, productive labor is "all labor which creates, modifies, or conserves use-values or which is *technically indispensable* for realizing them. . . ." (1971: 191–2) Productive labor becomes a category relevant in the course of discussions of class because it is this labor that is necessary to produce all that is produced, because this is the labor that is exploited, and because this is the labor that is capable of taking over and organizing the process of production without capitalists. It is productive labor that Marx expected to diminish in terms relative to the total supply of labor power, hence producing a "surplus population" that can "exist in every possible form."

The question thus becomes what labor is necessary for capitalist accumulation. Given capitalism at a particular stage of its development, what are the requirements for reproduction of capitalist social relations? The problem is not a definitional one; nor does it have anything to do with any interests, as O'Connor seems to believe (1976). Marx's hair-splitting over workers in storage houses constituted an attempt to answer precisely this question: are all warehouse workers necessary for capitalist accumulation or only those who store products that are perishable (Gough, 1972)?

We do not know what kinds of labor are necessary for the production of capitalist relations. We are today less inclined to believe, as Marx did, that capitalist relations, not only of production but also legal and ideological relations, reproduce themselves "of themselves," by mere repetition of cycles of production (1967, III: 694). We tend to suspect, therefore, that all those people employed in the "apparatuses" are actually necessary for continuing capitalist accumulation. But we have few, if any, specific answers. Actually, the tendency has been to jump into the abyss of functionalism; whatever happens seems to be a "function" that has the effect of reproducing capitalist relations, and all that happens is necessary to reproduce capitalism.

It does not matter that for Nicolaus *un*productive workers are *required* to fulfill the functions, but what is important is that certainly not all of the relative surplus population becomes so functionally employed. While Marx and Engels often emphasized the technical role of capitalists and their delegates as organizers of the process of production and while Marx explicitly mentioned engineers and others as part of the "global laborer," all those people who command, catalogue, manage, mediate, and serve are frequently treated as superfluous artifacts of *political* class relations of capitalism and not as a necessary outcome of capitalist accumulation (Engels: 107).[33] Moreover, Marx's "servants" were certainly not Nicolaus' "middle class." They are people who cannot find any productive employment, who are left to their own fate to "eke out a miserable existence." If they are to succeed in surviving, they can indeed do so only as "servants," and thus they include all those not "usefully" employed: domestic servants as well as policemen, lawyers and criminals, valets and politicians. These are the people

[33] Still in his "choreographic" stage, Marx referred to "an unemployed surplus population for which there is no place either on the land or in the towns, and which accordingly reaches out for state offices as a sort of respectable alms, and provokes the creation of state posts." (1934: 112). Also Gramsci: "The democratic–bureaucratic system has given rise to a great mass of functions which are not all justified by the social necessities of production, though they are justified by the political necessities of the dominant fundamental group." (1971: 13) In the 1970 postscript to "Ideology and Ideological State Apparatuses," Luis Althusser took a surprisingly intentionalist position with regard to this issue, arguing that: "The reproduction of the

whom Kautsky described as "parasites" and about whom Marx had only to say that "from whore to pope, there is a lot of such rubble."

Is the middle class technically indispensable for capitalist accumulation? "The economic machinery of the modern system of production," Kautsky wrote, "constitutes a more and more delicate and complicated mechanism: its uninterrupted operation depends constantly more upon whether each of its wheels fits in with the others and does the work expected of it. Never yet did any system of production stand in such a need of careful direction as does the present one." We would thus expect the author to continue by saying, exactly as Nicolaus and Urry do, that capitalism creates numerous places the function of which is to coordinate, direct, plan, manage, and administer this complicated system. But this is not Kautsky's conclusion. Instead, Kautsky continues, "the institution of private property makes it impossible to introduce plan and order into this system." (1971: 52)

Perhaps one has to go back to *Capital* and particularly to the more popular *Socialism: Utopian and Scientific* to appreciate more fully this emphasis on the anarchy of capitalist production, on the incompatibility of plan and order with the institutions of private property. Living in the post-Keynesian era, we may forget that Marx's theory was written during a time when even a census, not to speak of any encroachment by the state upon the capitalist's sovereignty within a factory, was treated by the bourgeoisie as synonymous with the end of all freedoms and with the advent of the dictatorship.[34] We must not forget the persistent emphasis on the anarchy of capitalist production characteristic of socialist thought of the late nineteenth century. "The contradiction between socialized production and capitalist appropriation," Engels wrote, "now presents itself as *an antagonism* between the organization of production in the individual workshop and the anarchy of production in society generally." (1959: 97–8) While production within each plant is purposeful and organized according to plan, capitalism as a system of production is incapable of overcoming its spontaneous, chaotic nature. Its anarchy leads to periodic crises, crises that accelerate the development of contradictions. And although capitalists respond to the contradictions by forming trusts and monopolies and although eventually

relations of production, the ultimate aim of the ruling class, cannot therefore be a merely technical operation training and distributing individuals for the different posts in the 'technical division' of labour. In fact there is no 'technical division' of labour except in the ideology of the ruling class: every 'technical' division, every 'technical' organization of labour is the form and mask of a *social* (= class) division and organization of labour. The reproduction of the relations of production can therefore only be a class undertaking. It is realized through a class struggle which counterposes the ruling class and exploited class." (1971: 183–4)

[34]   According to Toynbee a census proposed in England in 1753 was "rejected as subversive of the last remains of English liberty." (1956: 7) In an article in the *New York Daily Tribune* of July 22, 1853, Marx cited *The Times* to the effect that "if the parliament prohibited the capitalist to keep workers at work for 12, 16, or some other number of hours, 'England,' says *The Times*, 'would no longer be a country of free people.'"

the state must undertake the direction of production, the anarchy inherent in capitalist production can only be overcome by the abolition of private ownership of the means of production.[35]

In sum, the recent attempts at reinterpretation of Marx's theory of the middle class point to a new direction for the development of marxist theory. Yet thus far they do not advance much beyond Kautsky's analysis. Everyone agrees that, with varying speed, capitalist development leads to the separation of small producers from their means of production and that this process is accompanied by the growth of "surplus labor." Yet two crucial questions remain unresolved: who besides the immediate producers and the organizers of the process of labor is technically necessary for continued capitalist accumulation, and what is the class status of those who are not necessary?

Without imputing it to Marx, let us accept the assertion that some places that are neither those of immediate producers nor of organizers of labor are indeed indispensable for the process of capitalist accumulation to continue. For lack of a better term, let us think of these places as constituting a "reproductive" category — a category composed of such places in the social division of labor that do not involve direct participation in the work of transformation of nature into useful products but that are nevertheless technically indispensable if capitalist production is to continue at the social scale. Engineers as well as teachers of engineers will certainly be located among such places, and perhaps even television broadcasters, if the "ideological apparatuses" are indeed technically needed for the reproduction of capitalist relations of production.

But even if some places other than those of immediate producers and organizers of production are indeed necessary, there exists in each capitalist society a large quantity of labor power that is not used in the processes either of material production or of reproduction of social relations. This is the equivalent of Marx's "surplus labor," corrected for whatever might be the deficiencies of his analysis. The presence of such surplus labor power is manifest, and it becomes reflected in the difficulties that we encounter attempting to analyze the class structure of any developed capitalist society. It is characteristic that, for example, Wright's analysis (1976) of the class structure of American society is limited to the "economically active population," that is, it does not include housespouses, students, retirees, institutionalized population, those more or less permanently on welfare, and so on. In other words, it includes only about one-half of the adult population of the United States.

The capitalist system of production separates in the course of its development a certain quantity of labor power from participation in the process of production,

---

[35] One should also not forget Lenin's statement (in *State and Revolution*) that any cook can be taught to run a socialist society.

even most broadly defined. This separation is, as a tendency, a lawful effect of capitalist development, which implies that any analysis of surplus labor must again constitute a class analysis in the sense described above: it must link the place of surplus labor in concrete historical struggles with the development of the capitalist system of production.

The process of the generation of surplus labor power is a *tendency* in the following sense. While the logic of the capitalist system imposes upon the individual capitalist a rationale that calls for a constant search for increasing productivity, the actions of capitalists as individual rational entrepreneurs are mitigated by the effects of struggles, particularly those that lead to interventions by the state in the system of production. Given the complex model of causality drawn above, the role of struggles with regard to the processes of class formation is twofold. First, class stuggles taking place within each conjuncture have effects upon economic, political, and ideological relations and hence indirectly upon subsequent processes of class formation. Secondly, given the particular structure of economic, ideological, and political relations, class struggles affect directly the class organization of persons located differentially in the system of production. The indirect effects of class struggles have consequences for the entire class structure, since they modify the system of production out of which classes are formed. Thus the very process of the generation of surplus labor is affected by class struggles. Interventions by the state into the system of production have a general effect upon the structure of the economic system, and in several capitalist societies the state has a deliberate policy of class formation. Credit policy, for example, has a direct effect upon the survival of the petite bourgeoisie. On the other hand, the struggle of the unions against automation as well as the demands for full employment may have the effect of retarding the growth of productivity and slowing down the generation of surplus labor.

The central point of this argument is, however, the following: the capitalist system of production does not structure the forms of surplus labor; it generates surplus labor but does not distribute this surplus labor into places-to-be-occupied. It leaves surplus labor as "servants" in Marx's sense. The determination of places is limited to the broadly conceived relations of production, namely, all those relations that are necessary for the continued capitalist accumulation to take place. Beyond the broadly conceived relations of production – distribution, circulation, education, legitimation, and whatever – there are no "places," no positions structured prior to class struggles, no positions to be filled. Surplus labor may assume the form of employment in the state administration; it may assume the form of early retirement, of large standing armies, of ten million college students. It may assume the form of impediments to productive employment of women, it may assume the form of three-day weekends, and so on. The form of organization of surplus labor is not determined by the relations of production. It is directly an effect of class struggles.

What then are the forms that surplus labor may assume? The first is *underemployment*, particularly by the state. By this is meant the situation in which the surplus labor power is purchased for a wage but is not expended for any labor that is necessary either for material production or for reproduction of social relations. Secondly, the surplus labor power may assume the form of a *reserve army* in Marx's sense, that is, the regulator of wage levels. Thirdly, surplus labor may assume the form of a permanent exclusion from employment during the entire lifetime of an individual. Fourthly, it may assume forms *distributed over the life span* of particular individuals, mainly education and retirement. Finally, it may be distributed over the *work span* of an individual in terms of shorter work hours, long weekends, and so on.

Clearly, this list is to some extent arbitrary and its justification would require an extensive discussion. Let me just make a few comments that relate to Marx's own view. Although Marx argued that surplus labor may "exist in any form," including the time when the laborer is not expending his or her labor power, he tended to emphasize the regulatory impact of surplus labor with regard to wages. Marx viewed surplus labor as an undifferentiated quantity of labor power having the function of maintaining wages at the level of subsistence, albeit culturally determined. This model is no longer accurate, if it ever was, since as a result of class struggles a number of institutional barriers has been erected that regulate the access of persons to the system of production. Compulsory education and compulsory retirement are the most important mechanisms of this nature. The quantity of surplus labor that can enter the labor market and hence perform the wage-regulating function has been significantly reduced by such institutional mechanisms. This is not to say that such barriers are irrevocable: the recent attempt to extend the age of retirement in the United States demonstrates that they are not. Nevertheless, surplus labor does not appear in an undifferentiated form. Indeed, the regulatory function of surplus labor has been significantly reduced. Only the first two of the above five categories play this role, and we know empirically that the second category is to a great extent sectorally limited to services and commerce and to women. A varying quantity of surplus labor is in different capitalist societies more or less permanently separated from the system of production, particularly in the United States where it coincides to a great extent with racial lines. Some of the surplus labor is distributed over the life-span, as we have shown above. Finally, some *is* rationally distributed over the work time of particular individuals. Indeed, there have been recent attempts in various countries to "distribute work" along these lines.

The mere existence of surplus labor implies that class analysis of contemporary capitalist societies must not be limited to those places that are structured by the system of production. The argument may bear restatement. I argued that (1) the capitalist system of production structures the places of immediate producers, of the organizers of the process of labor, and perhaps of those who are neither immediate producers nor organizers but who are nevertheless necessary for capitalist reproduction; (2) this system of production in the course of development and under the indirect impact of class struggles generates a certain quantity of surplus labor, but it does not structure the forms of social organization of this surplus labor; and, (3) surplus labor assumes forms that are a direct effect of struggles.

Conclusion

Thus finally we must abandon even the title. It is not the proletariat that is being formed into a class: it is a variety of persons some of whom are separated from the system of production. Processes of forming workers into a class do not take place in a vacuum; rather, they are inextricably tied to the totality of processes through which collectivities appear in struggle at particular moments of history. And the outcomes of these processes, while not arbitrary, are not determined uniquely by the structure of social relations. More than one outcome lies within the limits set by those relations.

The immediate experience of social relations, the experience based on income, the character of the work, the place in the market, the prestige of occupations, and so on, does not of itself become transformed into collective identification since this experience is mediated by the ideological and political practices of the movements engaged in the process of class formation. But as Gough (1972) points out, neither does the distribution of carriers into categories of places in the capitalist relations. Even the relations of exploitation do not of themselves determine a unique pattern of class formation. In an indirect sense, the proletariat is exploited by all other categories with the exception of the petite bourgeoisie. Workers and the petite bourgeoisie are the only producers of all that is consumed. The surplus produced by workers is directly and indirectly (through the state) transferred as revenue to all other categories. In this sense even the poorest of the lumpenproletariat lives off the workers: given capitalist relations of production there are objective bases to the antagonism of workers to the "welfare class." Moreover, it is indeed in the interest of the workers, given again capitalist organization of social relations, that the largest possible share of surplus be retained by capitalists and allocated to accumulation, since in this way future total product is increased. Hence, there exist objective bases for a political alliance between the narrowly defined industrial proletariat and the modern, expansionist fraction of the bourgeoisie. This was true most likely for the 1924–8 alliance between the S.P.D. and the dynamic sector of German industry, not improbably for the Roosevelt "New Deal" coalition, and perhaps for the current alliance between the Communist Party and the Christian Democrats in Italy. This would also have been the nature of the often rumored agreements between the Communist Party and the Christian Democrats in Chile. Note that these are all principally political alliances in which the working class is defined narrowly.

Yet at the same time all categories other than the capitalists and the petite bourgeoisie are separated from the ownership of the means of production and forced to sell their labor power for a wage, unless they can subsist on so-called welfare. Moreover, in Marx's analysis the labor of commercial employees, while not creating surplus value, enables the merchant capitalist to appropriate surplus value without paying the employees the full equivalent of their labor (1967, III: 17). In this sense, both the reproductive and the service categories, while living off the surplus produced by workers, are separated from the means of production, forced to sell their labor power, and in a particular sense exploited by the capitalist. This produces a commonality of interests defined in terms of a number of secondary characteristics, particularly of a distributional nature, and leads to the notion of the working people, the modern equivalent of *les classes laborieuses*. Thus defined, the working class is sufficiently broad to constitute the "working-class majority."

Finally, the strategy can be extended to the formation of the working class defined as "the masses" or "the people," all those exploited and oppressed, poor and miserable. This strategy focuses on prices, taxes, and employment rather than on wages and conditions of work; and it incorporates under the umbrella of "the people" the petite bourgeoisie and the unemployed.

Each of these strategies of class formation, as well as other strategies that would emerge from a more systematic analysis, has consequences not only for the form of class structuring of surplus labor but also directly upon the manner of formation of the working class. The consequences were discussed above. In particular, strategies based on broad definitions of the working class decrease the salience of class and bring forth other cleavages as bases for collective identification and organization.

The limits of these strategies are constituted by the internal conflicts characteristic of each block, what Mao has called the "contradictions among the people." Recent histories of Chile and Italy are veritable laboratories of such practical experiments. Their feasibility can be examined only through political practice and only in terms of a concrete conjuncture. None of the above should be treated as an evaluation of such strategies. I have merely attempted to demonstrate that the multiplicity of strategies has objective bases in the conditions under which the processes of class formation develop under advanced capitalism. At the same time, I attempted to demonstrate the perpetual and discontinuous nature of the processes of class formation. Concrete analysis is incompatible with the view of classes as economically determined, spontaneously emerging subjects that simply march on to transform history. Classes are formed as effects of struggles; as classes struggle, they transform the conditions under which classes are formed.

Postscript: Methodological Individualism and the Concept of Class

The relation between social relations and individual behavior is the Achilles heel of marxism. I will not try to reconstruct Marx's own approach(es) nor try to find the moment when a particular view of this relation dominated marxism. Let me just note that Marx himself, particularly before 1857, and Engels in his nonexpository writings (see particularly the letter to Bloch of September, 1890) treated the society as a contingent product of strategically behaving individuals. As Marx put it in the *Poverty of Philosophy*, "What is society, whatever its form may be? The product of men's reciprocal action." (n.d.: 180) Yet at some time, I suspect under the influence of Engels' naturalism, which took over the marxism of the Second International, marxists began to think about history as if individuals didn't exist. This led to a preoccupation with a number of pseudoproblems, from Plekhanov's *The Role of the Individual in History* to Althusser's "Ideological Apparatuses."

Let me pose the problem analytically. Marxism is a theory that takes as the point of departure for understanding history "objective" social relations, that is, relations that are, in Marx's words, indispensable and independent of anyone's will. Indispensability I take to mean that people located at a particular stage of development of their productive capacities can survive as a species only if they establish a particular form of cooperation. Independence from individual will I interpret to mean that social relations are invariant relations among places-to-be-occupied-by-individuals rather than among specific individuals: the substitution of one individual for another does not alter these relations.[36] Even if Mr

---

[36] Needless to say this is the feature that distinguishes the marxist (or, generally, essentialist) approach to social structure from theoretical approaches in which structure is an attribute of recurrent interactions. In the latter conception, social structure may change as one individual leaves a particular place and is replaced by another, since the structure of interactions is thought to depend upon the particular traits of these

Ford rotated places with Mr Black, the worker with lowest seniority in his factories, after each cycle of production, capitalist relations would remain capitalist.

Given that the theory parts from social relations, the problem becomes to explain how and why does it happen that these social relations are lived by individuals, expressed in their conduct. Mr Black does something presumably *because* he occupies a specific place in the structure of a particular society. Any theory that takes as its point of departure the level of collective organization must account for the mechanisms by which social organization becomes manifested in individual behavior. We have two ways to proceed. One approach I will call "sociological," and the other I will call "economic," but these labels are only for a shorthand reference.

In the sociological approach something becomes "internalized." The society becomes internal to individuals who manifest this internalized society in their actions. Internalization is the key term, typically with mentalistic connotations, although sometimes the psychology is hidden in the black box of behaviorist agnosticism or Althusser's mysterious mechanism of *appellation*.

In the mentalistic conceptions, in which internalization represents a process by which individuals acquire certain states of mind or behavioral predispositions, the individual act is thought to consist of two steps. In the first step, typically associated with the process of "socialization," individuals acquire attitudes that they then carry within themselves throughout a variety of social conditions. In the second step, they act out these internalized patterns of behavior. Associated with a particular kind of an empiricist epistemology, this theory maintains that the internalized patterns can be indirectly observed as such, in their predispositional form, as "attitudes."

In this two-step vision of behavior, deviance appears as the opposite to socialization. Behaviors that deviate from the norm are explained by imperfections of socialization. Any variation of behavior of people exposed to the same norms and socializing agents is interpreted as deviance. To put it differently, from the perspective of internalization, all individuals exposed to the same social norms by the same socializing agents are expected to behave in the same way.

Most importantly, what is characteristic of all the versions of this approach (and there are versions, my description is a caricature) is that they treat all behavior as an *act of execution*.[37] Patterns of behavior are internalized and acted

---

individuals. Hence sociology seeks inductive generalizations, while marxism shares with structuralism the methodological distinction between essence and appearance. Note, however, that Parsons' sociology is dualistic in its treatment of structure.

[37] For a critique of this approach see Bourdieu (1976). My entire discussion owes a debt to Bourdieu.

out. Behavior is the acting out (note that this is also true of Althusser's "theatre") of the internalized society.

Let me immediately point out the consequences of this approach for the concept of class, as it is normally understood with marxism. One is classified as a member of a class by virtue of the position one occupies within social relations. The tautology is deliberate: one is a member of a class because one happens to be a member of this class. Class membership is *the point of departure* for the analysis of individual behavior. We encounter a Mrs Jones. She works as a salesperson in a department store, is an owner of a piece of land that she inherited from her farmer father, is married to a machinist, is the mother of a son studying to be an accountant, and is white and Catholic. We hesitate for a moment on how to classify her but resolve the problem by deciding she is a worker (or a "new petite bourgeoise," depending on whether one follows Wright or Poulantzas).[38] Mrs Jones is a worker, now we are ready to talk about Mrs Jones. She should behave like all other workers: vote Left, join a union, maybe even struggle for socialism.[39] To classify is to homogenize the determinants. As a worker she shares conditions and motivations with workers and thus shares behaviors with workers. The mode of explanation is: (1) Mrs Jones sells her labor power for a wage (observation). (2) Therefore, she is expected to act as a worker (prediction). One may complicate matters by introducing intermediate steps, the specific working-class culture, and say that (2a) the working-class culture is . . ., and (3) Mrs Jones calls herself a "Mrs" rather than "Ms" because such is the working-class culture.

But note that there is one behavior of Mrs Jones that has escaped the explanatory power of this paradigm: Mrs Jones sells her labor power for a wage. Presumably, she does so not because she has internalized the norms of being a worker but because that is what she does. The question of why Mrs Jones sells her labor power cannot be answered in this way. And this question is fundamental for the understanding of the relation between social structure and individual behavior. To make it less marxist-complex, imagine that an ad appears in the local paper that says, "The means of production cannot be put into motion unless someone (anyone; we assume homogeneous labor) will sell his labor power for a wage. Please apply to Mr Smith who already occupies a contradictory location in our company. Telephone number, and so forth." And there is Mrs Jones — a lady who owns some land, is married to a machinist, is a mother of a prospective accountant, and is white and Catholic. Mrs Jones

---

[38] Although my general points use workers as examples, they can be applied more generally as well.

[39] By evidence we may also decide that since Mrs Jones is a Catholic female worker she should be expected to join a union, vote Right, and adhere to the repressive minority, which she would call the "moral majority." The intellectual procedure would remain the same. We will only explain more variance of the observed behavior.

answers the ad and, in a Wonder Woman whirl, she enters into the social relations of production as a personification.

We could accept this kind of a theoretical posture: all the (relevant) behaviors of Mrs Jones are to be explained by the internalization of norms with the exception of her phone call to Mr Smith, which is to be explained differently. This is, I believe, what marxists have been doing as sociologists. The awkwardly dualistic aspect of this posture apart, we would still need to explain why Mrs Jones is a worker. One answer may be, and sometimes is, that the question is trivial since Mrs Jones has no choice. Dispossessed of the means of production and equipped with an instinct of self-preservation ("the first human need" of *The German Ideology* (Marx and Engels, 1964), although there, I think, it functions as a methodological postulate, not as a metaphysical assumption), Mrs Jones cannot survive but by offering her only endowment for sale.

But Mrs Jones does have a choice. After all, she owns some land, which she can perhaps sell; she is married to a machinist, who can perhaps work overtime; and she has, or will have, an accountant son, who might help her set up a resale shop. Many American workers eventually do succeed in owning their own business. Why could not Mrs Jones? If Mrs Jones becomes a worker, it is not because she was directed to do so by an internalized norm, nor because she has no choice; she becomes a worker because she *chooses* to become a worker.

Since I do not cherish being an object of ridicule, let me explain what I mean. Clearly, I do not mean that people decide to be workers at their pleasure, offended by a life sparkled by diamonds and rocked only by yacht decks. What I mean is the following. Mrs Jones has some goals;[40] for example, she seeks, with the assistance of her family, to maximize the current value of her consumption stream when she becomes a widow, which as a wife of a worker she is likely to become. She also has resources: her labor power, the unused labor power of her husband and son, some social connections (she may already know Mrs Smith; see Granevetter), and some credit (although she is probably a net debtor; see Kaldor, 1972). She now sits around a table with her family and friends and thinks how to realize her objective given the constraints of family resources. She enrolls in an optimization course and upon graduation she decides that the best thing for her to do is to become a worker. She has objectives and resources: she chooses to become a worker. Her objectives and her resources do not classify her as a worker; she decides to become a worker given her objectives and resources.

In what sense did Mrs Jones choose? Given her objectives and constraints and

---

[40] The fundamental weakness of the economic approach, and of economics, lies right here. Marx was the last thinker who simultaneously viewed behavior as a rational, strategic conduct and sought to explain how people acquire their historically specific rationality, including preferences. The effect of the marginalist revolution was to abandon this question and to introduce the separation between economics and sociology that I am reproducing here.

that she has the know-how acquired in the course, she will choose what is best for her. That is predictable. In that sense, perhaps, she did not have a choice. But she did go through a process of choosing – of perceiving, evaluating, and deciding. If choice is seen as simply an aspect of the *conditions* she faces in life, she has no choice. If choice is an aspect of *behavior*, she did choose. Indeed, it is possible to study choice behavior scientifically because outcomes can be predicted given conditions and objectives.

Let me now indicate some consequences of this approach. First, note that in this view social relations are treated as structures of choices available to actors, not as sources of norms to be internalized and acted. Social relations are the structures within which actors, individual and collective, deliberate upon goals, perceive and evaluate alternatives, and select courses of action. As a corollary, let me repeat what was said in the body of the text, namely, that social relations must themselves be viewed as a historically contingent outcome of, to use Marx's phrase again, "men's reciprocal actions." That is, while social relations constitute a structure of choices within which actors choose, their choice may be to alter social relations. Social relations are not independent of human actions. It is not in this sense that they are "objective." They are objective, indispensable, and independent of individual will only in the sense that they constitute the conditions under which people struggle over whether to transform their conditions.

Second, classes are no longer a given either. They too are historically contingent products of reciprocal actions. Existing conditions may hurl women into the labor (power) market; other conditions may prevent them from becoming workers. Conditions may swell the ranks of the petite bourgeoisie; other conditions may destroy it. And these conditions are themselves a product: of a land reform, of a welfare system, of old-age insurance, of distributional conflicts. Class structure can no longer be read from the relations of property alone, since the structure of choices that results in class formation is an outcome of conflicts also in the realm of politics. It was the French revolution after all, not the steam engine, that produced the French peasantry.

Finally, the central problem. We have had enormous difficulties in understanding politics in terms of class conflict. These difficulties are due to a number of assumptions, too complex and too numerous to be recounted. Until Olson, we thought that similarity breeds solidarity, and even in the face of his criticism one might find reasons why this would be true of workers (but not of capitalists).[41] But, I think, the problem remains, and its origins are still in Marx's

[41] Here are some reasons why the free-rider paradox might not be true of workers. Workers have no choice but to join ranks. See Roemer (1978). Since workers encounter the same situation recurrently, they may adopt long-term cooperative strategies even if these are inferior in the short run. See Edel (1979). The general approach is developed in Taylor (1976). Workers may modify each other's preferences through a process of "dialogue." See Offe and Wiesenthal (1980).

formulation of the transformation of the class-in-itself into the class-for-itself. Specifically, having been educated by Roemer (1982), I now think that the whole difficulty stems from taking class positions as a given from which to begin the analysis. Individuals face choices, and one choice might be to become a worker and another choice might be to cooperate with other workers. But they do have choices, and we must analyze the entire structure of choice as given to individuals, not to workers. For it may be that there exist conditions under which their choice is to become workers and cooperate with capitalists against other workers and the optimality of this strategy may be incomprehensible if we truncate the choice set by viewing individuals as ready-made workers. It may be that blacks and whites do not cooperate as workers because it is rational for capitalists to divide and rule (Roemer, 1979) but it still remains that they do not cooperate because they are black and white, not only workers. Segmented labor markets imply different structures of choice for people with different individual endowments, and segmented labor markets breed disunity among those who become workers. Let me thus join in the pleas for a methodological individualism.

3. Party Strategy, Class Organization, and Individual Voting*

Political Parties and the Voting Behavior of Individuals

Why is class important in molding individual voting behavior in some societies but not in others, during some periods of time but not during others? Why are Norwegians more likely to vote on the basis of class than the French? Why are Swedish workers more prone to vote Social Democratic today than they were sixty years ago?

These are not questions about individuals. For even if individual acts tend to coincide with individual traits, why do individuals endowed with some attributes vote the way they do? Reduction does not suffice as an explanation because the causal path from individual traits to individual acts passes through the totality of social relations. "The counting of votes," wrote Antonio Gramsci, "is the final ceremony of a long process." (1971: 193) This is a process of forming images of society, of forging collective identities, of mobilizing commitments to particular visions of the future. Class, ethnicity, religion, race, or nation do not happen spontaneously, of themselves, as a reflection of objective conditions in the psyches of individuals. Collective identity, group solidarity, and political commitments are continually forged — shaped, destroyed, and molded anew — as a result of conflicts in the course of which political parties, schools, unions, churches, newspapers, armies, and corporations strive to impose upon the masses a particular vision of society. The relation between places occupied by individuals in society and their acts is a contingent historical product of conflicts that confront interests and images, that involve preferences and strategies, that bring victories or defeats. Political behavior of individuals can be understood only in concrete historical articulation with these conflicts: particular traits become causes of individual acts when they are embedded within a definite structure that has been imposed upon political relations at a given moment of history.

The organization of politics in terms of class is not inevitable. There is nothing inherent in capitalism and nothing in the logic of history that would

* This chapter was written jointly with John Sprague.

make inexorable the emergence of classes as collective subjects. Class position structures the daily experience of individuals, generates a certain kind of knowledge, endows people with interests, and under some circumstances may even evoke an understanding of a shared lot, a feeling of similarity. But this experience does not become spontaneously collectivized as one of class. As Marx said, and Gramsci was fond of repeating, people become conscious of social relations in the realm of ideology, individuals become aware of conflicts of interest at the level of ideology. Roberto Michels put it sharply: "It is not the simple *existence* of oppressive conditions, but it is the *recognition of these conditions by the oppressed*, which in the course of history constituted the prime factor of class struggle." (1962: 228) Class relations are not spontaneously transparent at the level of the "immediate" (Gramsci, 1971), the "lived" (Althusser, 1971) experience — the experience which is simply a reflection upon everyday life. The spontaneous experience may be one of poverty, of compulsion, of inequality, of oppression. It may be one of similarity. But it is not an experience of class.

Even similarity need not breed solidarity. People who are in a similar situation and who have identical interests often find themselves in competition with one another. As Marx and Engels noted already in the *Communist Manifesto*, "the organization of the proletariat into a class, and consequently into a political party, is continually being upset by the competition among workers themselves." (1967: 144). "The simple objective condition of producer," Jean-Paul Sartre emphasized, "defines the concrete man — his needs, his vital problems, the orientation of his thought, the nature of his relationships with others: it does not determine his belonging to a class." (1968: 96)

Thus the division of a society into classes does not necessarily result in the organization of politics in terms of class. Nor is the experience of class the only one which is objective. If "objective" means experience that is inherited by individuals and independent of individual will, then being a Catholic today in Italy is an objective experience, as is being a Black in the United States, or a woman in France. The people who perpetuate their existence by selling their capacity to work for a wage are also men or women, Catholics or Protestants, Northerners or Southerners. They are also consumers, taxpayers, parents, and city-dwellers. They may become mobilized into politics as workers, but they may also become Catholic workers, Catholics, or Bavarian Catholics. Hence, in spite of the wealth of information we do have today about the patterns of individual voting, the question remains open: why do people vote the way they do?

The thesis of this study is that individual voting behavior is an effect of the activities of political parties. More precisely, the relative salience of class as a determinant of voting behavior is a cumulative consequence of strategies pursued by political parties of the Left. Hence, this is a study of voting but not of voters, predicated on a theory of the system of economic and political organization under which political parties formulate their strategies and individuals cast their votes.

Political parties – along with unions, churches, factories, and schools – forge collective identities, instill commitments, define the interests on behalf of which collective actions become possible, offer choices to individuals, and deny them. Political parties are not simply reflections of class structure or expressions of class interests. They are relatively autonomous from both the social structure and state institutions, and they play an active role with regard to both. The organization of politics in terms of class is always a result of conflicts in which multiple forces strive to maintain or to alter in various ways the existing social relations. Is the society composed of classes or individuals with harmonious interests? Are classes the fundamental line of social cleavages or are they subordinate to some other divisions? What are the classes? Are interests of classes antagonistic or do they encourage cooperation? Which classes represent interests more general than their own? Which are capable of leading the entire society? These are the issues in which political parties play a crucial role.

Different parties, however, play different roles. Conflicts over the political salience of class are characterized in any capitalist society by a basic structural asymmetry. The organization of politics in terms of class can be attempted at most by one specific class, workers. In any capitalist system, the principal competing visions of society are one of class and one of universalism, and both of these ideologies rationalize interests. The claims of workers as a class are particularistic, and when workers organize as a class they seek to impose upon the entire society the image of a society divided into classes, each endowed with particularistic interests. Specifically, to legitimize their claims, workers must show that capitalists are also a class, whose interests are also particularistic and opposed to other classes. Capitalists, in turn, cannot represent themselves as a class under democratic conditions and do so only in a moment of folly. The response to the particularistic claims of the working class is not a particularism of the bourgeoisie but ideologies which deny altogether the salience of class interests. Ideologies of the bourgeoisie do not emphasize its specific interests but propose a universalistic, classless image of society, composed of individuals–citizens, whose interests are basically in harmony. Hence, ideological conflicts concern rarely, if ever, the legitimacy or justice of particularistic claims made by various classes. Instead, they juxtapose a particularistic image of society put forth by organizations of workers and universalistic visions propounded by spokesmen of the bourgeoisie. And as a consequence, the relation between parties and classes is not the same for different classes. The bourgeoisie rarely, if ever, appears as a separate party, to promote its class-specific interests. Capitalists operate politically through all kinds of parties which claim to represent universal national interests.

This argument does not imply that organizations of workers never make universalistic claims, portraying interests of workers as those of the society, not only for the future but also at the present. This kind of universalistic stance is to be expected of any party seriously engaged in the competition for votes. Our argument is rather that class is important in a society if, when, and only to the extent to which, it is important to some political parties, which organize workers as a class. Workers are the only class which is a potential proponent of the class image of society: when no political party seeks to organize workers as a class, separately from and in opposition to all other classes, the class image of society is absent altogether from political discourse. Hence, historical variations in the salience of class as a determinant of political behavior can be attributed to the strategies pursued by political parties. To return to Gramsci, "One should stress the importance and significance which, in the modern world, political parties have in the elaboration and diffusion of conceptions of the world, because essentially what they do is to work out the ethics and the politics corresponding to these conceptions and act, as if it were, as their historical 'laboratory'." (1971: 213)

The Dilemma of Class-Based Parties

The historical experience of class-based electoral parties has been shaped by the combination of two structural features of their social and political environment: workers never were and would never become a numerical majority in their respective societies and the political institutions of democratic countries are based on majority rule. This combination of minority status with majority rule constitutes for party leaders the structure of choices within which they deliberate upon goals, perceive and evaluate possibilities, choose strategies, and act. Leaders of class-based parties must choose between a party homogeneous in its class appeal but sentenced to perpetual electoral defeats or a party that struggles for electoral success at the cost of diluting its class orientation. This is the alternative presented to socialist, social democratic, labor, communist, and other parties by the particular combination of class structure and political institutions in democratic capitalist societies.

Socialists entered into the electoral competition, in most Western European countries around 1890, deeply persuaded that they would eventually win the support of an overwhelming majority and legislate their societies into socialism. The syllogism was simple and persuasive. Since workers were to become an overwhelming majority of the population as capitalist development continued to destroy the petty property of farmers, merchants, craftsmen, and artisans, and since elections are an expression of numbers, socialists would obtain the electorate mandate of an "immense majority," to use Marx's phrase. As a young Swedish theoretician put it in 1919, democracy "contains an automatically operative device that heightens the opposition to capitalism in proportion to the development of capitalism." (Tingsten, 1973: 402)

Moreover, socialists entered into the electoral competition at the time when workers were separated from the rest of society not only economically but also socially and politically, through class-specific restrictions of suffrage, and when they saw themselves as a separate group (Rosenberg, 1965: 161 and 165; Bergounioux and Manin, 1979: 25). Workers distrusted any influences originating from the outside: socialist parties had to become workers' parties if they were to be supported by workers (Landauer, 1959, I: 457–8; Fusilier, 1954: 29). Necessity and hope coincided: socialists had to become the party of workers and they were to win elections as a party of workers.

Yet, even if socialist theoreticians were persuaded that the eventual proletarianization of the great masses is an inexorable tendency of capitalist development, they saw no reason to wait for history to take its course. As soon as they decided to compete for votes, some time between 1884 and 1892 (Haupt, 1980: 88), socialist parties sought to gain the electoral support of people other than workers. The two parties which faced a predominantly agrarian class structure, the French *Parti Socialiste* (Guesdists) and the Danish Social Democrats turned for support to small farmers as early as 1888 (Landauer, 1959, I: 447; Landauer, 1961). Appeals to other classes were formulated by the German S.P.D. at the Erfurt Congress of 1891 (Kautsky, 1971), the Belgian *Parti Ouvrier* in 1894 (Landauer, 1959, I: 468), the British Labour Party in 1918 (McKibbin, 1974: 95–7, a polemic with Beer, 1969). In Sweden, the multi-class strategy was debated as early as 1889 and was adopted in 1911 (Tingsten, 1973). Only Germans, as always theoretically minded, could not reconcile what they did with what they thought until 1927, when they finally decided that the law of concentration of capital does not apply to agriculture (Hunt, 1970).

Once they decided to compete for the votes of "allies" – some groups other than workers – socialists were appealing to an overwhelming majority of the population. And yet no party ever won the votes of an overwhelming majority. Socialist parties struggle to reach 50 percent of votes cast where they are most successful. They never win the support of 50 percent of those entitled to vote. Moreover, they cannot even obtain the votes of all workers – of the proletariat in the classical sense of the word. (For the history of this concept see Sombart, 1909; Furet, 1963; and above, Chapter Two.) In several countries as many as one-third of workers do not vote for socialist parties; in some, one-half of workers vote for bourgeois parties. Socialist parties appear condemned to minority status when they are a class party of workers and they seem relegated to the minority when they seek to be the party of the masses. They are in a dilemma.

Their experience is not uniform. By relative standards the Swedish Social Democrats have been quite successful electorally during most of their history while, say, the Dutch Party has been less so. But by invoking relative standards one often forgets that absolute standards exist as well; one proceeds as if the common fate did not require an explanation. And yet it is that which different histories have in common that illuminates the limits of our historically inherited possibilities. Before asking why this party has been more successful than that one, can we ignore the fact that none has been successful in terms of its own dreams and designs, that not one has brought to realization the very purpose of its foundation?

The Electoral Trade-Off

The choice of electoral strategy constitutes a dilemma for socialist and other left-wing parties if neither the strategy of relying exclusively on the support of workers nor the strategy of seeking votes regardless of their class origins is successful in conquering the support of that overwhelming majority which would be required for a socialist transformation. The strategy of keeping the party class-pure, of leaving the emancipation of the working class to workers themselves, could not be successful because, contrary to the expectations with which socialists initially entered electoral competition, workers never were, and would never become, the majority of the electorate in their societies.

Clearly, the validity of this assertion depends upon the definition of workers one adopts. We define workers in a narrow way, as manual wage-earners employed in mining, manufacturing, construction, transport, and agriculture, persons retired from such occupations, and inactive adult members of their households. This is the way socialists understood this concept before all the ambiguities resulting from the appearance of salaried employees began to appear. Moreover, even if some parties eventually used the term worker more broadly, as in "workers by hand or brain," they continue until today to distinguish workers as we define them from other groups of wage-earners in their strategic analyses. Hence, a narrow definition is the appropriate instrument for analyzing socialist strategies.[1]

---

[1]   Given this narrow definition, the proportion of workers in the electorate peaked in Belgium at 50 percent in 1920, in Denmark at 28 percent in 1960, in Finland at 23 percent in 1917, in France at 36 percent in 1928, in

But the specific definition also involves a bet on our part: a hypothesis that the line of sharpest divisions, of interest and values, lies between narrowly defined manual workers and other wage-earners. We test this hypothesis below.

On the other hand, the strategy of seeking electoral support among people other than the industrial proletariat could not be successful if this strategy were to lead to an erosion of socialist strength among workers. There are two reasons to expect that such a trade-off between the support by non-workers and the ability of the party to mobilize and hold the support of workers would indeed occur.

The first reason is that by broadening their appeal to the middle classes socialist parties dilute the general ideological salience of class and, consequently, weaken the power of class as a cause of the political behavior of workers. When political parties do not mobilize individuals as workers, but as the masses, the people, the nation, the poor, or simply as citizens, the people who are men or women, young or old, believers or not religious, city- or country-dwellers, in addition to being workers, are less likely to see the society as composed of classes, less likely to identify themselves as class members, and eventually less likely to vote as workers. Class identity ceases to be the only conceivable source of workers' political commitments: one can no longer recall, as Vivian Gornick did recently, that "before I knew I was a woman and I was Jewish, I knew I belonged to the working class". (Gornick, 1977: 1) As socialists appeal to voters in supraclass terms, they weaken the salience of class and either reinforce the universalistic ideology of individuals–citizens or leave room open for competing particularistic appeals of confessional, ethnic, or linguistic identities. As socialists become parties like other parties, workers turn into voters like other voters.

But the relation between political parties and workers is not only an ideological one. Class interest is something attached to workers as a collectivity rather than a collection of individuals. Individual workers and particularly workers of a specific form or sector have powerful incentives to pursue their particularistic claims at the cost of other workers (De Menil, 1971; McDonald and Solow, 1981; Wallerstein, 1982) unless some organization — a union confederation, a party, or the government directly — has the means of enforcing collective discipline.

When socialist parties extend their appeal to people other than workers they can no longer represent the interests that constitute the public goods for

Germany at 37 percent in 1903, in Norway at 32 percent in 1950, and in Sweden at 40 percent in 1950. Hobsbawm (1978), while presenting an argument similar to ours, refers to British data according to which workers would have constituted 75 percent of the population around 1870 but neither his definition of workers nor his definition of population is quite clear.

workers as a class but only those interests which workers share as individuals with other people. While supra-class-orientated socialist parties continue to be parties of workers as individuals, they cease to constitute the organization of workers as a class — an organization that would discipline individuals or groups of workers in their competition with one another by promoting confrontation with other classes. It is the principle of class conflict — of "stopping competition among the workers so that they can carry on general competition with the capitalist" (Marx, n.d.: 123) — that is compromised when class parties become parties of the people.

This is why the dilemma appears with a vengeance within the system of electoral competition. When socialists seek the support of other people they erode the very sources of their strength among workers. To be effective in elections they cannot remain class-pure and yet they can never cease altogether to be a party of workers. They seem unable to win either way.

It has been forcefully argued that the effect we hypothesize would occur only if a party were to appeal to the class interests of non-workers (such as, we suppose, credit for the petite bourgeoisie or land for peasants) but not if a party were to add to the working-class program non-class demands, such as, Erik Olin Wright's example, honest government. We agree that there are some demands, and the example is well chosen, which workers would support along with other individuals. But when parties call for cleaning up the government they are not propagating class ideology and when they organize town meetings they are not organizing workers as a class. Workers may be in favor of honest government and any and all parties that call for honesty, but mobilization around non-class issues does not reinforce the casual force of class as a determinant of individual behavior.[2]

The first hypothesis of this study asserts, therefore, that socialist parties did not win an overwhelming majority of the vote, not even of those whom they viewed as potential supporters, because their efforts to extend their electoral appeal diminished the salience of class as a determinant of the political behavior of workers. There exists a trade-off between the recruitment of middle classes and of workers: when socialist parties direct their efforts to mobilizing the support of allies they find it increasingly difficult to recruit and maintain the support of workers.

[2] Several other people, in addition to Erik Olin Wright, who commented on earlier versions of this chapter posed the same issue historically, pointing to the "new social movements" as the qualitatively new potential ally for the working class and arguing again that appeals by left-wing parties to such people mobilized by such movements would not have a negative effect upon the recruitment of workers. We continue to be skeptical, however, since we do not see these movements as qualitatively new. Socialists sought support from women, youth, various cultural movements, and in some countries even teetotalers and religious groups already sixty years ago. These are, of course, theoretically complex and politically crucial issues and we certainly do not think they are closed.

This trade-off need not be obvious. The socialist vote can grow during some periods simultaneously among middle classes and workers as it did in several countries. Electorally motivated strategies to gain the support of the middle classes have been successful in West Germany, where, according to surveys, the S.P.D. vote among *Beamte und Angestellte* increased from 27 percent in 1953 to 50 percent in 1972 while the proportion of workers voting socialist increased at the same time (in fact only from 1969 to 1972) from 58 to 66 percent (Pappi, 1973, 1977). In Sweden, the proportion of non-workers voting socialist increased from 23 percent in 1956 to 34 percent in 1968 while the proportion of workers hovered around 80 percent (Särlvik, 1977; Esping-Anderson, 1979). These experiences are not contrary to our theory.

The reason why the existence of the trade-off may not be evident during some, even long, periods is that the pool of workers available for socialist recruitment may be large in relation to the negative effects of the multi-class strategy upon them. Let $W(t)$ represent the proportion of the electorate consisting of workers voting socialist during the t-th election.[3] Let $\Delta W(t)$ be the change of this proportion between any two consecutive elections, from the t-th to the $(t + 1)$st, where $t = 0,1 \ldots$. Finally, let $X(t)$ represent the proportion of the electorate consisting of workers, defined throughout as manual wage-earners in mining, manufacturing, construction, transport, and agriculture, and their adult dependents. Given these definitions, the pool of workers from which additional socialist voters can be recruited for the $t + 1$st election consists of workers who did not vote socialist during the t-th election, or $[X(t + 1) - W(t)]$.[4] If a particular party recruits available workers with some average efficiency p, then the proportion of socialist voting workers in the electorate grows by the amount $p[X(t + 1) - W(t)]$ between two consecutive elections. But if the cumulative success of the party among the middle classes does in fact diminish its effectiveness in recruiting workers, then the growth of workers' socialist votes will be checked. Let $N(t)$ be the proportion of the electorate consisting of socialist voting allies: some specific groups other than workers to whom the party appeals for electoral support. Then the change of the socialist vote of workers between any two consecutive elections may be represented by

[3] By the electorate we mean all persons who have the legal right to vote (or register and vote) in a particular election. All of the vote shares in this analyses are defined to the base of the electorate, which means that workers who do not vote socialist either vote for bourgeois parties or do not vote. To transform shares of the electorate into shares of votes actually cast divide the former by the turnout.

[4] This pool is heterogeneous. At some moment, particularly in the aftermath of extensions of the franchise to workers (often first male and only later female), it consists mainly of non-voters. During periods of rapid industrialization this pool also might contain people who had just become workers and who had not yet had a chance to vote. Finally, it comprises workers who vote for bourgeois parties.

$$\Delta W(t) = p[X(t + 1) - W(t)] - dN(t).[5] \tag{1}$$

One can see immediately that even if d is positive the socialist vote can grow simultaneously among workers and other groups as long as the pool of workers available for recruitment is sufficiently large. This was clearly the case when socialist parties first entered electoral competition: workers constituted at that time a sizeable proportion of the electorate in many countries and few of them voted socialist, since many did not vote at all.[6] The trade-off becomes apparent only when the party has achieved some success among workers and allies. At some time, when a large proportion of workers and allies vote socialist, the mobilization of additional allies may result in a fall of support among workers. This will happen at the moment when the party's efforts to recruit new workers are exactly offset by the effect of the middle-class strategy upon them. This is the moment when $p[X(t + 1) - W(t)] = dN(t)$ and the socialist vote of workers is stationary at the level given by[7]

$$W^* = X - (d/p)N \tag{2}$$

where X is assumed constant. If an additional non-worker votes for a party that just won W^* of the workers' votes, the party's vote among workers will fall by the quantity (d/p).

In fact, a party may never win as many as W^* votes of workers and its support among workers may never decline. Hence the trade-off may never be immediately evident. But as long as d is positive, the party pays an opportunity cost for winning middle-class votes throughout its history.

Note that if an additional ally votes for a party that just won W^* of the workers' votes, the party will gain altogether $(1 - d/p)$ votes: the vote cast by the non-worker minus the loss among workers. If d is greater than p, the party will lose votes if it pursues a middle-class strategy past this moment. If the value of d/p is such that $0 < d/p < 1$, then the party will gain votes in the aggregate but at the cost of losing net support among workers. And if d were negative, and $d/p < 0$ our entire theory would be false: such a value would indicate that workers behave as bandwagon voters, more likely to vote socialist when the party is successful among non-workers.

We will refer to any value of $W(t)$ which satisfies equation (2) as W^* – the carrying capacity of the party among workers. The carrying capacity is the

[5] From the descriptive point of view it would have been better to write $\Delta W(t) = [p - dN(t)]$ $[X(t + 1) - W(t)] - dN(t)W(t) = p[X(t + 1) - W(t)] - dN(t)X(t + 1)$. But there are good reasons to avoid non-linearities and the qualitative conclusions are not affected.
[6] Only about one-half of eligible male workers (52 percent of group III) voted in the 1911 election in Sweden according to the official statistics (Särlvik, 1977: 391). More generally, Rokkan and Valen (1962: 158) point out that "new eligibles were mobilized after, rather than before extensions of suffrage."
[7] W^* is obtained by setting $\Delta W(t) = 0$ in (1) and solving for $W(t) = W^*$.

equilibrium value of the socialist vote among workers conditional on $N(t)$. If at any time the proportion of the electorate consisting of socialist voting workers happens to equal W^* then this proportion remains at W^*. Equation (2) specifies a linear trade-off between the vote of allies and of workers. The intercept of this line is $X(t)$ while the parameter (d/p) measures the severity of the trade-off confronting a party in equilibrium. As an illustration, Figure 1 shows the equilibrium trade-off for the Swedish Social Democrats under the 1964 class structure. The values of the parameter d and the measures of trade-off (d/p) are presented in Table 1 for all of the Left parties combined and for the major socialist parties separately. An explanation of how those numbers were calculated is provided in the Appendix.

The parameter d is positive in all cases: even if its values are at times quite low, every party faces some trade-off.[8] The differences among major socialist parties are highly pronounced. Wherever social democrats compete with a large communist party their trade-off is extremely steep: the German S.P.D. faced the loss of 16.7 workers per each ally it recruited and the French Socialists the loss of 9.3 workers. The reason why the middle-class strategies were so costly in pre-1933 Germany, in France, and in Finland is that in these countries workers had the alternative of moving as workers to the Communists. The German S.P.D. could not afford to depart very far from the stance of defending the narrowly defined corporate interests of workers when it faced the threat from the *Kommunistische Partei Deutschlands* but could, and did, move to embrace the middle classes after the war (Abraham, 1982; Green, 1971: 111; Hunt, 1970: 148). French Socialists remained resolutely *ouvrièrist* until the late 1940s (Touchard, 1977) and paid an electoral cost for the consequent strategic vacillations.

Yet the trade-off for the Left as a whole also shows important cross-national differences: almost negligible in Denmark and Norway, it is moderate in Sweden and Finland, and quite sharp in France, Belgium, and Germany. What accounts for these differences? Given that we are comparing only seven countries, which differ systematically in a number of ways, competing explanations cannot be eliminated. Two explanations are, however, quite persuasive theoretically. The trade-off is steeper in those countries in which parties propounding particularistic ideologies have competed for the loyalty of workers. In those countries where the choice of workers is class identity or the universalistic ideology of individuals—citizens the trade-off is weak or moderate; in those countries where confessional, linguistic, or ethnic identities are organized within the electoral system, left-wing parties face a sharp trade-off. The

---

[8] See Appendix, Table A2 for evidence that the estimates of d are quite sharp.

Table 1. *Equilibrium Trade-Off Between Recruitment and Allies and Workers*

Country	Total Left		Socialists only	
	d	(d/p)	d	(d/p)
Belgium	0.137	1.10	[a]	[a]
Denmark	0.002	0.05	0.017	0.13
Finland	0.095	0.53	0.058	1.41
France	0.090	1.05	1.182	9.31
Germany	0.130	1.41	3.571	16.70
Norway	0.009	0.27	0.001	0.02
Sweden	0.073	0.53	0.060	0.77

[a]The results for Belgian Socialists are unusable.

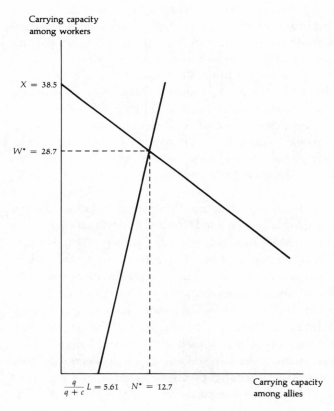

Figure 1. Carrying capacities of the Swedish Social Democrats, given the 1964 class structure, as proportions of the electorate

countries where the trade-off is milder are also the ones where trade-unions have been large and concentrated and the bargaining process has been centralized since an early date. The countries where the Left as a whole faced a sharper trade-off are those where unions are either numerically weak or divided or where the bargaining process is decentralized. Thus the trade-off is weaker in the corporatist systems, because in these systems trade-unions play much of the role of organizing workers as a class, while in the countries where corporatist arrangements are weaker political parties are alone in confronting the individualizing effects of supra-class strategies. Altogether, the severity of the trade-offs which left-wing parties face among workers as they seek support from other classes depends upon the other participants in the conflict over the causes of individual behavior: other political parties and other organizations capable of organizing workers as a class.

The existence of this trade-off constitutes one limitation of socialist growth. Faced with a working class which is a numerical minority, class-based parties seek electoral support from the people in general. They often win this support but they dilute the importance of class as a determinant of the political behavior of workers and they erode their strength among workers.

Party Strategies and Their Consequences

This analysis does not yet explain, however, why socialist parties failed to win a larger share of the electorate. They had to lose the votes of some workers as they turned to other groups but why did they not win enough votes from these groups to have obtained decisive majorities?

Clearly, other parties stood in the way, and whatever the socialists might have done, the counter-strategies of their competitors imposed limits upon socialist success. But part of the reason must be internal: there are prima-facie grounds for believing that socialist parties have not been willing to seek the support of other groups at any cost to their strength among workers. The socialist quest for electoral success was circumscribed by an autonomous concern for class loyalty. Socialists might have sought votes from allies but they seem to have valued the votes of workers above those of other supporters.

How do socialist parties choose electoral strategies? Once they determine who are the voters from whom socialists may obtain support, the decision must be made how the party should allocate its emphases and its efforts between workers and other potential supporters. A party may decide to emphasize the particular attention it devotes to interests and values of the middle class or perhaps some category identified in non-class terms, such as youth or women. Alternatively, the party may stress its uncompromising devotion to the working class and its interests, even to the point of deliberately discouraging middle-class support. And at times it may speak with more than one voice, offering a weighted, and ambiguous, mix of appeals.

The strategy that a party adopts under the particular circumstances depends upon the degree to which party leaders are concerned with the class composition of their electorate, which is to say the degree to which they value the support of workers autonomously from electoral considerations. Let $(N/W) = k$ be the class composition the leaders of a particular party would like to maintain. Then this party will opt for a multi-class strategy as long as the quantity $[kW(t) - N(t)]$ is positive and will pursue a working-class strategy as long as this expression is negative.[9] A party sensitive to its class composition will be characterized by a low value of k; indeed, a party with a $k = 0$ would always seek to discourage allies from voting socialist. A party not concerned about class composition would be characterized by a high, positive k. Our numerical results indicate major differences in concern with class composition. The Norwegian Labor Party was concerned about the class origins of its votes only when its support among the middle classes exceeded that of workers ($k = 1.11$). The leaders of the Danish (0.41), Swedish (0.29), Finnish (0.25), and French (0.22) socialist parties would have abandoned multi-class strategies when non-workers exceeded between a fourth and a third of each party's voters. And the German S.P.D., at least before 1933, persisted in the light of our result ($k = 0$) in an orthodox laborist stance.

Since the essence of competition is that the success of any one party is limited by the actions of its rivals, it would be unreasonable to suppose that socialist strategies are always effective. Let c stand for the effectiveness of a party in recruiting or discouraging additional non-workers. Then the effect of party strategies upon the change of socialist support among non-workers will be $c[kW(t) - N(t)]$.

To make this description more realistic we must also allow for the fact that some people vote Left independent of the strategies parties pursue with regard to them, typically as a protest vote (Braga, 1956; Allardt, 1964). Let $L(t)$ represent the proportion of the electorate consisting of people other than workers to whom the party may turn for support in the current election. Then the quantity $[L(t + 1) - N(t)]$ measures the pool of non-workers available for socialist recruitment. To represent protest vote, we simply assume that if a party did not formulate any specific strategies oriented to encourage or discourage non-workers from voting socialist, its vote among non-workers would change

[9] Since the party seeks to maintain class composition at $(N(t)/W(t)) = k$, it will do nothing if $kW(t) = N(t)$, or $kW(t) - N(t) = 0$. It will attempt to adjust toward non-workers if this difference is positive and toward workers if it is negative.

proportionately to the size of this pool, where q represents this proportion. Empirically, q turns out to be negligible for all the socialist parties (zero in Denmark, Norway, and France, 0.04 to 0.06 in Sweden, Finland, and Germany) and it exceeds 0.10 only for the French and Belgian Left parties treated together.

If some non-workers drift toward socialist parties in protest and if these parties choose their strategies in the manner described above, then the change in the proportion of the electorate consisting of socialist voting allies may be represented by

$$\Delta N(t) = q[L(t + 1) - N(t)] + c[kW(t) - N(t)].$$
(3)

Setting $\Delta N(t) = 0$, we can now determine the carrying capacity of each party among non-workers: the level of support a party can obtain and hold. This level, N^*, is given by

$$N^* = \frac{q}{q + c} \; L + \frac{ck}{q + c} \; W$$
(4)

where L, like X in equation (2), is assumed to be constant.

Barring the one case of extreme sensitivity to class composition – the German S.P.D. before 1933 with a k of zero — the slope of the function which relates N^* to W is positive. If a party is successful among workers then it can afford to devote itself to the mobilization of allies. Hence, the ultimate strength of a party among non-workers depends upon its strength among workers.

Since W^* depends upon N and N^* upon W, the carrying capacities of each party among workers, allies, and the electorate as a whole are determined uniquely given the class structure. Figure 1 shows the intersection of the functions $W^* = f(N)$ and $N^* = g(W)$ for the Swedish Social Democrats under the 1964 class structure. This intersection specifies the carrying capacities of the party at that time. Table 2 shows the carrying capacities of major socialist parties and left-wing parties combined for the last election used in calculating values of parameters and for a linearly extrapolated 1980 class structure. Note that the total Left or socialist vote is $Y(t) = W(t) + N(t)$.

The secret of the stagnation of the socialist vote is thus twofold: first, workers are less likely to vote socialist when parties turn for electoral support to other groups and, secondly, socialist leaders are willing to pursue supra-class strategies only if they enjoy sufficient support among workers. Where other parties do not appeal to workers on particularistic bases, where trade-unions assume some of the burden of organizing workers as a class, and where party leaders are not too sensitive to class composition, the Left is able to recruit and hold substantial support among workers and other groups simultaneously. But in those countries where other political parties appeal to workers on

Table 2. *Carrying Capacity[a] Among Workers, Allies, and the Electorate for the Last Estimated Election and an Interpolated 1980 Class Structure[b]*

Country	Date	W*	N*	Y*	Date	W*	N*	Y*
				Total Left				
Belgium	1971	1.6	15.8	17.4	1980		c	
Denmark	1971	26.7	32.4	59.1	1980	26.8	32.7	59.5
Finland	1972	5.5	27.1	32.7	1980		c	
France	1968	12.0	12.3	24.3	1980	9.8	11.6	21.4
Germany	1933	17.5	11.0	28.5	1980	17.9	11.2	29.1
Norway	1969	17.2	48.1	65.3	1980		c	
Sweden	1964	34.1	8.4	42.5	1980	31.9	8.0	39.9
				Socialists only				
Denmark	1971	26.9	11.1	38.0	1980	27.0	11.1	38.1
Finland	1972	5.2	10.4	15.6	1980		c	
France	1968	8.1	1.8	9.9	1980	7.0	1.6	8.7
Germany	1933	19.4	0.8	20.3	1980		d	
Norway	1969	29.7	33.1	62.8	1980		c	
Sweden	1964	28.7	12.7	41.4	1980	26.1	13.1	39.1

[a]Carrying capacity is the equilibrium vote share of the electorate.
[b]Straight-line interpolation from the last two censuses analyzed.
[c]Our analyses of class structure are too crude to warrant interpolations.
[d]German results can be sensibly interpolated for the Left as a whole but not S.P.D. alone.

particularistic bases, or where trade-unions are weak or divided, or where party leaders value class loyalty independently of electoral considerations, the Left has discovered that its capacity to conquer and maintain electoral support is highly limited.

Choice and Necessity

If history is not given uniquely, if under given historical conditions men and women have some room for choice and their choices have consequences, then historical analysis need not be limited to that unique sequence of events that happened to have transpired. A theory may lead to the rediscovery of opportunities that were lost, possibilities that were inherent at each juncture, and alternatives that remain open.

For party leaders the class structure and the intensity of the trade-off constitute conditions which, at least within some time span, are independent of their actions. These conditions impose limits upon political opportunities. But within these limits party leaders do choose and their choice may have consequences for socialist electoral performance.

Thus one set of questions concerns the range of choice that was available to leaders of left-wing parties. How much of a difference was there for them to make? Have they chosen the strategies that were best under the circumstances? Have they missed opportunities at specific and perhaps crucial historical moments?

We proceed as follows. Suppose first that party leaders choose a strategy for each election by selecting a criterion of class composition, $k(t)$, and follow the course of action implied by the chosen criterion under the circumstances. Now, the extreme alternative available to party leaders at each time is to opt either for a strategy of mobilizing as many non-workers as possible or a strategy of keeping the party as class-pure as possible. When the leaders opt for mobilization of the middle classes we will speak of the pure supra-class strategy and will denote all the quantities associated with this strategy by the superscript s. In contrast, when the leaders attempt to restrict their electoral support exclusively to workers we will speak of the pure class-only strategy and we will denote all the quantities associated with this strategy by the superscript c. Given these definitions, the difference between the time paths of the total vote associated with these pure strategies, $D(t) = Y^S(t) - Y^C(t)$, describes the realm of manoeuverability available to party leaders at a particular moment of electoral strategy choice.

Suppose now that once the leaders pick one of the pure strategies, they persevere in this strategy indefinitely into the future. Table 3 shows how much of a difference the choice of strategies could make in the long run. If our numbers are at all reliable, a caveat we do not repeat only to avoid repetitiousness, then the Left in Belgium and France had almost no difference to make in the long run. In Finland, Denmark, and Germany, the Left as a whole could have done better or worse depending upon the strategic choices but the margin is less than 10 percent of the electorate. In Sweden and particularly in Norway the choice seems to have been wide open.

These electoral choices translated into different political alternatives in different countries. In Denmark and Norway what was at stake was indeed an overwhelming electoral majority. For the Swedish Social Democrats the choice was one between a strategy that would keep them almost permanently in office and one that would not – an important difference, as Martin (1975) has shown. The French Socialists and the pre-1933 S.P.D. faced a less attractive alternative since for them the strategy choice was a matter of electoral survival. Thus choices of electoral strategies mattered and party leaders did have some difference to make.

Did socialist leaders try to make the most of the alternatives they faced? Did they try to maximize the vote? Note that in explaining the stagnation of the socialist vote we assumed that party leaders valued the votes of workers more

Table 3. *Long-Term Difference Between Vote Shares Resulting from Supra-Class and Class-Pure Strategies (Recent Class Structure)*

Country	Number of elections during which differences will increase	Number of elections when difference will equal zero	Long-term difference[a]
	Total Left		
Belgium	2	19	−0.2
Denmark	99	never	7.0
Finland	always	never	5.7
France	2	36	−0.9
Germany	7	21	−9.8
Norway	12	never	50.7
Sweden	14	never	17.6
	Socialists only		
Denmark	7	never	29.2
Finland	5	32	− 1.9
France	1	2	− 22.1
Germany	1	1	− 13.0
Norway	31	never	68.4
Sweden	6	never	7.3

[a]Difference is calculated $Y^s - Y^c$. Hence positive sign indicates that supra-class strategy is superior in the long run.

than votes cast by other people. But how do the strategies which were actually chosen compare with those that would have been best electorally?

First, we examine what party leaders should have done if they had wanted to win votes, as many as possible, regardless of all other considerations. The obvious answer turns out to be treacherous, since turning for support to non-workers would not always have been advantageous from the purely electoral point of view. Indeed, it can be shown that if the trade-off, as measured by (d/p), is greater than unity, the pure class-only strategy will turn out to be electorally superior after some finite number of elections. If the trade-off is less severe, then the pure supra-class strategy will always result in more votes for the party.[10]

Table 4 shows the carrying capacities associated with the strategies that best reconstruct the actual experience of socialist and Left voting, with the pure

---

[10] Since both the criterion – sum of party's vote over time – and the constraints – given by equations (1) and (3) – are linear, the solution to the maximization problem runs up to the descriptive bound imposed upon ^{c}the control variable k. Hence, either k^S or k^C will maximize the Lagrangean. It can be shown that

$$\text{sign } \frac{\delta L}{\delta k} = \text{sign } \frac{p - d}{p(q + c) + cdk} ,$$

which in turn depends exclusively upon the difference $(p - d)$. Hence the maximizing strategy is supra-class when $p > d$ and it is pure-class when $p < d$.

Table 4. *Comparison of Carrying Capacities Associated with the Actual, Supra-Class, and Class-Only Strategies (1970 Class Structure)*

Country	Actual[a] Carrying capacity	Workers/ socialist voters[c]	Supra-class Carrying capacity	Workers/ socialist voters[c]	Class only[b] Carrying capacity
			Total Left		
Belgium	17.4	87.8	17.3	0	17.5
Denmark	59.1	49.5	60.4	44.0	53.4
Finland	32.7	73.0	37.7	0	32.0
France	24.2	61.3	23.7	0	24.6
Germany	28.5	61.4	23.6	0	33.3
Norway	65.3	26.3	81.0	14.1	30.3
Sweden	42.5	80.7	56.3	33.3	37.8
			Socialists only		
Demark	38.0	72.5	57.6	41.4	28.4
Finland	15.6	80.0	14.1	0	16.0
France	9.9	81.8	2.7	0	24.8
Germany	15.0	100.0	2.0	0	15.0
Norway	62.8	47.3	98.7	29.4	30.3
Sweden	41.4	77.6	47.1	20.6	39.8

[a]Actual strategy is the strategy estimated to best fit the model.
[b]In the case of the class-only strategy the desired proportion of workers among socialist voters is always 100 percent.
[c]This is more precisely the proportion of workers among socialist voters which would result from following the particular strategy.
[d]As of 1933.

supra-class, and the pure class-only strategies. These numbers indicate what proportion of the electorate each party would be able to recruit and hold if the class structure were frozen at its 1970 levels. The table also shows the criteria of class composition that would characterize the particular strategies. Instead of presenting the value of k, however, we translated these values into proportions indicating how many workers there would be among party supporters if the party adopted the particular strategy.

Class-only strategies turn out to have been electorally superior for the Belgian, French, and German Left as well as for the Finnish, French, and German Social Democrats. Supra-class strategies are superior for the major socialist parties and for the Left as a whole in Denmark, Norway, and Sweden.

Within the realm of available choice, party leaders disappoint those who believe that their exclusive concern should be or is the maximization of the vote. Most parties would have improved their long-run performance had they pursued strategies different from those actually chosen. Among the major socialist parties, only the S.P.D. followed the electorally optimal policy, which was to keep the party class-pure. The French Socialists and the Swedish Social Democrats both pursued electorally inferior strategies but in different ways: the French by being insufficiently *ouvrièrist* and the Swedes by being excessively concerned about working-class support.

The three Scandinavian parties for which the supra-class strategy is electorally superior, by quite a wide margin in Norway and Denmark, nevertheless have opted to pursue strategies that kept them closer to their working-class base. In fact, they probably did not have a choice. The reason why these parties could have gained votes by following supra-class strategies is that they faced relatively mild trade-offs among workers when they diluted the emphasis on class in their organization and propaganda. But the reason, at least in part the reason, why the abandonment of class by these parties would have had relatively little effect on the voting behavior of workers was that workers were organized as a class by large, concentrated, and centralized unions. And here the circle closes rather viciously, for it is precisely because of their interdependence with the unions that Social Democrats in Denmark, Norway, and Sweden could not adopt strategies that would have maximized the vote. (For evidence see Elvander, 1979: 18; Heidar, 1977: 300; Hentila, 1978: 331–2; Martin, 1972: 15 and 168ff.; Scase, 1977: 323.)

In Belgium, Finland, France, and at least pre-1933 Germany the trade-unions did not take the burden of organizing workers as a class off the shoulders of political parties. The result was that class ideology and class organization were highly vulnerable to socialist electoral strategies and the electoral trade-off the left-wing parties encountered in these countries was so steep that any major turn for support to the middle classes would have been disastrous for their vote-getting power. The Danes, Norwegians, and Swedes were in a different predicament. The trade-unions in these countries grew rapidly and unified at an early stage. Class relations became institutionalized by a nationwide collective bargaining system. As a result, Social Democrats in these countries could have pursued middle-class-oriented strategies at a tolerable or even negligible cost. But the very same organizations which assumed the task of organizing workers as a class imposed constraints on the degree to which socialist parties could freely pursue their electoral opportunities.

Are Socialist Leaders Vote-Maximizers?

The previous analysis of long-term consequences places, however, an unfair burden on party leaders. It is unreasonable to expect leaders of electoral parties to pay much attention to anything but the proximate future. Politicians who maximize in the long run end up writing memoirs within a very short one. We should ask, therefore, whether party leaders attempted to win all the votes they could in the proximate elections, regardless of the consequences the particular strategy might have for the long run.

Two parties are particularly interesting since they represent the clearest contrast, although each is representative of others in the same situation. Figure 2 shows what would have been the consequences if the French Socialists and the Swedish Social Democrats chose at any moment either of the pure strategies and followed this strategy during just two consecutive elections. The points of origins — the dots — at each election time represent the vote share which the party actually obtained. The two lines which originate from each point represent the vote shares the party would have obtained had it adopted at the time the pure supra-class or the pure class-only strategy. For example, the French Socialists in the 1962 elections won 10.1 percent of the electorate. Had the Socialists adopted at this moment the pure supra-class strategy they would have gained 15.5 percent in the 1967 elections. Had they persevered with the same strategy for the 1968 elections, they would have won the votes of 8.9 percent of the electorate. In turn, if the Socialists had opted for the pure class-only strategy, they would have obtained 13.3 percent in 1967 and 13.5 in 1968.

The analysis of the alternatives available in the short run to the leaders of the Swedish Social Democratic Party confirms the conclusions derived from the long-run analysis. At each moment of history, the party would have improved its electoral performance by embracing a pure supra-class strategy. If party leaders did not choose such strategies, it is because of the constraints discussed above.

The French Socialists have been in a much tighter spot. Note in Figure 2 that the pure supra-class strategy was always superior for the next election and invariably inferior after two elections. Thus at each moment the party faced an inter-temporal trade-off — party leaders had to choose for which election they wished to maximize votes.

The case of the French Socialists, the Finnish Social Democrats, and the pre-1933 German S.P.D. show that one cannot speak of vote-maximization ahistorically: one must ask with what perspective party leaders view the future. But more importantly, the fiction of elections as a series of unconnected events is no longer tenable. The strategies which party leaders choose today produce the conditions under which they are forced to decide in the next election. The irrelevance of Downs' theory of party competition is due to the assumption that parties encounter an exogenous public. Once we look at party strategies in historical perspective, as a process, we cannot view each election as an event that had no antecedents and would have no subsequent consequences. The public opinion which parties encounter in each electoral campaign is, as Gramsci

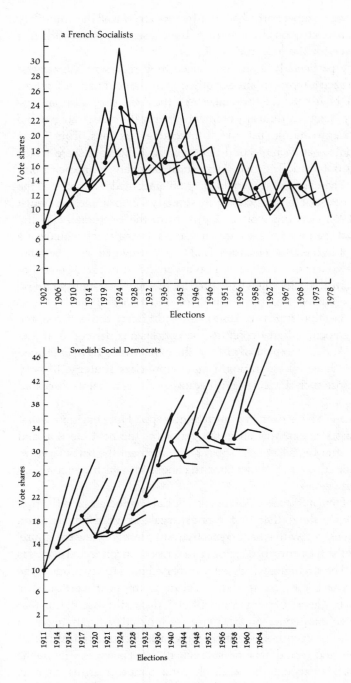

Figure 2. Counterfactual analysis of the French Socialist and the Swedish Social Democratic vote

emphasized, a result of past actions. The conditions which parties encounter at the present is a product of strategies chosen in the past. And many objective conditions of today are the errors of yesterday. Therefore, when party leaders choose strategies for the next election they must consider the conditions they will encounter as a consequence in the future.

Historical Patterns of Class Voting

Through a variety of means, ideological as well as organizational, conflicting political forces impose upon individuals particular images of society, mold collective identities, and mobilize commitments to specific projects for a shared future. Collective identity, group solidarity, and political commitments are continually forged, destroyed, and molded anew in the course of conflicts among organized collective actors, such as parties, unions, corporations, churches, schools, or armies. The strategies of these competitors determine as their cumulative effect the relative importance of the potential social cleavages for the voting behavior of individuals. Thus sometimes religion and sometimes language, sometimes class and at other times individual self-interest become the dominant motivational forces of individual behavior. The causes of individual behavior are produced in the course of history by conflicting political forces.

Individual voting behavior, individual behavior in general, is not ruled by natural causes — forces that would determine the course of individual action independent of human activity. This is why the discussions of whether class, religion, party identification, or the pursuit of self-interest is most important in determining voting behavior are not theoretically enlightening. In society causes are a product of reciprocal interactions. Causes of voting should thus be expected to vary across countries and to change over time.

But if the behavior of individuals is not ruled by natural causes, it is nevertheless lawful. We have seen that the salience of class as a cause of individual voting behavior is the effect of strategies pursued by political parties of the Left, by trade-unions, and by other parties and organizations that may seek to organize workers on the basis of identities and commitments other than class. We will now examine the effect of this process upon the voting behavior of individuals, specifically, upon the historical patterns of class voting.

Patterns of class voting should be expected to vary depending upon strategies pursued by left-wing parties, upon the severity of the trade-off, and upon the class structure. It is convenient to revert again to the analysis of comparative statics. Note that our argument about the way in which workers join and defect from the ranks of socialist voters entails the following assumption about the way in which individual workers make voting decisions: they are indifferent between voting and not voting socialist whenever exactly

$W^*(N)$ workers vote socialist in response to N allies voting for the party. In turn, our argument about leaders' strategic decisions is based on the assumption that leaders are indifferent whether additional allies vote or leave the ranks exactly when the class composition of the electorate is such that $kW = N$, or $W = N/k$. Workers and party leaders are thus simultaneously inert in their actions when $W^* = N/k$, which after some rearranging yields the proportions of workers voting socialist in equilibrium as[11]

$$\frac{W^*}{X} = \frac{1}{1 + k\left(\frac{d}{p}\right)} \tag{5}$$

where X is treated as a constant.

When the trade-off is mild and the party concerned about class composition almost all workers will vote socialist. Under such conditions few allies will vote socialist and the degree of class voting in the electorate, as measured by Alford-like indices, will be high.[12] When the trade-off is mild and the party less concerned about the class origins of its support, the proportion of workers voting Left will still be high but so will be the proportion of allies. When the trade-off is steep but the party very concerned about class composition, workers will still vote overwhelmingly socialist but few allies will. Finally, when the trade-off is steep and the party indifferent to class composition, the proportion of workers voting socialist will be low and the proportion of allies will be moderate. These conclusions can be conveniently summarized in tabular form:[13]

		d/p	
	severe	W/X: moderate N/L: low A: moderate	W/X: low N/L: moderate A: very low
trade-off			
	mild	W/X: high N/L: low A: high	W/X: moderate N/L: high A: very low
		high	low $\quad k$

Party's concern over class composition

[11] This derivation and the subsequent analysis assume that there is no spontaneous drift toward the party and $q = 0$. Qualitative results are not affected by this assumption and without it the algebra is messy.

[12] It can be also shown that $\dfrac{N^*}{L} = \dfrac{k}{1 + k(d/p)} \dfrac{X}{L}$, and the value of Alford's index is given by $A = \dfrac{W}{X} - \dfrac{N}{L} = \dfrac{1 - k(X/L)}{1 + k(d/p)}$

[13] To get an institution about these results, let k and (d/p) equal, in turn, 0 and 1, and calculate W/X, N/L, and Alford's index.

These analytical consequences of our theory concern class voting in the long run but the model can be used to open the black box of class voting throughout entire electoral histories, following a long line of methodological devices — recall surveys, cohort analyses, and ecological studies — that are being used to get a glimpse at patterns of voting during the period preceding survey studies. And to evaluate the model empirically we can compare its predictions with the reports of survey studies during the period when such reports are available.[14]

We must begin, however, by warning the reader not to expect a perfect fit. There are good reasons to expect that at best we should be able to provide ball-park comparisons: (1) definitional differences between the model and surveys, (2) errors in surveys, and (3) errors in our estimates.[15] In particular, we must avoid the intuition that we are comparing model estimates of an unknown validity with surveys which present the true state of affairs. Surveys are replete with error, sampling error is one obvious source. Most importantly, surveys report either intentions or recollections, not the vote itself. And we know that people sometimes change their voting decisions at the last moment and that they tend to overreport having voted for the winners. Indeed, we have found that our predictions of election results are frequently more accurate than those based on surveys.

With all these caveats, we present the results. Given all the potential sources of divergence and error, the overall results rest squarely within the realm of plausibility. The extrapolations derived from the model bear a statistical relation to survey results: correlations between model and survey proportions are significant at the 0.05 level for workers voting Left (at the 0.01 level without Norway), at the 0.01 level for workers voting socialist, and at the 0.01 level for allies voting socialist. Only in the case of allies voting for the left-wing parties combined are the predictions of the model statistically independent of survey results. Thus the model which characterizes the process of electoral recruitment since the beginning of the century reproduces results of surveys conducted since the 1950s. Clearly, the fit is closer in some countries than in others and the predictions derived from the model do not reproduce survey results with any exactitude. But the evidence seems sufficient to establish the validity of the theoretical principle: the importance of class varies historically and strategies of

---

[14] We also compared our estimates for Sweden with Lewin, Jansson, and Sorbom's (1972) cross-sectional results. They share 77 percent of variance.

[15] Our estimating algorithm is outlined in the Appendix. Definitional divergencies are frequent and not always specifiable. Survey researchers typically use categories of "manual" and "non-manual," both of which are broader than our "workers" and "allies." At times they classify respondents according to their own occupation and at times according to the occupation of the head of household, and this makes a difference (Michelat and Simon, 1975). They also treat retired people in different ways: sometimes on the basis of past occupation and sometimes as retired. What is worse, we were often unable to reconstruct from published sources the definitions that were used.

Table 5a. *Comparison of Model and Survey Results About Class Voting for the Left*

Country	Year	Proportion of workers voting Left		Proportion of allies voting Left	
		Model	Surveys	Model	Surveys
Belgium	1968	53	43[1]	20	18[1]
Denmark	1960	67	85[1]	73	62[1]
	1964	66	85[2]	69	65[2]
	1966	69	86[1]	63	58[1]
	1968	61	79[3]	63	
	1971	67	69[4], 75[5], 77[6], 78[1]	70	30[4], 33[5], 49[6], 60[1]
	1973	51	51[1], 65[5]	53	29[5]
	1975	57	59[1], 61[2], 64[7]	59	26[7], 43[1], 43[2]
	1977	65	67[7]	68	32[7]
	1979	66	65[1]	70	56[1]
Finland	1958	73	68[1]	23	14[1]
	1966	87	80[2]	31	23[2]
	1972	68	74[3]	28	21[3]
France	1956	63	56[1]	35	35[1]
	1958	52	45[1]	29	35[1]
	1967	65	41[2], 43[3], 44[4], 54[5]	34	28[2], 29[3], 29[4]
	1968	60	38[3], 43[4]	29	26[3], 29[4]
	1973	67	53[3], 63[6a], 68[5]	33	27[3], 28[6a]
	1978	73	47[7], 67[5]	35	30[7], 53[5]
Germany[b]	1953	51	48[1], 58[2]	32	27[1], 29[2]
	1961	63	56[1]	34	30[1]
	1965	66	54[1]	35	34[1]
	1969	69	58[1]	36	46[1]
	1972	77	66[1]	40	50[1]
	1976	70	53[2]	36	39[2]
Norway	1957	39	77[1]	31	
	1965	40	71[2], 77[1], 77[3]	44	30[2]
	1969	42	75[1], 80[4]	46	
	1973	35	69[1]	38	32[1]
	1977	36	70[3]	40	
Sweden	1956	76	73[1], 76[2d], 77[3], 85[4e]	19	23[2], 48[4e]
	1960	77	73[5], 78[1], 80[2d], 81[3] 84[4e], 87[6]	20	25[2d], 45[3], 54[4e]
	1964	88	75[1], 77[2d], 81[3], 84[7]	20	30[2d], 44[7]
	1968	99	75[1], 76[2d], 79[3], 81[6]	23	47[1]
	1970	93	72[2d], 75[3], 76[6]	22	32[2d]
	1973	93	73[2d], 75[3], 79[7]	23	29[2d], 37[7]
	1976	92	73[3], 76[8]	23	
	1979	93	75[3]	23	

[a]Includes *extrême gauche*.
[b]Vote for the S.P.D., predicted by extrapolating results for total Left.
[c]Using additional information, reported by Berglund and Lindstrom (1978: 180).
[d]Survey definition broader than model definition: typically shop assistants counted as workers and all persons other than manual workers counted as allies.
[e]Survey definition narrower than model definition: typically industrial workers only and allies without non-agricultural self-employed.

Table 5b. *Comparison of Model and Survey Results About Class Voting for Major Socialist Parties*

Country	Year	Proportion of workers voting socialist		Proportion of allies voting socialist	
		Model	Surveys	Model	Surveys
Denmark	1969	91	84[1]	31	
	1964	90	73[2]	30	
	1966	85	65[1]	29	
	1968	77	65[3]	26	
	1971	82	59[4], 60[3], 65[5], 65[6]	27	25[4], 29[5]
	1973	57	38[1], 48[5]	19	20[5]
	1975	68	45[1], 46[2], 47[7]	21	18[7]
	1977	83	55[7]	25	24[7]
	1979	83	52[1]	26	
Finland	1958	34	34[1]	12	6[1]
	1966	46	42[2]	17	15[2]
	1972	45	45[3]	15	15[3]
France	1956	30	39[1]	4	28[1]
	1958	32	10[8], 30[1]	4	5[8], 26[1]
	1967	41	15[3], 16[2], 16[4]	4	15[3]
	1968	37	14[3], 14[4]	4	13[3]
	1973	50	17[3], 22[6], 35[9]	6	13[6], 14[3], 40[9]
	1978	58	19[7], 27[5]	8	18[7]
Norway	1957	64	75[1]	26	
	1965	62	63[2], 69[1], 69[3]	25	44[2]
	1969	67	69[1], 73[4]	27	
	1973	48	55[1]	20	25[1]
	1977	60	64[3]	24	
Sweden	1956	57	69[1], 74[3]	27	
	1960	67	69[5], 77[3], 83[6]	31	44[5]
	1964	66	75[3], 78[7]	29	43[7]
	1968	81	73[1], 77[3], 79[6]	36	46[1]
	1970	73	64[2], 70[3]	32	41[2]
	1973	72	64[2], 69[3], 69[7], 73[2]	32	29[2], 34[7], 38[2]
	1976	71	68[3]	32	
	1979	71	70[3]	32	

Sources (Tables 5a and b):
Belgium   1 Hill, 1974: 48
Denmark   1 Esping-Anderson, 1984: 3–4. 2 Berglund and Lindstrom, 1978: 108. 3. Esping-Anderson, 1979: 276. 4 Damgaard, 1974: 121. 5 Borre, 1977a: 15. 6 Uusitalo, 1975: 39. 7 Borre, 1977b.
                   1 Allardt and Pesonen, 1967: 342. 2 Pesonen, 1974: 294. 3 Allardt and Wesołowski, 1978: 63.
France   1 Sondages, 1960: 18–19. 2. Rabier, 1978: 362. 3 Sondages, 1973: 18–19. 4 Braud, 1973: 32. 5. Jaffré, 1980: 41. 6 *Le Monde*, 1973. 7 *Le Matin*, 1978.
Germany   1 Pappi, 1973: 199. 2 Pappi, 1977: 217.
Norway   1 Valen and Martinussen, 1977: 51. 2 Martin, 1972: 92. 3 Esping-Anderson, 1984: 3–4. 4 Uusitalo, 1975: 41.
                   1 Särlvik, 1974: 398. 2 Särlvik, 1977: 95. 3 Esping-Anderson, 1984: 3–5. 4 Särlvik, 1966: 217. 5 Särlvik, 1967: 169. 6 Esping-Anderson, 1979: 276. 7 Petersson and Särlvik, 1975: 88. 8 Stephens, 1981: 167.

political parties and other organizations have cumulative consequences for the way people vote.

Further Evidence

Ever since the *Communist Manifesto*, one persistent tendency within the socialist and later communist movement was to insist that the people who sell their labor power for a wage but perform non-manual tasks in offices or stores are in fact proletarians, workers like other workers. "Educated proletarians," "workers by brain," "office workers" were the optimistic terms in which these people were repeatedly described. Time after time party theoreticians recognized that these "white-collar proletarians" failed as yet to behave like industrial manual workers but this lapse of their class-consciousness was to vanish imminently, perhaps as the result of exhortations by these theoreticians. Social scientists often fall victim to the same wishful thinking and one book after another is written about the "working-class majority."

Yet even if the conditions of work and life of lower-salaried employees become more and more like those of workers, even if they begin to be unionized at rates almost equal to manual workers, even if they are frequently married to manual workers, in elections these lower echelons of non-manual wage-earners do not behave like manual workers. Survey results show that the gap between salaried employees and manual workers has not been closing, at least certainly not because salaried employees began to vote for left-wing parties at a high rate.

The fact that lower-salaried employees vote less often for left-wing parties than manual workers confirms the validity of our definition but not necessarily the hypothesis concerning the behavior of workers, and this is what our theory is about. It might have been true that few salaried employees would vote Left, but very much to the regret of manual workers who might have liked to see their office class-mates within the socialist ranks. Neither does our statistical analysis thus far resolve the issue of the reaction of workers to party efforts to recruit lower-salaried employees. This statistical analysis demonstrated that in all cases and countries there existed a trade-off between the support of allies and the recruitment of workers: the parameter d was always positive as the theory predicted. But the allies are a heterogeneous category that includes middle-level salaried employees, artisans, craftsmen, and shopkeepers, and owners of family farms, in addition to lower echelons of non-manual employees. Thus far we do not know whether there is a trade-off specifically between support by the salaried proletariat and the recruitment of workers.

Survey results permit us to answer three questions, at least with the reference

Table 6. *Proportion of White-Collar Employees Voting Left According to Surveys and Their Distance from Manual Workers*[a]

Denmark	1960	1964	1966	1971	1973	1975	1977	1979
E-A	62		58	60	45	43		56
B&L		65						
Damgaard				40				
Borre				43	44	42	51	
Uusitalo					49			
Distance[b]	− 23	− 20	− 28	− 28	− 13	− 18	− 16	− 9
Finland	1958	1966	1972					
Various	19	38	32					
Distance[b]	− 49	− 42	− 42					
France	1956	1958	1967	1968	1973	1978		
Sondages	47	43	32	29	37			
Braud			36	38				
Rabier			34					
Le Matin						40		
Jaffré						47		
Distance[b]	− 9	− 2	110	− 8	− 26	− 13		
Germany	1953	1961	1965	1969	1972	1976		
Pappi, 1973	27	30	34	46	50			
Pappi, 1977	29					39		
Distance[b]	− 25	− 26	− 20	− 12	− 16	− 14		
Norway	1957	1965	1969	1973				
E-A	53	56	54	46				
Distance[b]	− 24	− 18	− 23	− 23				
Sweden	1956	1960	1964	1968	1970	1973	1976	1979
E-A	51	54	53	56	51	51	46	45
Särlvik	32	37	42	47				
P&S				47		40		
Distance[b]	− 34	− 34	− 30	− 25	− 23	− 29	− 27	− 30

[a]Lower white-collar employees in Denmark and Norway. All white-collar employees or "new middle class" in Finland. *Employés* and *cadres moyens* in France. *Angestellte* and *Beamte* in Germany. Lower and middle white-collar employees in Sweden. See Table 5 for source key.
[b]*Distance* is measured as the difference between average survey reports for lower-salaried employees and average reports for workers.

to the last thirty years or so. First, is the hypothesis concerning the existence of the trade-off between the support by allies and the recruitment of workers confirmed by survey studies? Secondly, is there a trade-off specifically with regard to salaried employees? Finally, is the trade-off with salaried employees distinct from the trade-off between the support of other groups and the recruitment of manual workers?

Survey results are far from reliable and observations are scarce, so scarce that we can answer these questions only in a very simple form and only by using the crudest statistical techniques. The answers are, however, unambiguous: survey studies confirm that there exists a trade-off between the support by allies and the

Table 7. *Statistical Relations Between the Proportion of Lower-Salaried Employees and Allies Voting Left and the Change of the Proportion of Workers Voting Left[a] (Based on Published Survey Results)*

Country	Lower-salaried employees Correlation	N	All allies combined Correlation	N
Total Left				
Pooled	-0.36^b	25	-0.36^b	19
Denmark	-0.03	7	-0.76	4
Finland		2		2
France	-0.89	5	-0.49	5
Norway	-0.47	4		2
Sweden	-0.23	7	-0.49	6
Socialists only				
Pooled	-0.46^c	28	-0.27	23
Denmark	-0.39	7	-0.23	4
Finland		2		2
France	-0.88	5	-0.89	5
Germany	-0.34	5	-0.38	5
Norway	-0.65	4		2
Sweden	-0.43	6	-0.43	5

[a]Correlation is for fitting a linear regression of the form $\Delta[W(t)/X(t)] - a + b[N(t)/L(t)] + e(t)$, where N and L are defined first as lower-salaried employees and second all allies combined. For the listing of lower-salaried employees see Table 6. Allies are a weighted sum of groups listed in the text.
[b]Significant at the 0.05 level.
[c]Significant at the 0.01 level.

recruitment of workers, that there has been a trade-off specifically with regard to salaried employees, and that the intensity of the trade-off with salaried employees cannot be distinguished with the available information from the trade-off with other groups (Table 7).

Thus, for manual workers, clerical and sales employees are not workers. Class membership becomes less important as a cause of voting behavior for manual workers when left-wing parties try to lump them together with "workers by brain."

Conclusion

"Models," Henri Theil teaches us, "should be used, not believed" (1976: 3). They are not simplified descriptions of a complex reality but instruments to be used together with knowledge of complexities in analyzing real situations. Hence we do not pretend that a few simplistic assumptions are sufficient to reconstruct the entire historical experience of electoral socialism. While we would have certainly abandoned the theory if it did not withstand a confrontation with the entire set of observations, we are undaunted by a lack of descriptive accuracy here and there, now and then. None of the numbers presented above can be taken as exact, but the theory and analyses considered as a whole carry some force.

Let us look at the implications of this analysis from a distance. We think we have demonstrated the following. Whether parties deliberately restrict their appeal to a specific base of support or attempt to conquer the entire electorate, their opportunities are limited by the real conflicts of interests and values that divide the society at any particular moment. If classes are classes, that is, if their interests qua collectivities are to some degree competitive and at times in conflict, then no party will be able to win the support of everyone without losing the support of someone. And the existence of such trade-offs implies that the distribution of electoral support must tend to become stable, even in the face of profound social and economic transformations. In a society in which there exist real divisions, no political party will be able to win elections overwhelmingly, in a way that could be taken as a clear mandate. Elections are just not an instrument for radical transformation. They are inherently conservative precisely because they are representative, representative of interests in a heterogeneous society.

In retrospect, the error of the early socialists was to have thought that one could precipitate radical social transformation through the electoral process. This belief was based on the assumption that capitalist societies would become almost homogeneous in class terms (Birnbaum, 1979) – dominated by the immense majority of workers. Instead, the class structure has become increasingly heterogeneous, and under such conditions elections would not and could not provide a clear mandate for grand projects for a better future.

APPENDIX

All of the empirical results presented in the text are based on estimating the system of equations given by

$$\Delta W(t) = p[X(t + 1) - W(t)] - dN(t) \qquad (1)$$
$$\Delta N(t) = q[L(t + 1) - N(t)] + c[kW(t) - N(t)] \qquad (2)$$
$$Y(t) = W(t) + N(t) + a[1 - X(t) - L(t)] \qquad (3)$$

This system could not be estimated directly because the states W and N are not observable from the existing historical sources. We know only how many people in total voted socialist but not how many workers and allies. Estimating the reduced form was also unfeasible since the parameters occur in highly non-linear combinations and are not identified.

In the practical situation we faced, only X, sometimes L, and Y are measurable. Hence, the descriptive quantities of central interest, W and N, must be constructed somehow during the estimating procedure itself. Our strategy has been to fit to the sum, Y, which is observable, by direct use of equations (1), (2), and (3). As a consequence, the initial conditions for W and N become parameters of the distribution to be fitted, along with the parameters p, d, q, c, k, and a. The subsequent values for $W(t)$ and $N(t)$ were then computed according to the logic of the model. Our criterion of fit has been to minimize the means squared error in prediction of the observed Y series.

Several constraints were imposed on the search. Parameters p, q, and a were restricted to the positive unit interval on descriptive grounds, while c and k were kept non-negative. The parameter d was not restricted, to allow the crucial test of its sign. Finally, the initial conditions were constrained by $W(0) + N(0) = Y(0)$ and $W(0) > N(0)$.

Subject to these constraints, repeated optimizations were computed for randomly selected starting points. A number of different algorithms have been used, but the workhouse has been the method of steepest descent in the parameter space. Experience revealed that starting values for parameters chosen within the unit hyper-cube or in an even smaller portion of that cube in the neighborhood of zero avoided pathological computational problems. After several thousand records were examined, we obtained estimates of the parameters and the best fitting paths for W and N.

Not all of these best-fitting paths were accepted, however, since some of the series which fitted well were descriptively unreasonable. The model must describe a possible world, hence we accepted only those time series in which all the quantities that constitute proportions behaved as such during the period on which the estimation was based as well as during the foreseeable future of the forthcoming five elections. In the case of the Belgian Socialist Party we could not obtain a series that would satisfy this criterion.

The essential differences between our procedure and typical regression techniques is that the series we estimate is conditional only upon the initial values $W(0)$, $N(0)$, while in regression the prediction depends on each preceding value in the sequence. To generate an equivalent series, we recomputed the prediction for $W(t)$, $N(t)$, and the residual vote in a way such that their sum would equal exactly $Y(t)$, adjusting the error in proportion to the magnitude of the contribution from each source, and then we calculated a new prediction for $W(t + 1)$, $N(t + 1)$, and the residual vote, this time conditional upon the just computed and adjusted error-free value. The values of fit given in Table A3 are for this adjusted series and the values in Figure 2 and Table 3 of the text are based on the error-free series.

We attach three tables. The first presents the fit of the smooth (fitted) and adjusted paths. The second table shows the sensitivity of the fit with regard to minor perturbations of the theoretically crucial parameter, namely, d. The last table compares the fit of our model with that of its potential competitors. Note that getting a good fit is not a claim to fame. But we call the competitive models naive because they are not based on a theory and their parameters are often theoretically meaningless and descriptively impossible.

The data concerning class distribution of the electorate were reconstructed for the purposes of this project from national censuses and other sources. For Denmark, France,

Table A1. *Model Fit (Smooth and Adjusted Paths)*

Country	Fit	
	Smooth path[a]	Adjusted path[b]
Total Left		
Belgium	0.16	0.30
Denmark	0.92	0.94
Finland	0.15	0.73
France[c]	0.75	0.84
Germany	0.87	0.92
Norway	0.98	0.98
Sweden	0.87	0.89
Socialist only		
Denmark	0.84	0.86
Finland	0.17	0.16
France	0.65	0.40
Germany	0.70	0.74
Norway	0.93	0.92
Sweden	0.85	0.85

[a]Path that was optimized in estimating routine.
[b]Path which mimics regression procedure. See text.
[c]Optimized to adjusted path.

Table A2. *Sensitivity Analysis: Proportion of Variance Explained When the Parameter* d *is changed by* − 0.05, − 0.01, + 0.01, *and* + 0.05 *from the Best Fitting Value*[a] *(Smooth Series)*

Country	− 0.05	− 0.01	Best	+ 0.01	+ 0.05
Total Left					
Belgium	− 0.65	0.10	0.16	0.18	0.22
Denmark	0.24	0.89	0.92	0.89	0.33
Finland	0.71	0.72	0.73	0.73	0.71
France	0.83	0.84	0.84	0.84	0.83
Germany	0.83	0.87	0.87	0.87	0.84
Norway	− 2.02	0.90	0.98	0.92	0.13
Sweden	0.85	0.87	0.87	0.87	0.85
Socialists only					
Denmark	0.68	0.83	0.84	0.84	0.74
Finland	− 3.10	0.03	0.17	0.07	− 2.19
France	0.64	0.65	0.65	0.65	0.64
Germany	0.70	0.70	0.70	0.70	0.70
Norway	0.72	0.93	0.93	0.93	0.78
Sweden	0.75	0.85	0.85	0.84	0.75

[a]Fit is calculated by subtracting the ratio of error variance to vote variance from unity.

Table A3. *Fit of the Model and Some of Its Naive Competitors*[a]

The naive models are:

I: $Y(t) = m_0 + m_1 x(t)$
II: $Y(t) = m_0 + m_1 Y(t - 1)$
III: $Y(t) = m_0 + m_1 X(t) + m_2 Y(t -_1)$
IV: $Y(t) = m_0 + m_1 X(t) + m_2 L(t)$
V: $Y(t) = m_0 + m_1 X(t) + m_2 L(t) + m_3 Y(t - 1)$
VI: $Y(t) = m_0 + m_1 X(t) + m_2 L(t) + m_3 Y(t - 1) + m_4 t$
Where $Y(t)$ is the socialist vote share of the electorate
        $X(t)$ is the proportion of workers in the electorate
        $L(t)$ is the proportion of allies in the electorate
        $t = 0, 1, 2 \ldots$ represents time.

The fit is as follows:

Country	Our Model	Naive Models					
		I	II	III	IV	V	VI
Total Left							
Belgium	0.30	0.05	0.11	0.13	n.a.	n.a.	0.08
Denmark	0.94	0.56	0.93	0.92	0.84	0.93	0.95
Finland	0.73	0.04	0.71	0.70	n.a.	n.a.	0.77
France	0.84	0.42	0.77	0.76	0.38	0.74	0.74
Germany	0.92	0.67	0.90	0.93	0.92	0.93	0.93
Sweden	0.89	0.65	0.87	0.87	0.70	0.86	0.93
Socialists only							
Denmark	0.86	0.37	0.84	0.83	0.82	0.86	0.88
Finland	0.16	0.00	0.22	0.20	n.a.	n.a.	0.21
France	0.40	0.00	0.16	0.20	0.00	0.14	0.14
Germany	0.74	0.81	0.73	0.83	0.81	0.82	0.82
Norway	0.92	0.02	0.91	0.90	n.a.	n.a.	0.92
Sweden	0.85	0.59	0.83	0.82	0.70	0.82	0.89

[a]Fit is measured as R^2 corrected for degrees of freedom for all the naive models.

Germany, and Sweden we were able to reconstruct the historical evolution of class structure in terms of about twenty categories cross-classified by sex and position within households. With regard to Belgium, Finland, and Norway, however, we could count workers but could not distinguish among different categories of non-workers. The results for these two groups of countries are thus not strictly identical since in the latter case all non-workers are treated as allies, $L = 1 - X$. The Norwegian series is not homogeneous through 1930, but probably still reliable. The Belgian data are likely to contain more errors and the early Finnish data most likely border on being worthless.

4. Material Bases of Consent

Introduction

Marx thought that capitalist democracy is an inherently unstable form of organization of society. It could not last. Writing in 1851, he expressed the belief that capitalist democracy is "only the political form of revolution of bourgeois society and not its conservative form of life". (1934: 18) Twenty years later he still viewed democratic organization of capitalist societies as "only a spasmodic, exceptional state of things . . . impossible as the normal form of society". (1971: 198)

This inherent instability resulted, in Marx's view, from the fact that the combination of private ownership of means of production with political democracy generates a basic contradiction:

> The classes whose social slavery the constitution is to perpetuate, proletariat, peasantry, petty bourgeoisie, it puts in possession of political power through universal suffrage. And from the class whose old social power it sanctions, the bourgeoisie, it withdraws the political guarantees of this power. It forces the political rule of the bourgeoisie into democratic conditions, which at every moment help the hostile classes to victory and jeopardize the very foundation of bourgeois society. From the ones it demands that they should not go forward from political to social emancipation: from the others that they should not go back from social to political restoration. (1952a: 62)

Underlying this theory was the assumption of the fundamental political importance of the objective conflict of material interests. Objective interests in satisfying material needs in the short run – the interest of wage-earners in wages and of capitalists in profit – place the two classes of individuals, "classes-in-themselves," in a situation of objective conflict. The objective conflict of interests is, for Marx, due to the "general law which determines the rise and fall of wages and profit in their reciprocal relation." According to this law, wages and profit "stand in inverse ratio to each other. Capital's share, profit, rises in the same proportion as labour's share, wages, falls and vice versa." Moreover, Marx thought that no improvement of the material conditions of workers would mitigate this conflict:

Even the most favourable situation for the working class, the most rapid possible growth of capital, however much it may improve the material existence of the worker, does not remove the antagonism between his interests and the interests of the bourgeoisie. Profit and wages remain as before in inverse proportions. (1952b: 35, 37)

This argument is based on a tautology: since wages and profits are considered as shares of the value added by living labor (i.e. conflict is always at the margin), no absolute improvement is sufficient to moderate the conflict over distribution. Capitalism is thus a zero-sum system by definition, and no material improvement can have legitimizing effects.

Since the distributional conflict is for Marx irreconcilable, the barriers to the realization of short-term interests are systemic: only when capitalism is abolished can short-term material interests of wage-earners be realized. Hence, the long-term (political) interest in socialism is a direct consequence of the objective conflict of short-term (economic) interests under capitalism. This conflict is the basis of class organization; this conflict becomes pronounced politically during economic crises, and is finally expressed in revolutionary upheavals.

Three central conclusions, all false, follow from these analyses of Marx. First, conflicts over material interests in the short run inevitably lead to conflicts between classes over the form of organization of society. Second, since democracy (universal suffrage more exactly) "unchains class struggle," capitalism can be maintained only by force. Finally, the road to socialism leads through and is an immediate result of economic crises of capitalism.

The historical experience of several societies shows that capitalism can survive for extended periods of time under democratic conditions, even in the face of acute and prolonged economic crises. Contrary to repeated predictions, in several societies universal suffrage has not become an instrument for abolishing capitalism and did not force the bourgeoisie to seek protection under an autonomous dictatorship. Capitalist relations of production can be perpetuated under democratic conditions; exploitation can be maintained with the consent of the exploited.

These observations constituted Gramsci's point of departure.[1] His central problem concerned the strategy of the revolutionary movement under the conditions in which prospects for a transition to socialism through a revolutionary insurrection are absent.[2] He rejected the notion that the

[1] All references to Gramsci, unless otherwise noted, are to the writings collected in *Prison Notebooks* (1971).
[2] See the commentary by Hoare and Smith to the 1971 edition of the *Prison Notebooks* and the beautiful biography by Fiori (1973). Since the Gramsci bibliography is already large enough to fill an entire library, nothing is any longer noncontroversial. Nevertheless, there seems to exist some consensus around the following account of the origins of Gramsci's thought: Lenin, in Gramsci's view, led a successful revolution without understanding why it would have occurred. This revolution was one "against Marx's *Capital*": its

revolution is permanent or that its possibility is universal. Faced with the resilience of capitalism, in the aftermath of a series of defeats, he asked the crucial question which must precede any choice of strategy, any political practice, namely, how does capitalism persist? Marxism may be a theory of revolution, as Lukacs once thought,[3] but only on the condition that this theory comprehends an analysis of the system against which and hence within which it is a revolution. A theory of revolution calls for a theory of capitalism.

This theory must account, in Gramsci's view, for the fact that capitalism survives economic crises, that it becomes "entrenched" against the effects of exploitation, that it reduces conflicts to those played by the rules of capitalist institutions, and finally, that it enjoys "active consent" of the exploited. Gramsci's answers emphasized the function of ideology in maintaining what he called the "hegemony" of the dominant classes. Indeed, we are told at times that Gramsci is the marxist theoretician of "the superstructures," of "cultural domination," of "ideological hegemony."[4] Anderson goes as far as to maintain that "in analysing the contemporary social formations of the West, we can substitute . . . 'culture' or 'ideology' for his 'political struggle' — as the mode of class rule secured by consent." (1977: 42) Since, as Marx said, the means of production owned by the bourgeoisie include the means of production and propagation of ideas, cultural domination can be directly deduced from the economic structure. In the light of these cultural interpretations, capitalism persists because of ideological or cultural domination, and this domination is due to the monopoly of the bourgeoisie over the "ideological apparatuses." (Althusser, 1971) Consent to capitalist relations is a mass delusion, a hoax.

Such interpretations render Gramsci's thought intellectually trivial and politically misdirected. Moreover, they are not sustained by the texts. Gramsci insisted that hegemony must rest on material bases. Objective conditions (which, by the way, "can be measured with the systems of the exact or physical sciences") (Gramsci, 1971: 180) provide a basis for the establishment of hegemony. "The level of development of the material forces of production

---

possibility could not be found in prior marxist theory, particularly as it became interpreted within the Second International. Hence the question was what theoretical bases are needed to establish the possibility of the Bolshevik Revolution. Nevertheless, Gramsci's times were different than those of Lenin: in the "West" a surprise insurrection could not be successful. Hence the theory must find a new road to socialism. See Canbareri (1973) and particularly Paggi (1977).

[3] Lukacs actually opened his *Notes on Lenin* with the assertion that "historical materialism is the theory of the proletarian revolution," an assertion which he was to describe forty-four years later as one which "demonstrates the prejudices of the time" (1971: 9, 90).

[4] See in particular Bobbio (1967: 97), according to whom Gramsci introduced into marxism two "inversions" of which "the first consists of giving the superstructure a privileged place over the base, the second of giving the ideological moment a privileged place over the institutional one within the superstructure." Other similar interpretations are reviewed by Piccone (1977) in the context of their role in contemporary Italian politics. A good critique of these interpretations is given by Texier (1968).

provides a basis for the emergence of the various social classes, each of which represents a function and has a specific position within production itself" (Ibid.: 18). Repeatedly, Gramsci emphasized that hegemony can be organized only if specific objective conditions are present:

It may be deduced that the content of the political hegemony of the new social group which has founded the new type of state be predominantly of an economic order: what is involved is the reorganization of the structure and the real relations between men on the one hand and the world of the economy or production on the other. (Ibid.: 263, 133)

Gramsci was not a determinist: the objective conditions, he thought, are necessary if hegemony is to be established, but they are by no means sufficient. Objective conditions may be present and yet hegemony may not be established because of autonomously political or ideological reasons, as in the case of the Italian bourgeoisie. Yet the objective economic basis is necessary not only to establish hegemony; it is necessary to maintain it continually, "for though hegemony is ethical–political, it must also be economic, must necessarily be based on the decisive function exercised by the leading group in the decisive nucleus of economic activity." (Ibid.: 161)

Hegemony, or more precisely consent to exploitation, can be maintained if the ideology in terms of which "men become conscious of social relations" makes their daily experience intelligible to the masses of people. Interests of the dominant groups must be "concretely coordinated" with those of the subordinate groups (Ibid.: 182). No ideology, marxism included, can perform its function of coordinating individual wills unless it is validated continually by daily life, by what Althusser (1971) calls "the lived experience." If an ideology is to orient people in their daily lives, it must express their interests and aspirations (Gramsci, 1971: 105). A few individuals can be mistaken, but delusions cannot be perpetuated on a mass scale (Ibid.: 327). Ideological hegemony can be maintained only if it rests on a material basis.

The question, thus, is under what material conditions can hegemony be organized and maintained? If hegemony must always be "real," if the ideology that expresses this hegemony must correspond to real interests and aspirations, then some material conditions must be present. In fact, Gramsci paid scant attention to these material conditions of hegemony. They can be reconstructed only if we proceed deductively by searching for the assumptions upon which any analysis of hegemony must be based.

Capitalism, Hegemony, and Democracy

A hegemonic system is, for Gramsci, a capitalist society in which capitalists exploit with consent of the exploited. Consent does not imply an absence of force: for Gramsci physical force, which is permanently organized, always underlies consent. Yet a hegemonic system is one in which this force is not manifest precisely because its utilization is rarely necessary to maintain the capitalist organization of society.

Gramsci's description of the hegemonic system is summarized in two passages which are cited here at length because they will guide much of the subsequent analysis:

> Undoubtedly, the fact of hegemony presupposes that account be taken of the interests and the tendencies of the groups over which hegemony is to be exercised, and that a certain compromise equilibrium should be formed — in other words, that the leading group should make sacrifices of an economic–corporate kind. But there is also no doubt that such sacrifices and such a compromise cannot touch the essential; for though hegemony is ethical–political, it must also be economic, must necessarily be based on the decisive function exercised by the leading group in the decisive nucleus of economic activity.

> The development and expansion of the particular group are conceived of, and presented, as being the motor force of a universal expansion, of a development of all the 'national' energies. In other words, the dominant group is coordinated concretely with the general interests of the subordinate groups, and the life of the State is conceived of as a continuous process of formation and superseding of unstable equilibria (on the juridical plane) between the interests of the fundamental group and those of the subordinate groups — equilibria in which the interests of the dominant group prevail, but only up to a certain point, i.e., stopping short of narrowly corporate economic interest. (1971: 161, 182)

Hegemony must thus be economic in the sense that it can be maintained only by a group that occupies a definite place within the system of production: "the decisive function" in the "decisive nucleus." Hegemony implies that the interest of this group is "correctly coordinated" with the interests of groups over which hegemony is exercised: concrete coordination means here that interests of the "subordinate" groups are to some extent realized. The mechanism by which these groups realize their interests is not completely clear: in the first passage, and in many other places, the reference is to "sacrifices," "compromises," and "concessions" which are made by the bourgeoisie, while the second passage implies that politics ("the life of the State") is organized in such a manner that groups struggle for the realization of their interests within the established institutions ("on the juridical plane"). Finally, hegemony can be maintained only if compromise outcomes can be found within well-defined limits: profits cannot fall below the level which is "essential" for accumulation, yet they cannot be so large as to make capitalists appear to be defending particularistic ("narrowly corporate economic") interest.

In what sense does the capitalist system of production provide the economic foundations for the hegemony of the capitalist class or a segment thereof? Capitalism is a form of social organization in which the entire society is dependent upon actions of capitalists. The sources of this dependence are twofold. First, capitalism is a system in which production is oriented toward the satisfaction of needs of others, toward exchange, which implies that in this system the immediate producers cannot survive on their own. Second, capitalism is a system in which part of the total societal product is withheld from immediate producers in the form of profit which accrues to owners of the means of production. Those who do not own the means of production must sell their capacity to produce to a capitalist, although they are free to choose the capitalist. They obtain a wage, which is not a title to any part of the product which they generate, but a medium for acquisition of any goods and services. They must produce a profit as a condition of their continued employment.

The product is appropriated privately in the sense that wage-earners qua immediate producers have no institutional claim to its allocation. Capitalists, who are profit-takers, decide under multiple constraints how to allocate the product, in particular what part of the profit to invest, where, how, and when. These allocations are constrained by the fact that capitalists (persons and firms) compete with each other and that this competition is regulated at the level of the capital as a whole.

It is a technical fact of any economic system that development cannot take place in the long run unless a part of the product is withheld from immediate consumption and allocated to increase productivity.[5] What distinguishes a system as a capitalist one is that the part withheld from current consumption is derived to a great measure from the part withheld from the immediate producers and is allocated to uses on the basis of the preferences of private capital.[6] As Morishima (1973: 621) put it, "three propositions (i) that capitalists exploit workers . . . (ii) that the capitalist system is profitable . . . and (iii) that the capitalist system is productive are all equivalent." While in any economic system (re)investment is necessary for continued production, employment, and consumption, in a capitalist system profit is a necessary condition for

[5] Investment is not the only source of increased output. Learning may lead to a better organization of production without any additional investment (Arrow, 1962). The under-utilized capacity can be activated. For a discussion of this issue which nevertheless concludes by emphasizing the essential importance of investment see Maddison's (1964) account of the economic development in the West after World War II.

[6] This assertion raises the question whether in a capitalist system saving and investment, even if still directed by capitalists and their delegates, cannot take place mainly out of wages. This question has been a subject of heated theoretical and empirical controversies, since many standard neo-Keynesian results depend upon the assumption that the rate of savings out of profit is higher than that out of wages. See Harcourt (1972: ch. 5) for a review of this controversy and Kaldor (1970) for the demonstration that the rate of savings out of wages is actually negligible, if not negative.

investment. If capitalists do not appropriate profit, if they do not exploit, production falls, consumption decreases, and no other group can satisfy its material interests. Current realization of material interests of capitalists is a necessary condition for the future realization of material interests of any group under capitalism.

This organization of the capitalist system of production provides the basis for the organization of ideological and political hegemony of the capitalist class or some fractions of it. Under capitalist organization of production, capitalists appear as bearers of universal interests. Demands of any group to improve its present life conditions are inimical to the future interests of the entire society, and this trade-off between the present and the future is institutionalized as the conflict between wages and profit. Moreover, since capital is a necessary condition of production, profits appear as reward of capital, without any further obligation concerning future distribution.[7] Finally, since the authority to organize the process of production rests with the legal title to the means of production, relations of authority associated with the division of labor appear as a technical necessity of any production.[8]

The conflict between current wages and current profit constitutes under capitalism not only a societal trade-off between the present and the future, not only a choice between consumption and investment, but even a trade-off between present and future wages. If wages are to increase in the future, a part of the societal product and the associated authority to organize production must pass out of the control of immediate producers. Capitalists are thus in a unique position in a capitalist system: they represent future universal interests while interests of all other groups appear as particularistic and hence inimical to future developments. The entire society is structurally dependent upon actions of capitalists.

Yet at the same time the realization of interests of capitalists is not a sufficient condition for the satisfaction of future interests of anyone else. Wage commitment is made now and for a specified duration (whether wages are paid ex ante or ex post), production takes place now, and profit is now appropriated by capitalists. Profit may be transformed into future increases of the societal product but, under certain constraints, it may also be consumed by capitalists, invested unproductively, or exported elsewhere. Moreover, even if profit is efficiently allocated to increase productivity, no particular group is assured under capitalism to benefit from the past exploitation. There is nothing structural about the capitalist system of production that would guarantee that

---

[7] For an analysis of the ideological function of the very concept of capital see Nuti (1972).

[8] Gramsci: "For the individual workers, the junction between the requirements of technical development and the interests of the ruling class is 'objective'". (1971: 202)

future interests of any particular group be satisfied. *Appropriation of profit by capitalists is a necessary but not a sufficient condition for the future realization of interests of any group.*

Yet hegemony presupposes, Gramsci says, that interests of some groups other than the dominant one be to some degree satisfied. And if interests of the bourgeoisie are to be "concretely coordinated" with the interests of other classes or their fractions, then some mechanisms must be organized through which these interests can find some realization. "Concessions" could constitute one such mechanism, if the bourgeoisie could indeed decide as a unified actor what degree of compromise is necessary for hegemony and if it could impose the self-discipline upon the individual capitalists. An autonomous dictatorship could also force the capitalists into such concessions. Concessions or sacrifices are indeed the terms that Gramsci used in such contexts. Nevertheless, in most Western countries, it is democracy which constitutes this mechanism.

Hegemony becomes organized as institutional conditions which permit those whose labor is extracted at any moment in the social form of profit to struggle in some particular ways for the distribution of the product, the increase of which was made possible by this profit. Specifically, hegemony becomes constituted when struggles over the realization of material interests become institutionalized in a manner rendering their outcomes to some extent indeterminate with regard to positions which groups occupy within the system of production. It is this kind of organization of social relations which constitutes "democracy." Capitalist democracy is a particular form of organization of political relations in which outcomes of conflicts are within limits uncertain, and in particular, in which these outcomes are not uniquely determined by class positions.

In a democracy conflicts have outcomes, since democracy is a system by which they can be terminated (Coser, 1959). Particular institutions, such as elections, collective bargaining, or the courts, constitute mechanisms for terminating, even if at times only temporarily, whatever intergroup conflicts emerge in a society. In the absence of collective bargaining arrangements, strikes are terminated only when one of the parties can no longer afford to continue the conflict. In the absence of elections, competition among elites assumes the form of "power struggles" which may last for an indefinite duration. Moreover, in the absence of such institutions, conflicts which are important to group interests often become terminated only after a physical confrontation. Democracy allows such conflicts to be terminated in a previously specified manner, according to explicit criteria, and often within a specified time. Physical force, although permanently organized, is reserved to those instances when a party to conflicts does not observe the rules or accept the outcome.

Like any system, democracy constitutes a relation between actions of particular groups and the effect of these actions upon them. Conflicts are organized: their outcomes are related to the particular combinations of strategies pursued by various groups. Wildcat strikes confronted with repression result in a different outcome than those to which the response is to accept the wage demands and limit employment. The outcomes are different when strikes concern the very right to organize than when they concern wage demands.

Some courses of action are excluded as admissible strategies. They are excluded in the sense that physical force can be used legitimately if any group reverts to them. Such uses of force are regulated by norms which specify ex ante and universalistically the contingencies in which it can be applied. They are considered legitimate in a particular system if they are limited to the contingencies specified by norms established as outcomes of prior conflicts. Legitimacy thus refers here not to any states of mind of the executors or the victims of repression, but merely to the correspondence between the uses of force and the rules which specify when it can and should be used. Nevertheless, since physical force is organized permanently in anticipation of such contingencies, the potential that this force will become autonomous is inherent in a democratic system.

The exclusion of some courses of action is inherent in any institutionalization of conflicts. When collective bargains acquire the status of contracts, some strikes become illegal and as such subject to the potential use of force. Where elections become organized, all other methods of choosing political leaders become "anti-parliamentary." To cite Gramsci: "It is not true that armies are constitutionally barred from making politics: the army's duty is precisely to defend the constitution – in other words the legal form of the State together with its related institutions." (1971: 212) At the same time, however, democracy cannot be organized in such a manner that strategies are predetermined for each participant. Some freedom of choice – that is, more than one course of action – must be available to any participant.

There is no reason to suppose that the ordering of outcomes upon a configuration of strategies is so strong that each combination uniquely determines the outcome. Conversely, the same outcomes may be associated with multiple configurations of strategies. Some regularity must exist, however, if strategies are to affect outcomes. Democracy cannot be organized in such a manner that all combinations of strategies lead to one and only one outcome, which would render outcomes completely predetermined and independent of the courses of action pursued by participants.

Outcomes of conflicts are thus to some extent indeterminate because each participant has a choice of strategy and all strategies do not lead to the same outcome. Specifically, these outcomes are uncertain. Since any organization of conflicts constitutes an ordering of outcomes upon actions, associated with each set of institutions must be also a distribution of the probability that conflicts will result in particular outcomes. Hence any system attaches prior probabilities to the realization of interests of particular groups. Electoral arrangements, judicial systems, collective bargaining mechanisms, mass media, even the system of university admissions or the regulation of land use – all constitute distributions of prior probabilities of the realization of group specific interests. Democracy thus constitutes an organization of political power in the sense of Poulantzas (1973: 104–14): as a system it determines the capacity of groups to realize their specific interests.

Hence, while the likelihood that interests of a particular group be satisfied to a given extent and in a particular manner is given a priori, outcomes of conflicts are not determined uniquely by places occupied by participants within the system of production. These outcomes are to some extent uncertain. Given a distribution of economic, ideological, and organizational resources, the manner in which conflicts are organized determines which interests are likely to be satisfied, which are unlikely to be satisfied, and, importantly, the variety of interests that are at all likely to be satisfied. The range of the likely outcomes is what characterizes a system as a democracy.

In a democracy, therefore, no group is ever certain that its interests will be realized. As a Chilean newspaper put it in the aftermath of Allende's election to the presidency, "Nobody expected that a marxist president would be elected by means of a secret, universal bourgeois franchise" (El Mercurio, October 17, 1970). All must struggle continually. Their chances are uneven, but they are neither predetermined nor immutable. Democracy condemns all groups to political impotence, since none is able to guarantee its interests once and for all. Before its outcomes all have to bow. Democracy generates outcomes which seem contradictory: once in favor of one group, once in favor of another. It strengthens the causes of the economic power of capitalists while it continually counteracts the political effects of this power. It stands above the society, not with a sword, but with probabilistically distributed opportunity.

These last few sentences paraphrase what Marx had to say about the Bonapartist dictatorship. Marx, who thought that capitalist democracy could not last, saw dictatorship as the only form of capitalist state in which capitalists could pursue their private interests while being politically protected from themselves and from other classes. But where democracy has lasted, it has become a relatively autonomous form of capitalist state: autonomous, that is, up to the probability distribution that constitutes the power of groups located within the system of production. Democracy is the modern Bonaparte.[9]

The indeterminacy inherent in a democratic system constitutes for all the opportunity to realize some of their material interests. Democracy is a social mechanism by which anyone as a citizen can express claims to goods and services which have expanded because a part of the societal product was withheld in the past from the immediate producers. While as immediate producers, wage-earners have no institutional claim to the product, as citizens they can process such claims through the democratic system. Moreover, again as citizens as distinguished from immediate producers, they can intervene in the very organization of production and allocation of profit.

This opportunity is limited but nonetheless real. It is the opportunity to influence the rate of accumulation, to mitigate the operation of the market, to escape the competition for wages, to compensate the effects of increased productivity upon employment, to equalize individual access to some services, to gain some security for old age. And even if this opportunity is limited, it is the only one that is organized, the only one that is available collectively.

It is the uncertainty that draws various groups into democratic institutions. Since outcomes of conflicts are within limits indeterminate, participation becomes an instrument for the collective realization of interests. To participate is to act as if particular courses of action had an impact upon the realization of one's interests. Uncertainty is thus a necessary condition of participation. If outcomes were predetermined, either by the distribution of economic resources or by corporatist arrangements or anything else, there would be no reason for any group to organize and to remain organized as a participant. Neither would there be any reason to participate if outcomes of conflicts were completely indeterminate, that is, if they bore no relation to the courses of action pursued by participants.[10]

At the same time, participation is oriented toward the realization of material interests within the confines of capitalism. In a society in which withholding from current consumption is not a sufficient condition for the improvement of material conditions of any particular group, the opportunity inherent in democracy focuses political activities on material issues.

Conflicts over material interests are not confined to struggles over

---

[9] Hence Poulantzas (1973) is right when he maintains that the state is under capitalism relatively autonomous with regard to classes, but he erroneously attributes to Marx the general character of this autonomy. For Marx the capitalist state had to be dictatorial to be autonomous.

[10] Hence if it is indeed true that Mexicans participate in politics less actively than Americans (Almond and Verba, 1965), it may only indicate that the policies of the state are in Mexico less dependent upon participation. Participation is not an expression of culture but of instrumentality.

distribution. Since the capacity of any group to satisfy material needs in the future depends fundamentally upon decisions of capitalists concerning the volume and the direction of investment, democracy is a system through which these decisions can be influenced by anyone qua citizen. Since the probability that interests of a particular group will be realized to some extent depends upon the manner in which conflicts are organized, conflicts over material interests must extend to the very organization of politics.[11] Hence while in a capitalist democracy politics is indeed the matter of "who gets what, when, and how" (Lasswell, 1936) or a process of establishing the priority of claims to the national product (Bottomore, 1966: 92), conflicts concern as well the direction of production and the organization of politics.

The reduction of politics to material interests is inherent in capitalist democracy. Material needs must be obviously pressing if their satisfaction generates conflicts. But the reason for this reduction is structural: it is the very uncertainty whether material conditions would improve in the future that leads to the search for the immediate security. If profits were a sufficient condition for a future improvement of material life, any group could engage in the kind of relatively certain trade-offs that are available to rentier capitalists: it could choose between investing a portion of its income for five years at 6 percent, ten years at 8 percent, etc. Any individual or group could assume with certainty that their material conditions would improve at a definite time and to a definite degree. Indeed, the purpose of various "social pacts," principally those that tie increases of wages to increases in productivity, is to create this kind of certainty while maintaining profit as the form in which withholding from current consumption is organized.

Yet such social pacts cannot last unless they are coercively enforced because capitalist democracy places any group in the situation of a prisoner's dilemma. It is advantageous for any group to have the security of advancing its interests at the present and only then to participate with others in the uncertain future. Any group is best off in this system if it obtains a wage increase and if other groups pay for the increases of productivity, since in this way it maximizes both its current income and the probability of increasing it in the future. Hence each group enters into politics attempting to maximize its own current consumption and the aggregate volume of investment. But someone must pay for the costs of accumulation. Satisfaction of material interests can thus neither be postponed nor delegated to others since democracy offers only the opportunity but no

---

[11] As Kautsky (1971: 186) wrote in his commentary on the Erfurt Programme. "The economic struggle demands political rights and these will not fall from heaven. To secure and maintain them, the most vigorous political action is necessary."

guarantees. As long as material needs are present, political conflicts focus on material issues.

Capitalist democracy is thus a system in which the dependence upon privately appropriated profit as the form in which a part of product is withheld from current consumption is the basis for somewhat indeterminate conflicts over the realization of material interests. Capitalist democracy at the same time structures political activities as political participation and reduces political conflicts to short-term material issues. It simultaneously generates conflicts over material issues and reduces conflicts to such issues. As Bonomi (1975: 993) points out, the price of hegemony is that certain conflicts must be tolerated, but at the same time the effect of hegemony is that only certain conflicts become organized. In this sense democracy provides the "trenches":

The massive structures of the modern democracies, both as State organizations, and as complexes of associations in civil society, constitute for the art of politics as it were "trenches" and the permanent fortifications of the front in the war position: they render merely "partial" the element of movement which used to be "the whole" of war, etc. (Gramsci, 1971: 243)

Reproduction of Consent of Wage-Earners

In a capitalist society, the realization of interests of capitalists is a necessary but not a sufficient condition for the realization of interests of any other group. This objective correlation between the organization of a society as a capitalist system and the interests of capitalists opens the possibility for establishing a hegemonic system in which the capitalist class becomes perceived as embodying universal interests and in which political conflicts become structured as conflicts concerning the realization of material interests within the confines of capitalism. Organized as a capitalist democracy, this hegemony system constitutes a form of class compromise in the sense that in this system neither the aggregate of interests of individual capitals nor the interests of organized wage-earners can be violated beyond specific limits.

This compromise can be reproduced only on the condition that wage-earners "consent" to the capitalist organization of society. The term "consent" is used to avoid the mentalistic connotations often associated with the concept of legitimacy. *The consent which underlies reproduction of capitalist relations does not consist of individual states of mind but of behavioral characteristics of organizations.* It should be understood not in psychological or moral terms. Consent is *cognitive* and *behavioral.*[12] Social actors, individual and collective, do not march around filled with "predispositions" which they simply execute. Social relations constitute structures of choices within which people perceive, evaluate, and act. *They consent when they choose particular courses of action and when they follow these choices in their practice.* Wage-earners consent to capitalist organization of society when they act as if they could improve their material conditions within the confines of capitalism. More specifically, they consent when they act collectively as if capitalism were a positive-sum game, that is, when they cooperate with capitalists as they choose their strategies.[13]

Gramsci asserts that consent becomes reproduced on the condition that the hegemonic system, which is based on the private ownership of the means of production, yields outcomes that to some degree satisfy short-term material interests of various groups. Thus, in this view *the reproduction of a particular form of social relations is conditional upon the outcomes of conflicts organized within these social relations.* This is theoretically a radical answer. Its far-reaching implications become apparent when this view is contrasted with those theories which attribute the particular form of social arrangements, whether the market or democracy, to some kind of a mysterious prior agreement, contract, or consensus about these forms of organization.[14] No prior consensus is necessary for Gramsci. Only the a-posteriori consent lies at the foundation of the capitalist social order. This consent is socially organized: the entire edifice of social and political organizations becomes erected to generate it. Yet this consent cannot be maintained interminably unless it corresponds to the real interests of those consenting. Legality, in Gramsci's view, is not a sufficient condition of consent.[15] Even if legitimacy constitutes a "generalized readiness . . . to accept decisions of still undetermined content" (Luhmann, 1975: 28), this readiness must be continually reinforced by the content. *"Legitimacy" is just a suspension of withdrawal of consent.* It merely provides a time horizon beyond which this consent, regardless how thoroughly it is organized, will no longer be granted if it does not find real corollaries in material interests.

Consent to the existing social relations is thus always tentative. The "end of ideology" is never possible: no social order is given once and for all. The consent to capitalism is permanently conditional: there exist material limits beyond which it will not be granted, and beyond these limits there may be crises.

[12] Gramsci: "The thesis which asserts that men become conscious of fundamental conflicts on the level of ideology is not psychological or moralistic in character, but structural and epistemological. . . ." (1971: 164, 365)

[13] "Cooperation" consists of making strategies and threats known to the opponent in the course of negotiations. See Luce and Raiffa (1958: ch. 6).

[14] See Godelier (1972) for a devastating critique of social contract theories.

[15] For a summary of a German discussion about the relation between legality and legitimacy see Habermas (1975: Part 111, ch. 1).

Reproduction of consent of wage earners requires that their material interests be to some extent satisfied within the capitalist society. Wage-earners view capitalism as a system in which they can improve their material conditions: they organize as participants and act as if capitalism were a positive-sum system when they benefit at a particular time from the fact that a part of societal product was previously withheld from current consumption in the form of profit. Capitalists retain the capacity to withhold a part of the societal product because the profits they appropriate are expected to be saved, invested, transformed into productive potential and partly distributed as gains to other groups.

These clearly are not "savings" in the sense in which economists use this term when workers loan some of their wages to capitalists as bank deposits. When workers save out of wages, they decide whether to do so and they know a priori at least the nominal rate of return. When, on the other hand, wage-earners consent to a capitalist system, they neither decide whether some of the product will be withheld from them, nor do they decide how much, nor are they in any way assured of some set rate of transformation of present profits into future wages.

Criticizing a model of economic growth developed by Kaldor (1970), Pasinetti observed that there is a logical slip in the model since workers save – in the economist's sense – but do not obtain any return on their investment. Pasinetti continues:

And since ownership entitles the owner to a rate of interest, if workers have saved – and thus own a part of the stock of capital (directly or through loans to capitalists) – then they will also receive a share of total profits. . . . By attributing all profits to the capitalists it [Kaldor's theory] has inadvertently but necessarily implied that workers' savings are always totally transferred as a gift to the capitalists. Clearly this is an absurdity. (Pasinetti, 1970: 96)

But why stop there? Is it not an absurdity that wage-earners would obtain less than the product without expecting that profits will be eventually transformed into an improvement of their material conditions? Is it not an absurdity that they would consent to capitalist relations, that they would not use their political rights for "social emancipation" if there did not exist a real possibility for realizing their material interests in some foreseeable future? But if it is true that reproduction of consent requires that profits be transformed in the course of time into improvements of material conditions of wage-earners, then given the past history of profits *there must exist at any time a level of wage increases which is minimally necessary to reproduce consent.* This level is not given uniquely by the past history of profits since it depends upon the economic militancy of wage-earners' organizations. Nevertheless, a minimal level of realization of material interests is necessary to reproduce consent, and this level is a function of past profits.

This minimal level can be thought of in the following manner. Let $P(t-v)$, $v = 0, 1, 2 \ldots, t$, represent the history of profits appropriated by capitalists during the sucessive periods of time in the past. Let r indicate the economic militancy of organized wage-earners; specifically, let it show what proportion of current profits must be transformed into wage increases if consent is to be reproduced. Then the increase of wages between the time t and the time $(t + 1)$ must be at least $\Delta W(t)$ if consent is to be reproduced. In a simple case it may be true that:

$$\Delta \hat{W}(t) = rP(t), \; r > 0; \; t = 0, 1, 2 \ldots \tag{1}$$

Given the definition of the difference, Δ, the level of wages necessary to reproduce consent at time t is given by

$$\hat{W}(t) = W(t-1) + rP(t-1). \tag{2}$$

This rule asserts that if consent is to be reproduced, wages must equal at least a given proportion of past profits, where this proportion depends upon economic militancy of wage-earners' organizations.

What this rule describes are the a-posteriori material conditions of consent, i.e. the manner in which wage-earners react to wages that they already have obtained. Specifically, the quantity $\hat{W}(t)$ is supposed to represent the level of satisfaction of material interests of wage-earners below which their consent to the capitalist system breaks down. Conversely, as long as wages exceed this level, consent can be reproduced.

Accumulation and Legitimation

Hegemony consists of exploitation with consent. This consent is not manufactured artificially. Consent must be based on a material basis: if wage-earners are to act as if capitalism were a positive-sum system, their material conditions must be improving as a consequence of past exploitation. Hence material interests of wage-earners must be realized at each time to some definite extent if hegemony is to be maintained.

Legitimation constitutes, therefore, a perpetual constraint upon accumulation in hegemonic capitalist societies. The question to be examined is under what conditions reproduction of consent must necessarily result in crises of accumulation.

As is well known, Marx thought that the rate of profit and hence the rate of capitalist accumulation must tendentially fall in the course of capitalist development even when wages remain at, albeit historically determined, subsistence levels. Marx's argument had nothing to do with distribution between capitalists and workers (although it relied on the distribution of surplus value as profit among capitalists) precisely because it was based on the assumption of endogenously determined wage levels. Yet regardless of the validity of Marx's argument concerning the rate of profit, there is today sufficient evidence that wage levels are not determined endogenously by the system of production alone and, actually, that wages have grown more during the past one hundred years than any nontautological definition of a changing subsistence would allow.

Hence the question to be examined is whether the rate of profit (and of accumulation) must fall if wages are formed at the consent-reproducing, rather than the subsistence, level. More specifically, we will inquire whether the rate of profit must fall because of the requirements of legitimation, even when it does not fall for reasons immanent to capitalist organization of production. Conversely, the problem is whether consent can be reproduced in a capitalist society in which accumulation continues, i.e. whether continuing accumulation necessarily generates crises of consent.

In order to examine these questions it is necessary to introduce some assumptions concerning at least the short-term dynamic of capitalist economic systems. Given the focus on the fall of the rate of profit induced by requirements of legitimation, it seems sensible to simplify the analysis by choosing a model of the economy in which this rate does not fall for Marx's nondistributional reasons and in which wages are exogenously determined. Let us first suppose, with a fair degree of simplification, that the entire gross national product is divided during each period into gross profits (i.e. costs of replacement of capital plus surplus) and wages, so that

$$Y(t) = P(t) + W(t), \tag{3}$$

where $Y(t)$ represents the gross product, $P(t)$ the gross profits, and $W(t)$ represents wages. With some simplification again, profit represents capitalists' share of the gross national product, including both the costs of reproduction of capital used up during each cycle of production and surplus or net profit, while wages represent all of the incomes derived from employment.

Secondly, we will assume that the dynamic of gross product is ruled by

$$Y(t + 1) = (1 + s/c)P(t) + W(t), \tag{4}$$

where s represents the rate of savings out of (gross) profit and c is the (gross) capital/output ratio.[16] The rate of savings out of wages, which is typically negligible (Kaldor, 1970), is taken to be zero. The logic of this description is the following: capitalists save a proportion s of their (gross) profit and invest it in an economy in which c units of capital are necessary to generate an additional unit of output. Note that both parameters, s and c, characterize the behavior of capitalists: their abstemiousness and efficiency in allocating investments. Wages are taken to be exogenous, representing the neo-Ricardian aspect of the model. They are thought to be partially determined by the democratic mechanisms described above, so that we can think in general of the actual level of wages as being characterized by a prior probability distribution $W_i(t)$.

Now, the question is what will happen in such a capitalist system when wages are at all times equal to the level at which consent is reproduced, i.e., when

$$W(t) = \hat{W}(t) \text{ for all } t, \, t = 0, \, 1, \, 2 \ldots \tag{5}$$

Since the consent-reproducing level of wages depends upon the economic militancy of wage-earners, r, now this parameter determines the actual level of wages.

With these assumptions, we can now examine the dynamic relation between accumulation and legitimation. The general results are the following. When wage-earners are not militant economically relative to the abstemiousness and efficiency of capitalists, then profits grow exponentially, wages and the total product grow exponentially, and distribution becomes altered in favor of wages up to a certain point. When wage-earners are moderately militant economically, always in terms relative to the behavior of capitalists, then profits decline at an ever-decreasing rate, wages and the total product grow at the ever-decreasing rate, and the share of wages tends to unity. Finally, when wage-earners are highly militant economically, wages increase temporarily and then fall almost to their original level, while profits fall sharply during the time when wages increase. The total product increases briefly and then declines almost to its original level.

These results imply, therefore, that continual capitalist accumulation is possible, on the condition that wage-earners are not militant economically, even when wages are at all times sufficient to reproduce consent. In other terms, distributional conflicts do not necessarily lead to a falling rate of profit, even

---

[16] The standard way to derive this dynamic equation is to assume that

(1) a part $S(t)$ is saved out of profits
$$S(t) = sP(t),$$

(2) investment, $I(t)$, is ruled by the expectation of aggregate demand,
$$I(t) = c\Delta Y(t),$$

(3) savings are made to invest and in equilibrium
$$S(t) = I(t).$$

Using this accounting equation (3) and solving this system yields (4). See Harrod (1970).

when wages are sufficient for legitimation. A capitalist system in which consent is at all times reproduced and in which accumulation proceeds smoothly is conceivable from the distributional point of view.

A fall in the rate of profit and the concomitant arrest of accumulation result, however, from distributional conflicts when wage-earners, whose consent is being reproduced, are at least moderately militant. When they are moderately militant, a secular tendency of the rate of profit to fall ensues as the result of legitimation. When wage-earners are highly militant, consent can be reproduced only when costs of reproduction of capital are not returned to capitalists, i.e. when the basic conditions of capitalist accumulation are not reproduced.

Wage-earners who are not militant end up materially best-off after a sufficiently long time. Since consent-reproducing wages follow past profits, and since profits expand rapidly when wage-earners are not militant, actual wages continue to expand as accumulation proceeds. Moreover, wages increase typically as a proportion of gross national product. In the illustration presented in Figure 3 the share of wages climbs from the initial 50 percent of the product to 74.12 percent at the end of the thirty-second cycle, and eventually reaches 86.31. This is still an unequal society, not only in terms of control over the process of production, but even in terms of distribution of personal income. Assuming that (noninstitutional) capitalists constitute 3 percent of all households, their per-household personal income is still 5.66 times greater than the income of an average household of the remaining 97 percent of the population at the end of the thirty-second cycle, and it would still be 2.55 times greater if the process continued forever. Indeed, as long as profits (and product) continually expand, capitalists are personally better off than the rest of the people and some of them are likely to be much better off. Since under capitalism even poverty tends to be unequally distributed, such inequalities may be sufficiently annoying, but they do continue to decrease until wages reach about 84 percent of the total product. Most importantly, a redistribution of personal income would have little effect upon the improvement of life conditions of wage-earners. If personal incomes were equalized at the end of the thirty-second period, the total gain in the wage fund would have been 33.64: a gain equivalent to that generated by growth in the previous five periods.

The fact that when wage-earners are not militant personal consumption of capitalists remains at high levels, $(1 - s)P(t)$ in terms of our model, signifies, however, not only inequality but also inefficiency. The part of profit consumed by capitalists, about one-half, is a part withdrawn from accumulation. If capitalists were personally only as well off as the rest of the people, or more precisely, if the same part of the total product was allocated to investment as is withheld from the immediate producers, the rate of growth would be much

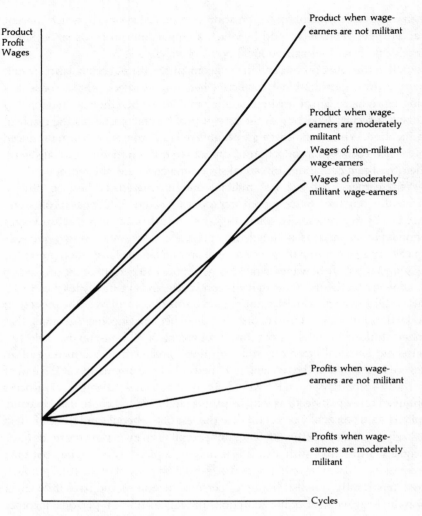

Figure 3. The dynamic of profit, wages, and product when $s/c = 0.10$ and $r = 0.08$ and 0.10

higher. In general, the inquality between personal incomes derived from profits and from wages means that growth of consumption over time is inferior to one that would have been achieved in an egalitarian society when other conditions are the same. If present consumption always takes place at the cost of the future, the consumption of capitalists is exceptionally costly. Even when wage-earners are not militant economically, and accumulation is as rapid as is possible, capitalist growth is suboptimally efficient.

Although in a long run the wage-earners who are not militant are better off, a moderate level of economic militancy is the dominant strategy, in the game-theory sense of this term, over a medium run. Figure 3 shows that when wage-earners are moderately militant they are better off during the first twenty-two periods than their less militant counterparts. This is a long period of time, whether it is measured in durations of collective contracts, electoral intervals, or even years: it represents at least one generation. Hence, the pressure toward militancy is built into the structure of the intertemporal trade-off. Note again that the consequence of moderate levels of militancy is a secular fall in the rate of profit and of accumulation.

Moderate militancy, however, dominates a more militant posture over any period of time longer than a few years. When wage-earners are highly militant, wages first increase rapidly at the expense of profits. It can be shown that when r is at least as large as $(1 + s/c)$, then consent can be reproduced only on the condition that entire profits, including the capital used up in the particular cycle of production, pass into the hands of wage-earners. In an economy in which the rate of savings out of (gross) profits is about 0.40 and the (gross incremental) capital/output ratio is about 4, an r equal to 1.1. will be confiscatory in this sense. Hence there exists a strategy on the part of wage-earners which is anticapitalist while being purely economic. When wage-earners are so militant as to reject cooperation with capital unless at least 110 percent of current profits are immediately transformed into increases of wages, a crisis is imminent. Unless, however, this sudden increase of incomes of wage-earners is accompanied by a socialist transformation of the very process of accumulation, it will lead to an economic crisis. With the fall of profits, investment will also decline, and eventually the total product, employment, and consumption. Economic crises, when not accompanied by political transformations, fall on the shoulders of wage-earners. the costs of recovery become expressed in terms of wages or employment or both.

Figure 4 shows the evolution of wages associated with different strategies on the part of wage-earners. The least militant wage-earners, whose consent can be reproduced when only 1 percent of current profits becomes transformed into wage increases, are best off after almost 50 cycles, but earlier they are not as well off as their more militant counterparts. Wages still continue to grow indefinitely when wage-earners are satisfied with 8 percent of current profits, but again such wage-earners are worse off for a long period of time, twenty-two cycles as we have seen earlier, than the slightly more militant wage-earners whose consent can be reproduced only at the cost of 10 percent of current profits. When they become highly militant, however, wage-earners are better off, under capitalism, for only a few cycles, and they continue to be worse off in the future. *The moderately militant strategy is thus dominant over any reasonable period of time: high*

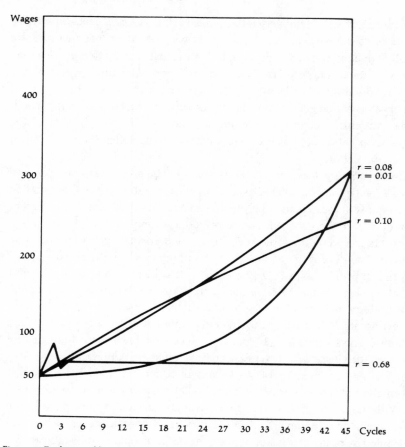

Figure 4. Evolution of legitimizing wages associated with different degrees of militancy of wage-earners, when $s/c = 0.10$

militancy generates economic crises, low militancy puts off the gains into the distant future. Hence, in spite of the fact that a sustained rate of profit (and accumulation) is possible under capitalism, one should expect wage-induced or, more precisely, legitimation-induced cyclical behavior. Legitimation of capitalism when wage-earners are moderately militant results in a "profit squeeze" (Glyn and Sutcliffe, 1972) and a slowdown of accumulation.

Note, however, that all statements concerning the effects of wage-earners' militancy upon the evolution of profits and wages are conditional upon the behavior of capitalists with regard to saving and allocation of investment. When capitalists invest in such a manner that less capital becomes necessary to produce an additional unit of output, and, in particular, when they save a higher proportion of profits, wages can grow faster without resulting in a slowdown of

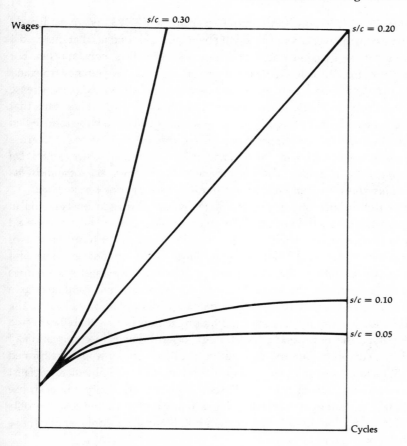

Figure 5. Evolution of legitimizing wages when $r = 0.1708$ and the rate of saving out of profits increases

accumulation. Figure 5 shows the dynamic of legitimizing wages when reproduction of consent requires that 17.08 percent of current profits be immediately transformed into wages increases and when s/c increases from 0.05 to 0.10, 0.20, and eventually to 0.30.

Since wages can grow faster when s/c is higher, which means practically that capitalists' rate of saving out of profits is higher, wage-earners have a profound interest under capitalism in influencing, in their status as citizens, this aspect of behavior of capitalists. Investment tax credits, differential taxation of undistributed and distributed profits, and accelerated depreciation schedules are among the more or less effective instruments by which saving behavior of capitalists can be influenced. The game between wage-earners and capitalists is not limited to distribution since, contrary to Lancaster (1973), wage-earners do have some control over capitalists' saving behavior. This implies that there exist trade-offs between wage-earners' militancy and capitalists' consumption. For example, the effect upon legitimizing wages of a decrease of militancy from an r equal to 0.10 to an r equal to 0.08 is compensated over four cycles by an increase of s/c from 0.10 to 0.125. If we assume that c is equal to 2, this means that legitimizing wages of the less militant wage-earners will remain the same when the rate of capitalists' consumption is reduced from 80 to 75 percent of gross profits. *The game is therefore cooperative in the sense that wage-earners bid legitimizing levels of wages while threatening with militancy and capitalists bid increased investments out of profits while threatening to increase consumption.*

But the fact that the total "pie" increases under capitalism is inconsequential in itself, since if workers did not obtain any part of the increase, the game would remain a noncooperative one. It would still be in the short-term interest of workers to "expropriate the expropriators," since they could not be worse off if profits became negative. The positive-sum nature of the capitalist system does not in itself constitute the game between wage-earners and capitalists as a cooperative one. If and only if wage-earners regularly obtain some part of the increase made possible by the past exploitation can they be reasonably expected not to pursue the noncooperative strategy of an immediate confiscation of capital. The conflict becomes a cooperative one if and only if wages are formed at a legitimizing level and when political conditions for an immediate socialist accumulation are absent. Under those conditions, but only under those conditions, the strategy of increasing wages in the short run at the cost of profits is dominated by the strategy of moderate militancy, and only under those conditions is cooperation possible.

Needless to say, wage-earners would always be better off if they could obtain higher incomes and allocate these incomes to a socialist accumulation, since then they would have direct control over the rates of investment. No trade-offs of wages for capitalists' willingness to invest would then be necessary. Nevertheless, the fact that socialist accumulation is more efficient in the longer run does not imply that wage-earners interested in the short-run improvement of their material conditions would necessarily opt for a socialist transformation. Such a transformation is likely to generate an economic crisis during which material conditions of wage-earners would be adversely affected. Hence, political conditions for a socialist transformation are not always present.

Conjunctures and Crises

Since outcomes of conflicts are indeterminate by virtue of the organization of a system as a democracy, the conclusions drawn above establish only the possibility of continuous capitalist accumulation. Accumulation free of crises caused by distributional conflicts is possible if wage outcomes resulting from these conflicts happen at each time to be exactly sufficient to reproduce the consent of economically nonmilitant wage-earners. But precisely because democracy must allow uncertainty if it is to be effective in generating participation, crises may occur even if they can be avoided. Crisis-free accumulation is thus by no means certain, or likely, even if wage-earners are not militant.

The notion of a distributional crisis of accumulation was implicit in the preceding deterministic analysis of the long run. A crisis of consent occurs any time when actual wages fall below the level $\hat{W}(t)$ necessary to reproduce it. In order to characterize a concrete historical situation as a crisis, it remains therefore to determine the minimal requirements of the system with regard to profits. Let the current level of profits necessary for accumulation to continue at a fixed rate be $\hat{P}(t)$.

A distributional crisis occurs, therefore, when the sum of wage and profits requirements is larger than the total product:

$$\hat{W}(t) + \hat{P}(t) > Y(t). \tag{6}$$

If wages were fixed to always equal the level necessary to reproduce consent, then the occurrence of crises would depend only upon the economic militancy of wage-earners and the behavior of capitalists. But outcomes of distributional conflicts are uncertain and a crisis may occur even if it can be avoided given s, c, and r, that is, even when wage-earners are not militant relative to the rate of saving and the efficiency of the technology.

Wage-earners consent to capitalist relations because they expect profits to be transformed into improvements of their future life conditions. This implies that there exists a level of wages necessary to reproduce consent. In turn, as long as wage-earners consider profits obtained in the past, there also exists a minimal level of profits which is necessary if reproduction of consent is to be possible in the future while accumulation continues. *Future legitimation requires current accumulation.* If wages fall below the minimal level and/or profits are not sufficient to reproduce consent and to allow future profits, a crisis must ensue.

The analysis of concrete situations is best conducted geometrically. A crisis can be portrayed as in Figure 6.

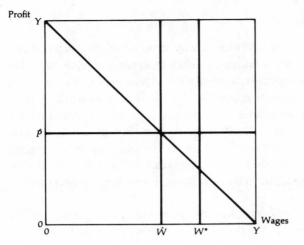

Figure 6.

Think of Figure 6 in the following manner. The side of the square represents the gross product at the particular time, $Y(t)$. Wages and profits are measured, respectively, on the horizontal and the vertical axes. Given that the product is partitioned into wages and profits, any distribution that satisfies this condition must lie on the diagonal for which it is true that

$$P(W) = Y - W. \tag{7}$$

Any distributional outcome can thus be represented as $[W(t), \hat{P}(t)]$ or $[W(t), P(W)]$. The point of intersection of $\hat{P}(t)$ and $P(W)$ is projected vertically upon the $W(t)$ axis. This point represents maximal wage level at which the condition (6) will be satisfied if it can be. This level of wage is

$$W^*(t) = Y(t) - \hat{P}(t). \tag{8}$$

It can be seen immediately that the situation represented in Figure 6 represents a crisis: there is no segment of the diagonal $[W(t), P(W)]$ which does not violate one of the two minimal requirements. If the level of wages is $0 < W < W^*$, then wages are lower than $\hat{W}$. If the level of wages is $W^* < W < \hat{W}$, then both profits and wages are below the minimally required levels. If $\hat{W} < W < Y$, then profits are lower than $\hat{P}$.

A crisis would be avoidable, however, if the sum of the minimal requirements of consent and accumulation was lower than the total product. In the situation portrayed in Figure 7 a wage outcome $0 < W < \hat{W}$ results in a breakdown of consent, and an outcome $W^* < W < Y$ threatens accumulation. But any

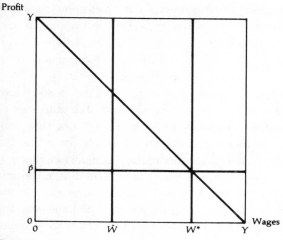

Figure 7.

outcome in the segment $\hat{W} < W < W^*$ satisfies both requirements. Hence this is not a crisis conjuncture even if crises may occur.

Note that the total product is the same in both the crisis conjuncture and the conjuncture in which crises can be avoided. If consent is conditioned by the past history of profits, then crises are not manifest at the level of economic indicators. They are more likely to occur when profits were high in the past, that is during periods of rapid expansion.

Before proceeding any further, let us reflect upon what has been described. We have seen that each historical moment is constituted by the past actions of wage-earners and profit-takers in such a manner that the total product, the level of wages necessary to produce consent, and the level of profit necessary to maintain the rate of accumulation are given at this moment by past history. They are inherited from the past and given at the present as conditions which are objective in the sense that they are independent of the actions pursued under these conditions. People do make history, but they make it under conditions inherited from the past. What exactly are these conditions? They constitute any moment of history, any concrete situation, or "conjuncture," as

Conjuncture (t): $Y(t)$, $\hat{W}(t)$, $\hat{P}(t)$, r, s, c.   (9)

But these conditions inherited from the past determine the consequences of distributional outcomes that occur at a particular moment for the preservation or transformation of social relations. While actual distributional outcomes are indeterminate from the point of view of conditions inherited from the past, these conditions determine the mapping of distributional outcomes upon crises that result from them. A crisis conjuncture is one in which the mapping of the consequences for the preservation or transformation of social relations is wage crisis/wage and profit crisis/profit crisis. The mapping in the conjuncture in which crises can be avoided is wage crisis/no crisis/profit crisis.

A conjuncture can thus be characterized as the mapping of the consequences for transformation or preservation of social relations upon the outcomes of conflicts which occur within it. A conjuncture, always identified concretely with regard to time and place, is the set of conditions which determine the consequences of actions feasible under these conditions. A conjuncture is simply "the situation," "a historical moment," a particular state of affairs. But, as we have shown, the conditions characterizing a concrete historical situation are at the same time empirical and theoretical: as Althusser put it, "simultaneously the existing conditions and the conditions of existence of the phenomena under consideration." (1970: 207) They are empirical in the sense that they are the concrete conditions at a given moment, and they are theoretical precisely because they determine the consequences of actions which occur at this moment.

While the consequences are thus determined, outcomes of conflicts are uncertain. The distribution of the probability that a particular distributional outcome $[W_i, P_i]$ will result at a particular time from intergroup conflicts is determined by the manner in which these conflicts are organized at this time. This distribution can be, for example, the one portrayed in Figure 8.

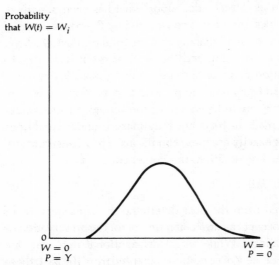

Figure 8.

This probability distribution W_i constitutes one of the elements constituting a conjuncture, since it determines the likelihood that a crisis will occur, conditional upon all the other elements specified above. Let us superimpose the distribution $W_i(t)$ from Figure 8 upon the conjuncture portrayed in Figure 7 (see Figure 9). It is apparent that the shaded area gives the probability that a crisis will occur, given the conjuncture as specified by equation (9). Even if crises can be avoided, they may be quite likely if W_i is flat relative to the segment $\hat{W} < W < W^*$.

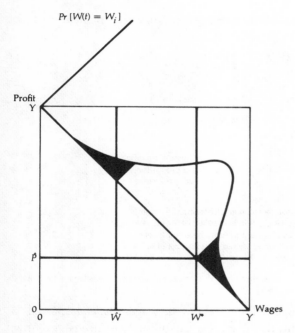

Figure 9.

If consent is to be reproduced continually while profits are not falling, capitalist democracy must be organized in such a manner that, on the one hand, outcomes of conflicts cannot be so uncertain as to make it likely that basic material interests of wage-earners or capitalists will be violated but, on the other hand, they must be sufficiently uncertain to absorb wage-earners as participants. If outcomes are determined enough to guarantee that when it can be, consent will be reproduced continually at nondecreasing levels of profits, this certainty may reach the point at which participation becomes eroded.

The general trend of historical development of capitalist democracies has been in the direction of reducing the uncertainty. The prior distribution has evolved from one which was biased toward profits and highly uncertain, as in Figure 8, to one which is more favorable to wages and at the same time very narrow, as in Figure 10 which portrays the a-posteriori, empirical distribution in Western Europe between 1953 and 1964.

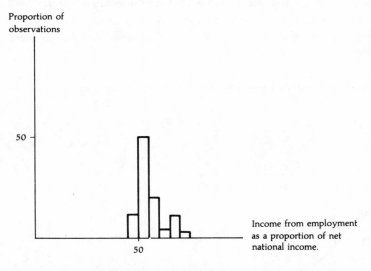

Four observations were given for each country, consisting of mean proportions between 1953 and 1955, 1956 and 1958, 1959 and 1961, and 1962 and 1964. Income from employment includes here employers' contributions to social security. Source: United Nations Economic Commission for Europe (1967, part 2, chapter 2, 30–1).

Figure 10. A-posteriori distribution of outcomes in 11 Western European countries between 1953 and 1964

Within a very narrow range, at the time between wages that equal 50 and 55 percent of total product, this distribution is flat, but its variance is very low. Within this range all outcomes are equally possible, outside of this range they are nearly impossible. The flavor of conflicts organized in this manner is nicely conveyed by the following account of a convention of the S.P.D.:

In one important respect a majority of delegates outdid the Eppler Commission. They voted to increase the top rate of income tax – now 53 percent – to 60 percent, while the Commission proposed the rate of 58 percent. This caused Professor Schiller [then Minister of the Economy and heir apparent to party leadership] to remark to his Cabinet colleagues: 'Obviously these people are trying to get quite a different sort of Republic from the one we have.' (*Guardian*, November 27, 1971)

This trend is not due to any "functions" of the state, even if it is functional for avoiding crises of consent (and dysfunctional for participation). It constitutes a cumulative effect of reforms which have resulted from past crises. One way in which the conflicts that appear during crises can be terminated is when wage-earners agree to tolerate wages below the consent-reproducing level in exchange for an increase in the probability of obtaining higher wages from this moment on. This probability is none less than power, and reforms are precisely those changes in the organization of conflicts which alter the power of specific groups. Extensions of franchise, proportional representation, the right to organize, countrywide collective agreements, and public financing of elections are among many such reforms which typically resulted from crises of consent. Capitalists did lose power in the course of history of capitalism.

Yet a cumulative effect of these reforms is a crisis of participation. When conflicts over the realization of material interests, as well as about organization of conflicts, are organized in such a manner that their outcomes are independent of the actions undertaken by participants, organizations representing wage-earners on the terrain of democratic institutions lose their support. As long as these outcomes are uncertain and depend upon actions of the masses, wage-earners must be organized to participate. But when election results and collective bargaining outcomes have no visible impact upon the material conditions of wage-earners, masses become dissociated from their representatives. Problems faced by the society are lived as acute and urgent; institutions organized to resolve conflicts are the representative institutions; and yet, election after election, collective agreement after collective agreement, nothing is resolved. The institutional crisis of several advanced capitalist societies is a crisis of participation: there is no reason for wage-earners to act as if their participation made a difference if it is becoming increasingly clear that it does so less and less. And the withdrawal of groups from the representative institutions has a profound destabilizing effect upon these institutions (Przeworski, 1975). When groups cease to participate, "parties" become "movements": politics becomes focused on the organization of society because economic issues become replaced by social, cultural, and ideological conflicts which cannot be easily resolved in a cooperative fashion (Habermas, 1975). Participation is necessary to reproduce the organization of a society as a capitalist democracy because participation reduces political activities to material issues, and these can be resolved under capitalism in a cooperative manner. The "postindustrial society" is not one in which everyone has what they want, but one in which the capacity of democratic institutions to absorb conflicts has been undermined by the growing independence of outcomes from mass actions.

Breakdown of Consent and Force

Gramsci persistently emphasized that economic crises do not lead automatically to "fundamental historical crises," that is, to revolutionary situations. The civil society, he said, "has become a very complex structure and one which is resistant to the catastrophic 'incursion' of the immediate economic element (crises, depressions, etc.)." (1971: 235) To put it differently, a breakdown of either the material or political basis of consent does not become necessarily manifested in a revolutionary upsurge of the dominated classes. A breakdown of consent is not a sufficient condition for a breakdown of capitalism, since its effect is first to bring to the fore the coercive mechanisms which underlie the reproduction of capitalist relations. Hegemony is "protected by the armour of coercion," and when consent breaks down coercion can still hold the system together.

When writing about hegemony, Gramsci typically attributed the coercive function to the "superstructures," either the state or the "civil society," where the latter does not include the system of production. Nevertheless, his analyses of capitalist economic relations imply that elements of coercion are to be found even at this level. Economic relations are of themselves coercive, in the sense that, regardless of individual states of mind, anyone who does not own the means of production must subject him or herself to the wage relation as a condition of physical survival. Counterhegemony cannot be exclusively ideological, for as long as coercion operates at the level of the economic structure, individual actions must express this structure. But even at the collective level, the economic structure of capitalism has a coercive effect upon wage-earners' organizations.

A breakdown of the material basis of consent becomes expressed within the working class as a transformation of the relation between the masses and the leaders who are during normal times simultaneously their representatives in the existing institutions. It is the task of working-class organizations to secure the realization of material interests of the masses. When they have failed in this task, the relation of representation, internal to the class, becomes affected first. At this moment the road bifurcates and the leaders—representatives face a sharply defined choice. Either they adopt a strategy of participating in democratic institutions to transform the capitalist system of production or the relation of representation breaks down. Hence, either the democratic system becomes the arena of conflicts over the organization of the system of production or the entire representative system becomes weakened as wage-earners withdraw from their organization of a society as a capitalist democracy is threatened: under such circumstances participation no longer expresses consent while withdrawal from participation is a threat to the democratic organization of conflicts.

Yet as long as accumulation is financed out of profits, private profits are necessary for accumulation. Crises of capitalism are in no one's material interest. In particular, crises of capitalism are a threat to wage-earners since capitalism is a system in which economic crises must fall eventually on their shoulders. No one drew the blueprint and yet the system is designed in such a way that if profits are not sufficient, then eventually either wages must fall, or employment, or both. If anyone is to be better off under capitalism, wage-earners cannot obtain more than that which is warranted by the abstemiousness and the efficiency of capitalists. Decisions by capitalists to save and to choose techniques of production constitute the parameters which constrain the possibility of improvement of material conditions of anyone. When profits are too low, when capitalists do not save, or when they invest inefficiently, the rate of growth of product falls and the opportunity of anyone to improve material conditions falls with it. And under capitalism there are no ways to get out of a crisis other than to increase the rate of savings out of profits, increase the input/output efficiency of production, and/or reduce wages (or force savings, which is the same). The brunt of the cost becomes expressed either in terms of unemployment or a fall of wages. Unless one of these occurs, and quite likely both, the crisis must get deeper and, under capitalism, the recovery more costly to wage-earners.

An element of coercion is thus built into the economic structure of capitalism. Unless the capacity to institute socialism is organized economically, politically, and ideologically within the capitalist society, wage-earners are better off avoiding crises and cooperating in the reproduction of capitalist accumulation. It is therefore understandable that the secretary of the Spanish Communist Party would maintain that:

One must have the courage to explain to the working class that it is better to give surplus to this sector of the bourgeoisie than to create a situation which contains the risk of turning against us. (Carillo, 1974: 187)

That is why "the fundamental forces of the working-class and popular movement do not stake their fortunes on a worsening of the crisis. They are working for a positive democratic solution to the crisis." (Chiaramonte, 1975) Conditions for the hegemony of capital cannot be abolished unless the system of production is transformed for, to repeat, "the content of the political hegemony of the new social group which has founded the new type of state must be predominantly of an economic order. . . ."

Moreover, material deprivation is not always the final consequence of economic crises. If history teaches any lesssons, it is that "bringing the system down" by means of economic militancy alone imports the danger of fascism. Faced with a threat to the institution of private profit, capitalists, or at least some capitalists, seek a secure pursuit of their private business under the protection of force. This is not to imply that capitalists are always capable of utilizing the permanently organized physical force as an instrument of repression whenever capitalism is threatened.[17] The characteristic dynamic of crises consists of the renunciation of the masses of their representatives in the institutions of capitalist democracy (Marx, 1934: 87–94; Gramsci, 1971: 210; Poulantzas, 1974a). As a result, relations of physical force become decisive during periods of crises.

Force, permanently organized physical force, is for Gramsci a constitutive element of consent, in the sense that any breakdown of consent activates the mechanisms of coercion which are inherent in all realms of social life and which remain latent as long as consent is sufficient to reproduce capitalist relations. Breakdown of consent bares coercion – coercion which is ubiquitous and which rests ultimately, but only ultimately, upon the monopoly of the state in organizing permanent physical force.

In order to understand this dynamic of consent and force we must clarify Gramsci's conception of the relation between the state and the civil society – a source of undue difficulties for several interpreters, most recently Anderson (1977). For Gramsci, all institutions that participate in reproducing capitalist social relations constitute elements of the state:

> every State is ethical in as much as one of its most important functions is to raise the great mass of the population to a particular cultural and moral level, a level (or type) which corresponds to the needs of the productive forces for development, and hence to the interests of the ruling classes. The school as a positive educative function, and the courts as a repressive and negative educative function, are the most important State activities in this sense: but, in reality, a multitude of other so-called private initiatives and activities tend to the same end – initiatives and activities which form the apparatus of the political and cultural hegemony of the ruling classes. (1971: 258)

This definition is exclusively functional: *any and every institution which participates in the production of capitalist relations is a part of the state.* Institutional distinctions of public and private are internal to bourgeois ideology. When Gramsci asks, to Anderson's bewilderment, whether the parliament might not under some circumstances be outside the state, the decisive question is "In other words, what is their real function?" (Ibid.: 253) The state is defined depending upon "the end" of various initiatives and activities, not by bourgeois legal distinctions.

Moreover, in all these institutions education, the positive aspect, and repression, the negative one, are inseparable. They constitute precisely "aspects," that is, twin characteristics of the same activities. "The Law," Gramsci says, "is the repressive and negative aspect of the entire positive, civilizing

---

[17] See Gramsci's analysis of the class composition of the army and its political effects (1971: 210–17). O'Donnell (1977) points out that capitalism is a system where the economically dominant class is separated from the organized means of coercion. His 1976 analysis of the political propensities of armed forces is the best I know.

activity undertaken by the State." (1971: 247; also 195, 242, 246, and 259) Consent and coercion cannot be treated as opposites: coercion is the, normally latent, element inherent in consent. It is true that coercion is possible without consent, but consent always contains an element of coercion.

Coercion is thus ubiquitous; it is not reserved to any particular institution. Gramsci would have rejected, and here Anderson's interpretation of his view is correct, the assertion that "the exercise of repression is juridically absent from civil society." Moreover, this element of coercion does not originate exclusively, or even mainly, from "conformity" or "custom," and certainly never from a self-imposed restraint, "consensus." Anderson confuses the monopoly of the state in organizing and threatening with the permanent physical force with the monopoly of exercising coercion. The state, precisely because of its monopoly in organizing force, enjoins other institutions, including the "private" ones, with the capacity and the legal right to exercise coercion *on its behalf*. Thus a school can force students to follow certain courses, to wear a particular type of clothes, to bend up and down for 45 minutes each day, or to jump into icy pools. Let me put it differently: I may stop at a red light because I believe that this is the best way of organizing traffic, I may stop because this is the custom, but if I do not stop and get caught I will get a fine, and if I do not pay the fine I will go to jail. Am I thus stopping as an act of *consensus,* a voluntary agreement, or *consent* which is protected by the armor of coercion? I think Gramsci says the latter: that even if I internalized the necessity as freedom, the element of coercion — coercion guaranteed by the monopolized force — is latent in the act. The repressive function is as ubiquitous as the educational one: it extends to schools, churches, parties, families, and so forth. *The "ideological state apparatuses" are the same as the repressive ones.*

Under "normal" circumstances when hegemony is not threatened, this exercise of coercion is masked by the appearance of "voluntary" conformity with the requirements of capitalist development. Even when force is used, "the attempt is always made to ensure that force will appear to be based on the consent of the majority, expressed by the so-called organs of public opinion. . . ." (Gramsci, 1971: 80n) Indeed, underlying the coercive function is:

The apparatus of the state coercive power which "legally" enforces discipline on those groups who do not "consent" either actively or passively. The apparatus is, however, constituted for the whole of society in anticipation of moments of crisis of command and direction when spontaneous consent has failed. (Ibid.: 12)

Is Gramsci inconsistent, therefore, when he speaks of the state in the narrow sense of coercive apparatus, when he allocates the repressive function to particular institutions, and when he emphasizes the pivotal role of permanently organized physical force during periods of crises? Gramsci vacillates in his ordering of functions to institutions because functions of institutions change. They are not simply different in different societies (East and West); they do not simply evolve in the course of history. Yet *underlying the seeming inconsistency is a completely consistent theory of the dynamic of the state.* This dynamic allocates functions to institutions depending upon the conjuncture of class struggle and specifically depending upon the modality and the degree of the threat to capitalism. All institutions combine consent and force, because there is no consent which is not supported by force. Under normal circumstances, however, no force is apparent anywhere in the society, since its uses are limited to at most individual transgressions. The only institution in the society which is force alone — the army — is hidden completely: it does not intervene in the normal exercise of hegemony and it appears to have been actually organized for the contingency of an external threat. Hence, during normal times no institution seems to perform a coercive function, not even the repressive apparatus of the state in the narrow sense.

What distinguishes the particular institutions, those which appear private as well as those which appear directly political, is not their function under the normal exercise of hegemony, but the order and the manner in which they reveal their coercive functions when hegemony is threatened. Gramsci gives only a few precise indications of this dynamic and he asserts, misleadingly in my view, that it is the state (in the narrow sense) which is the outer layer of defense. His specific analyses would indicate that it is the *inner* layer; that the institutions of the civil society reveal first their coercive functions and only when they have been conquered by the contesting forces is the coercive core of the state also revealed. If schools socialize people to work, there is no need for anything else; if schools are taken over, market discipline must be intensified; if people do not work in factories and offices in spite of this discipline, new laws must be passed to make them do it. Only when such laws cannot be passed does naked force becomes manifest in all realms of social life. It is thus perfectly conceivable that at some moment the parliament may not be a part of the state: when it is controlled by forces hostile to the hegemony of capitalists in general or a particular class block in particular. A social formation is weak when schools or families do not generate consent because the access to the core, i.e. the parliament, the executive, and ultimately the army, is more direct. In such formations a case-to-case intervention of physical force is necessary to maintain capitalism, which makes such systems much more exposed.

Hence while it is true that the organization of permanent physical force is monopolized in most societies, this force becomes activated only when other lines of defense have failed. The few historical instances in which revolutionary forces came to the verge of destroying these defenses make it apparent that they are indeed highly complex. The question which Gramsci formulated and for which we still have precious few answers concerns precisely the dynamic of the breakdown of consent as it systematically bares coercion.[18]

[18] "For Gramsci," writes Paggi, "the issue with regard to force is clearly more complex than the respective strength of the armies in the field. It is rather a matter of grasping the complex way in which a class society is structured from the economic to the political sphere, and to represent its movement as a succession of the various outcomes of the confrontation between the struggling forces." (1977: 59)

5. Material Interests, Class Compromise, and the State*

Introduction

This chapter examines the conflict between capitalists and wage-earners over the realization of material interests in advanced capitalist societies. The central question is whether wage-earners' pursuit of their material interests will necessarily lead them to opt for socialism.

This is an old question and the responses to it are familiar, emphatic, and confused. One response is attributed to Marx and is, in fact, found in some of his writings, particularly in *Wage Labour and Capital*. There Marx maintained that since the national product generated by the capitalist sector of the economy is divided into a part appropriated by capital as profit and a part paid in exchange for labor power as wages, the shares of capital and labor are inversely related. That much is obviously true, since the product is by definition constant at any instant of time. But Marx went much farther. He claimed that even when accumulation is viewed in dynamic terms, in fact even when workers' conditions are improving, the conflict over distribution retains an essentially noncooperative character. For Marx this conflict is irreconcilable within the confines of the capitalist society.

The political conclusion Marx and most of his followers drew from this analysis is that workers' pursuit of material interests must lead them to realize that these interests can be advanced if and only if the entire system of wage labor is abolished. As Luxemburg (1970b: 30) put it in 1900, "as a result of its trade-union and parliamentary struggles, the proletariat becomes convinced of the impossibility of accomplishing a fundamental social change through such activity and arrives at the understanding that the conquest of political power is unavoidable." From the "objective conflict of material interests" one can proceed to the political, equally objective, "fundamental interest in socialism" by means of a syllogism.

The response found a mirror image among those defenders of capitalism who claim that the capitalist system is essentially cooperative, that it constitutes a

* Parts of this chapter were written jointly with Michael Wallerstein.

171

"non-zero-sum game," and that workers are better off when they cooperate with capitalists to increase the size of the pie rather than fight over relative shares. Marx is said to have been blinded to see only the seamy side of history, the grim side of conflict rather than the radiant promise of cooperation (Boulding, 1970: ch. 5). The alleged deradicalization of working-class movements constitutes in the eyes of anti-marxist proponents of economic determinism a sufficient proof that in the course of economic development workers have themselves discovered the advantages of compromise and abandoned all thought of transformation.

The issue is ideological, which is to say important, and it would be naive to expect that we can reach a consensus. Nevertheless, I will show immediately that its present formulation is muddled and that if we can agree to some assumptions we will arrive at unambiguous answers. I will, therefore, proceed deductively, from assumptions to their logical consequences.

The Problem Defined

I will approach the issue in its narrowest possible formulation since it is in such a narrow formulation that the question has been traditionally posed. Specifically, I will assume that workers under capitalism have an interest in improving their material welfare, and I will base the entire analysis of their political preferences and strategies on this narrow assumption.

Note that it might be true that workers are, in fact, endowed under capitalism with some needs that transcend this system and that by definition can be realized only under socialism, for example, "an eternal striving for freedom and justice." (Fromm, 1961) This kind of an assumption, however, would reduce the question of workers' preference for socialism to an immediate tautology. The question here is not whether human kind is endowed as a species with some kind of a transcendental need for socialism but only whether the needs that workers seek to satisfy under capitalism would necessarily lead them to opt for socialism as a better system for satisfying these needs.

Secondly, even under capitalism workers may have many needs: a need for autonomy in the work place, for free time, for sex, or for beauty. The quest for satisfaction of these needs may lead workers to reject capitalism. I will return to such eventualities, but for the moment the analysis will be limited to material interests, that is, those needs that can be satisfied through the consumption or use of objectifications of socially organized activities of transformation of nature, which, under capitalism, are commodities. Again, the question is not whether under capitalism workers experience any need that would lead them to opt for socialism but only whether those needs that in principle can be satisfied as the result of the socially organized process of production would inevitably lead them to opt for a socialist organization of this process.

Furthermore, not all material needs become organized as interests. Following Heller (1974), I will treat as interests such needs that can be satisfied by consuming or using commodities and for which the barriers to satisfaction are (in a particular society) external to the needs of a particular individual. If I cannot consume more cake and wine because I want to be beautiful, that is if the only barrier to satisfying a need consists of my other needs, then this need is not a referent of interest. Hence, needs that can be satisfied by objectifications turn into interests under conditions of scarcity.

I assume, therefore, that workers under capitalism have an interest in improving their material conditions. The question is whether the pursuit of this interest, and only of this interest, would necessarily lead workers to opt for socialism as a superior system for satisfying material needs. Writing at the turn of the century, John Mitchell, President of the United Mine Workers, posed the following choice for organized workers: "Trade unionism is not irrevocably committed to the maintenance of the wage system, nor is it irrevocably committed to its abolition. It demands the constant improvement of the condition of the workingmen, if possible, by the maintenance of the present wage system, if not possible, by its ultimate abolition." (Sombart, 1976: 19) The question is whether the demand for "the constant improvement of the condition of the workingmen" would necessarily lead workers to opt for the ultimate abolition of the wage system as a whole.

Imagine a situation in which capitalists appropriate profit and consume it entirely. Under such conditions workers would certainly be better off – immediately or at some time in the future – if they did not consent to the private appropriation of profit. They would be better off immediately if they were the ones who consumed this part of the product; alternatively, they would be better off in the future if they withheld this part from current consumption and invested it. Or suppose, more realistically and in the spirit of Marx's analysis, that capitalists do invest some part of profits they withhold and that they themselves consume the remaining part of the increment that resulted from past investment. In this situation the process of accumulation would continue, but workers would not at any time be the beneficiaries of it. Hence, although the game would no longer be a zero-sum one, workers would perpetually be as badly off as they could physically be. Under these conditions workers would again be better off if they did not tolerate the private appropriation of profit but instead kept the entire product and either consumed it or invested it for their own future consumption. That the game is not zero-sum does not yet imply that it is a cooperative one: a point always missed by Marx's critics.

These conditions, however, are still too restrictive. All that is needed for workers to rationally opt for socialism out of their material interests are two conditions: that socialism be more efficient in satisfying material needs than capitalism and that moving toward socialism would immediately and continually improve workers' material conditions. It does not matter whether workers' conditions are deteriorating or improving under capitalism as long as the move in a socialist direction is always immediately and permanently superior for workers' welfare. These conditions are portrayed in Figure 11. Even if the situation of workers would have improved under capitalism from level a to level b, workers would be better off by the amount c-minus-b if they had taken the socialist path at time $t = 0$. Hence, even if their material conditions were improving under capitalism, rational workers would opt for socialism as a necessary consequence of the pursuit of their material well-being. In this situation, it is indeed true that "even the most favorable situation for the working class, the most rapid possible growth of capital, however much it may improve the material existence of the worker, does not remove the antagonism between his interests and the interests of the bourgeoisie, the interests of the capitalists." (Marx, 1952b: 37)

The very possibility that such a situation may exist is sufficient to demonstrate that empirical studies that relate the improvement of workers' conditions ("embourgeoisement") to their "deradicalization" rest on invalid epistemological premises, as do all empirical studies that do not specify the possible alternatives to the observed history. Even if it were empirically true that workers' organizations become deradicalized at the same time as improvements of their material welfare occurred, one could not draw from this observed historical covariation any causal inferences unless it was possible to prove at the same time that a better alternative was not available. If workers are said to have been deradicalized *because* their conditions improved, then one must admit the possibility that they would have become more radical if these conditions would have improved even more by making a step toward socialism. Empiricist epistemology is intrinsically ideological since it implicitly denies the existence of any historical alternatives: while the proposition that deradicalization coincided historically with embourgeoisement is capable of being judged true or false, the proposition that workers became deradicalized *because* their material conditions improved is not subject to such a test unless the other possibilities are explicitly denied. The observation that workers' conditions improved in the course of the history of capitalism is not sufficient in itself to draw any inferences about their preference for a particular form of social organization. For, if Marx was right, workers are always better off by moving in the direction of socialism.

Before going any further, it might be useful to clarify what moving toward

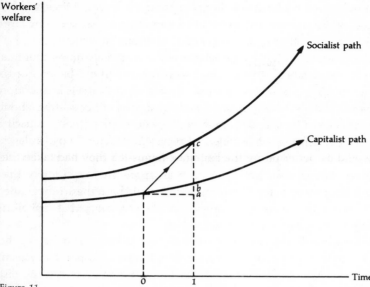

Figure 11.

socialism means here and what other options we have. As a first approximation, suppose that workers have three options. One, they can claim the entire capital stock ("means of production") from capitalists and reorganize the system of production in such a way that the directions of investment and the decision to withhold from current consumption would be made by all citizens rather than by owners of capital or their delegates. Investment funds would thus be deducted directly from the gross product, profits being abolished as a juridical and as an economic category. This claim for reorganizing the process of accumulation I consider to be a step toward socialism.

Two, workers can claim the entire current product or even a part of the capital stock without reorganizing the process of withholding from current consumption. This is a purely economicist strategy.

Three, they can claim less than the entire product, thus leaving a part in the hands of capitalists as profit. This strategy opens room for class compromise and cooperation with capitalists.

The hypothesis that material interests lead necessarily to a preference for socialism asserts that *if* workers are interested in a continual improvement of their material conditions and *if* they are rational, they must opt for socialism. This hypothesis would be false if its premises are true and one or both of the following could be shown to be also true: socialism is inferior to capitalism in efficiently allocating resources to socially preferred uses (uses to be chosen by all citizens through some reasonable balloting system), à la von Mises and his followers, and/or conditions exist under which a move in the socialist direction makes workers worse off than a move along the capitalist direction.

I will immediately reject the first possibility and will assume throughout that as a system of organization of production socialism would not be inferior to capitalism in satisfying material needs. Let me only note that this assumption does not refer to the historically realized performance of either system, about which there has been a fair amount of discussion, but to the potential capacity inherent in both systems, again a subject of recurrent debates. In particular, it would be a mistake to compare the historical record of capitalism with the potential envisioned in socialism, since such an approach would imply that workers are at all times as well off as they possibly could be at these times under capitalism. Hence, this procedure would exclude the possibility that capitalism could be reformed to improve workers' welfare.

Suppose, therefore, that socialism is superior to capitalism. The crux of the problem is whether this superiority is sufficient for workers to opt for socialism. If it can be shown that conditions exist under which a move in the socialist direction would be inferior to a move along the path of capitalism, then one could no longer deduce workers' socialist orientation from their material interests.

Let us first imagine what such conditions would be like and only then inquire about their existence. Suppose that socialism is potentially superior to capitalism at any moment of capitalist development (or at least after some threshold, if one believes that conditions must be "ripe") but that immediate steps toward socialism leave workers worse off than they would have been had they advanced along the capitalist path.[1] The equivalent of Figure 11 would then look like Figure 12. Under these stipulated conditions, moving from the full potential capitalist path to the full potential socialist path involves a temporary deterioration of workers' welfare. During the period $t=0$ to $t=1$, the conditions of workers deteriorate below their past level and below the level that they would have attained under capitalism, c_1, and only then they begin to improve. Although the level of welfare eventually attained on the socialist path, s_3, is higher than the level workers would have reached along the capitalist path, c_3, during the entire period until $t=2$, these workers would have been better off following the capitalist path. Between the capitalist path and the socialist one there is a valley that must be traversed if workers move at any time toward socialism. If such conditions indeed exist and if workers are interested in a continual improvement of their material welfare, then this descent will not be

[1] This is true whether this path is upwardly or downwardly sloped. Even if workers' conditions are deteriorating under capitalism, the transition path may still deepen the crisis.

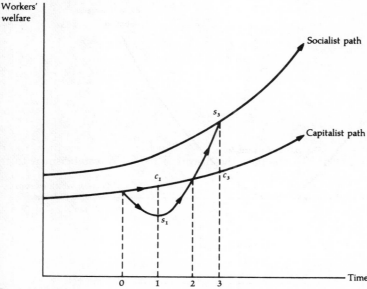

Figure 12.

undertaken or, if it is undertaken, will not be completed by workers under democratic conditions.

At any time workers would thus face a choice between climbing upward toward the best situation they could obtain under capitalism and a temporary deterioration of their conditions on the road to socialism. At a fixed moment of time, we could portray this structure of choices as in Figure 13. As long as their current state is above the indifference level corresponding to the bottom of the transitional valley, any move in the socialist direction involves a temporary deterioration of workers' welfare.

Now, if the transition to socialism involves a deterioration of workers' welfare and if workers have an option of improving their material conditions by cooperating with capitalists, then the socialist orientation cannot be deduced from the material interests of workers. I will now demonstrate that this is indeed the case.

The Form of Class Compromise

Thus far we have only defined the issue. The question now is whether conditions for class compromise do in fact exist under capitalism. This is a twofold question. Can workers improve their material welfare by cooperating with capitalists, and does a step toward socialism necessarily involve a temporary deterioration of

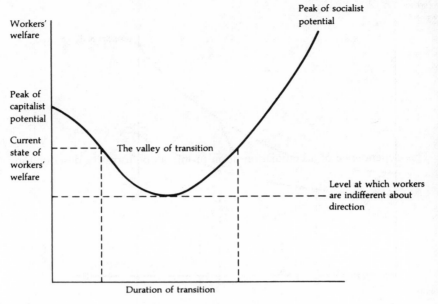

Figure 13.

workers' welfare? Before we answer this question, however, it is necessary to understand what class compromise would look like under capitalism.

In a capitalist society profit is a necessary condition of investment, and investment is a necessary condition of continued production, consumption, and employment. As Chancellor Schmidt put it, "the profits of enterprises today are the investments of tomorrow, and the investments of tomorrow are the employment of the day after," and in place of "employment" he might as well have said "production" or "consumption" (*Le Monde*, July 6, 1976, p.5). In any society some part of the product must be withheld from current consumption if production is to continue and consumption is to increase, but the distinguishing characteristic of capitalism is that most of the investment occurs out of profits, that part of the product that is withheld from the immediate producers. Hence under capitalism private profit is the necessary condition for the improvement of material conditions of any group in the society. Unless capitalists appropriate profits, the capital stock becomes depleted, production falls, and employment and consumption fall with it. In fact, capitalists increasingly justify the very institution of profit exactly in these terms, as the following paid advertisement by Mobil Oil Company beautifully illustrates.

Corporate earnings have to rise to levels substantially above those of recent years if our country is not to get into even deeper trouble. [If this does not occur] every group will begin fighting for a larger piece of that static pie. Women, blacks, and other racial movements, and young people of all backgrounds will be hardest hit. College graduates will find job hunting even tougher. More and more of them will have to take jobs lower in the economic scale. This will further squeeze every minority and everybody else. Economic growth is the last, best hope for the poor and for all the rest of us. Sheer redistribution of income cannot do the job. We must create a steadily larger income pie. This can be done only through economic growth. And only profitable private businesses can make the capital investments that produce economic growth and jobs and tax revenues. (*New York Times,* May 6, 1976, p.17)

This dependence of accumulation upon profit can be formally described in many ways, among which I will choose a very simple macroeconomic model of the form:

$$Y(t + 1) = (1 + s/c)P(t) + W(t),\qquad(1)$$

where $Y(t)$ stands for the net national product, $P(t)$ for net profit, $W(t)$ for wages, s for the rate of saving out of profit, and c for the capital/output ratio, and where the rate of saving out of wages is assumed to be negligible. At any time t the part s of profits $P(t)$ is saved and invested into an economy in which c units of capital are needed to produce one unit of output. The rate of growth of such an economy depends upon the rate of profit and the rate of saving out of profit:

$$\Delta Y(t)/Y(t) = sP(t)/cY(t) = sP(t)/K(t) = sp(t),\qquad(2)$$

where $\Delta Y(t)$ stands for the increase of the product between time t and $(t + 1)$, $K(t) = cY(t)$ for the accumulated capital stock, and $p(t) = P(t)/K(t)$ for the rate of profit. Hence the rate of growth varies proportionately to the rate of profit and the rate of saving out of profit. The rate of saving, s, characterizes the behavior of capitalists, since, given the share of profit in the national product, their decisions to invest and thus to save determine the rate of growth of the economy.

While profit is a necessary condition of development, it is not a sufficient condition for the improvement of material conditions of any particular group. First, capitalists may not invest the profits to increase productivity: despite constraints they may instead consume profits, invest them unproductively, hoard them, or export them elsewhere. Second, even if capitalists do invest profits to increase productivity, no particular group can be in any way assured that it will be the beneficiary of this investment. Capitalists may themselves retain the increment, or they may enter into a number of alternative political alliances. Their market relation with workers ends as the cycle of production is completed and the wages are paid, and there is nothing in the structure of the capitalist system of production that would guarantee that workers would be the ones to benefit from any part of the product being withheld from them as profit.

These structural conditions limit any possible compromise between capitalists and workers. Since the appropriation of profits by capitalists is a necessary but not a sufficient condition for any improvement of the material welfare of workers, a class compromise is possible only on the condition that workers have a reasonable certainty that future wages will increase as a function of current profits. Any compromise must have the following form: workers consent to the perpetuation of profit as an institution in exchange for the prospect of improving their material well-being in the future. In terms of such a compromise capitalists retain the capacity to withhold a part of the product because the profit they appropriate is expected by workers to be saved, invested, transformed into productive potential, and partly distributed as gains to workers.

The general logic of cooperation is not always stated explicitly. Indeed, during the early period of the development of the working-class movement this compromise was based only on the right of workers to associate, to bargain collectively, and to strike. Eventually, explicit norms did appear pegging wages to prices, to the competitive position of an industry in the international system, and, especially during the expansionist period between 1950 and 1970, to increases of productivity. Nevertheless, whatever the explicit norm cementing a particular "social pact," the underlying logic of cooperation must relate future wages to current profits. The only conceivable reason for workers to consent voluntarily not to claim the entire social product is to treat current profits as a form of workers' "delegated" investment.

Hence a class compromise must rest on some norm of the form:

$$\Delta \hat{W}(t) = F\,[P(t - i)], \; i = 0, 1 \ldots k \ldots ,$$

where $\Delta \hat{W}(t)$ stands for the increase of wages between time t and time $(t + 1)$ expected under a particular agreement, $P(t - i)$ for the history of profits, and F for the rule that relates past profits to current wage increases under a particular agreement. For the sake of simplicity, and without much loss of generality, let the rule be simply of the form:

$$\Delta \hat{W}(t) = rP(t). \tag{3}$$

The coefficient r represents, therefore, the proportion of current profits that must be immediately transformed into wage increases in the light of a particular agreement.

Note that a compromise is possible only on the condition that $0 < r < (1 + s/c)$. Clearly, r must be larger than zero if this rule is to have any meaning. It may be less obvious why it should be less than $(1 + s/c)$ rather than simply 1 if the compromise is to be at all tolerable for capitalists. If $r = 1$, then at time $(t + 1)$ capitalists pay as wage increases all of the profits they appropriated at time t. In the meantime, however, they would have invested these profits with the marginal rate of return s/c, and after one period they would still be left with the amount $(s/c)P(t)$. Hence only when $r = 1 + s/c$ are the entire profits confiscated at $(t + 1)$. This level of r is thus immediately "confiscatory" with regard to the reinvested current profits, although it still leaves in the hands of capitalists the accumulated capital stock.

The coefficient r indicates the rate of transformation of profits into wage increases under which workers enter into a specific compromise. This coefficient can be treated, therefore, as representing the economic militancy of organized wage-earners.

An agreement concerning the rate of transformation of profits into wage increases, however, would be still too tenuous from the workers' point of view because it leaves open the question whether capitalists will save and invest enough to make wage increases at all possible. The perennial complaint of working-class movements is that capitalists are too lazy or too inefficient to be entrusted with control over investment. Already in 1910, a French socialist noted the "timidity," the "uncertainty," the "lack of initiative" of capitalists. "We ask the French employers," he continued, "to resemble the American employer class. . . . We want a busy, active, humming country, a veritable beehive always awake. In that way our own force will be increased." (Griffuelhes, 1910: 331) And again, in 1975, Chiaramonte complained in an official report to the Central Committee of the Italian Communist Party (P.C.I.) about a "disconcerting lack of ideas on the economic and industrial future of the country and on the productive prospects for their [capitalists'] own industries. They continue to cling to productive, technical, and organizational policies adopted several dozen years ago. . . ." (1973: 31)

Investment cannot be left to the control of capitalists: this is the second condition of a full-fledged compromise. While in the early stages of the development of capital–labor relations the conflict focused narrowly on the right to struggle for wage increases, the essential feature of the social democratic, Keynesian compromise has been the attention of working-class organizations to the actual investments out of profits. Having announced the austerity policy, having repeated that the P.C.I. is "not aiming at a worsening of the situation, . . . or an aggravation of the crises," Chiaramonte continued, "this does not mean that we in any way think it would be sufficient to limit the workers' pay claims and demands for greater control over working conditions to automatically obtain an increase in investment and productive reconversion." (1975: 34) What the P.C.I. demands in exchange for "austerity" is control over investment. Or, as the 1973 Conference of the Irish Trade Union Confederation put it, "all workers must be guaranteed that their wage restraint will lead to productive and beneficial investment and not towards even further increases in the personal incomes of the privileged section of society. . . ." (Jacobsen, 1980: 268)

Given the uncertainty whether and how capitalists would invest profits, any class compromise must consist of the following elements: workers consent to profit as an institution, that is, they behave in such a manner as to make positive rates of profit possible; and capitalists commit themselves to some rate of transformation of profits into wage increases and some rate of investment out of profits.

Conditions of Class Compromise

Thus far we have only specified what a class compromise would look like if one was to be concluded. We can now proceed to the central question of this chapter, namely, whether organized workers pursuing their material interests would opt for such a compromise or choose to struggle for a transformation of the system of production.

How would organized workers rationally make such a decision? There are two considerations: the wages they expect in the future if the compromise holds and the risk that the compromise will not hold. Suppose first that actual wages follow the path stipulated by a compromise, that is, $W(t) = \hat{W}(t)$ for all $T \leqslant t \leqslant T + h$, where h is the horizon with which workers consider the future. If capitalists invest at the rate s in the economy characterized by the productivity of capital $1/c$, then the time path of compromise wages will depend upon the relation between r and s/c. Recall that

$$\Delta Y(t) = \Delta P(t) + \Delta W(t) = (s/c)P(t), \qquad \text{(from 1)}$$

and

$$\Delta W(t) = \Delta \hat{W}(t) = rP(t). \qquad \text{(from 3)}$$

It then follows that

$$\Delta P(t) = (s/c - r)P(t), \qquad (4)$$

or

$$P(t + 1) = (1 + s/c - r)P(t). \qquad (5)$$

There are three cases to consider (Figure 14):[2]

If workers choose an r such that $r < s/c$, then wages will grow exponentially,

---

[2] Equation (5) is a first-order linear difference equation of the form $Y(t + 1) = aY(t)$, with the solution $Y(t) = a^t Y(0)$. For any $Y(0) > 0$, $Y(t)$ will be a monotonically increasing function of time if $a > 1$; it will monotonically decrease to zero if $0 < a < 1$; it will oscillate around zero if $a < 0$ (Goldberg, 1973).

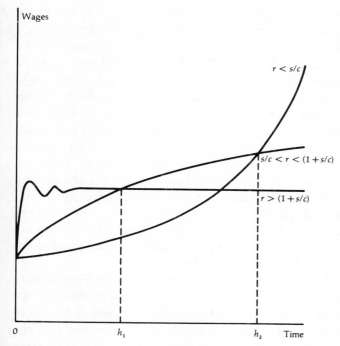

Wages

$r < s/c$

$s/c < r < (1 + s/c)$

$r > (1 + s/c)$

0   h_1 h_2 Time

Figure 14.

following the exponential growth of profits. In this case we will say that workers are not militant or that they offer wage restraint.

If workers choose an r such that $s/c < r < (1 + s/c)$, then wages will grow rapidly at first and then stagnate at a fixed level as net profits decline to zero. Such a strategy we will call moderately militant.

If workers choose an r such that $r > (1 + s/c)$, then workers are highly militant. Wages will then experience a sharp increase as net profits immediately become negative. Since this strategy cannot lead to a compromise, there is no reason to expect that subsequent wages would bear any relation to profits. If they did, wages would oscillate henceforth around a fixed level while profits would oscillate around zero.

One way to review these consequences of the workers' strategies is to observe that the nonmilitant workers would be best off after some time h_2, about a generation if time is measured in years; moderately militant workers would be best off during the period between some time h_1 and h_2; and highly militant workers would be best off during the initial period until h_1. The values of h_1 and

h_2 depend upon the particular relation between r and s/c. The time span h_2 can be as short as a couple of years, whereas h_2 can be as long as thirty years.

In considering the effects of their actions workers cannot be certain, however, that the compromise would hold. Hence, their decision must depend upon the likelihood that capitalists will observe the terms of a compromise if one were to be concluded. Since the future becomes increasingly less predictable the further one looks into it, the wages workers would obtain at each moment in the future would weigh progressively less in the workers' decision, the further in the future they would occur. Hence, I assumed that even if workers valued wage increases equally regardless of the magnitude of current wages and were indifferent between certain consumption today and certain consumption in the future, they would nevertheless discount the future on the grounds of uncertainty.

Since I assume below that capitalists also discount their future welfare on the grounds of uncertainty, we can treat similarly the determinants of risk facing each class. The risk is associated with the political and economic conditions at the time when a decision is made, specifically:

(1) The degree of bilateral monopoly. Unless workers are monopolistically organized, they cannot be certain that particular groups among them would not conclude their own agreements with their respective employers at the cost of other workers. Since capitalists cannot completely avoid competing with one another, each firm faces the danger that other firms would ride free on the costs of compromise.

(2) The institutionalization of labor–capital relations and the likelihood that a compromise would be enforced by the state. The question is whom the state would be capable and willing to coerce to prevent deviations from the compromise: capitalists, workers, or both? Partisan control over the state and the electoral prospects would constitute an important consideration in evaluating the risk.

(3) The ordinary risks inherent in investment owing to domestic and international economic fluctuations, domestic and international competition, technical change, and other economic factors.

Furthermore, the degree of risk borne by capitalists when they invest depends in part upon the rigidity of their wage commitment. If wages are highly rigid, capitalists face the risk inherent in investment alone. If the wage bill can be reduced below the terms of the compromise when times are bad, much of the risk is borne by workers. To some degree, therefore, the uncertainty faced by capitalists is inversely related to the uncertainty confronting workers.

Let a, $a > 0$, be the rate at which workers discount the future on the grounds of uncertainty. The higher the a, the less certain it is at $t = 0$ that a compromise would hold in the future and the faster workers discount the future wages stipulated under a compromise. Given the level of wages associated with a particular compromise and the degree of workers' uncertainty, the workers' problem is to find a level of economic militancy that maximizes the current value of their discounted future wages, or

$$\max_{r} W^* = \sum_{t=0}^{t=h} (1 + a)^{-t} \hat{W}(t), \; a > 0, \tag{6}$$

where the anticipated path of wages, $\hat{W}(t)$, is given by equations (3) and (5).[3]

Note that W^* depends upon workers' militancy, r, their horizon, h, their discount rate, a, the productivity of capital, $1/c$, and the saving behavior of capitalists, s. Thus $W^* = F(r; h,a,c; s)$. The productivity of capital, the horizon, and the rate of discount are fixed; they constitute the objective conditions of the moment. The behavior of capitalists with regard to saving is something workers must adjust to. Economic militancy is the strategic variable of workers, whose problem is to choose an r that maximizes W^* in the face of the investment strategy of capitalists, represented by s. Let $r^*(s)$ be the solution of the equation (6); that is, the value of r which maximizes W^* given that capitalists invest at the rate s, when h, a, and c are given. Then $r^*(s)$ is the best reply strategy of workers (Harsanyi, 1977: 102).

Workers must weigh the gains of immediate wage increases against the expected gains that would result in the future from less militant demands. Profits appropriated by capitalists who are investing at the rate s will increase output by s/c, or $\Delta Y(t)/P(t) = s/c$. Note also that the maximal return to output of a unit of profit, when all profits are invested, is given by the productivity of capital, $1/c$. We have, then, the following theorem: When the horizon is sufficiently long, workers' best reply will be a compromise level of r if their rate of discount, a, is less than the rate of return s/c. Otherwise they will be highly militant. Stated formally:

Workers' Best-Reply Theorem
For all $h > H$, where H is some positive number,

$r^*(s) > (1 + s/c)$ if $a > 1/c$ for any s,
$r^*(s) > (1 + s/c)$ if $a > s/c$ or $s < ac$,
$r^*(s) < (1 + s/c)$ if $a < s/c$ or $s > ac$.

In the case of an infinite horizon, the workers' best-reply strategy is given by a bang-bang function. When $a > s/c$, the workers' best reply is maximal militancy. When $a < s/c$, the workers' best reply approaches zero.[4]

---

[3] Note that workers solve this problem repeatedly at each $T, T = 0,1 \ldots$, and we should have written W^*_T as a sum going from $t = T$ to $t = T + h$. For convenience, we assume that we are examining one such decision, at $T + 0$.

[4] For the proof of this and other theorems see Przeworski and Wallerstein (1982: 236–7).

What occurs when h is some finite number? Our numerical experiments indicate that for $c = 4$, H is approximately equal to 12; that is, for any $h > 12$, a maximally militant strategy will be best when $a > s/c$ and a compromise strategy will be best when $a < s/c$. (If $h < 12$, the best-reply strategy is to be maximally militant in all cases.) But, for any finite horizon, the workers' best-reply strategy does not suddenly jump from maximal militancy to zero. Rather, for $s > ac$, $r^*(s)$ is a continuous, monotonically decreasing, positive function. The higher the rate of saving above the product ac, the lower will be the workers' best-reply level of militancy.

One way to explain this theorem is that workers today would value equally the wages they anticipate receiving in each year of a compromise if for any two successive periods, the compromise wages would grow at such a rate that $W(t + 1) = (1 + a)W(t)$, or equivalently, $\Delta W(t) = aW(t)$. Now, we know that if a compromise were observed exactly, the wage path would follow the rule $\Delta W(t) = rP(t)$ for all t. Hence, the present value to workers who discount the future at the rate a of the wages they would obtain in any period of a compromise characterized by the level of militancy r, would be exactly constant if and only if $rP(t) = aW(t)$. The present value of each period's wages would be growing if $rP(t) > aW(t)$; otherwise it would be declining.

Suppose that $rP(t) = aW(t)$ for all t. Taking differences of both sides and dividing by $P(t)$ yields $r\Delta P(t)/P(t) = a\Delta W(t)/P(t)$. But $\Delta P(t)/P(t) = (s/c - r)$ and $\Delta W(t)/P(t) = r$. Hence, the present value of future wages stipulated under a compromise would remain constant if $a = (s/c - r)$. If $a < (s/c - r)$ or $r < (s/c - a)$, they would be growing over time. If $a > (s/c - r)$ or $r > (s/c - a)$, they would be falling.

Now, if workers are to benefit at all from current profits, r must be positive. The question then is whether there exists, under the conditions given by s/c and a, a positive value of r such that the present value of future wages is growing. Such an r exists only if $(s/c - a) > 0$, or $s/c > a$. Under these conditions, workers will compromise for any $h > 12$. If the horizon is sufficiently long (where the sufficient length depends upon s/c and a), workers will opt for a strategy of wage restraint such that $r < (s/c - a)$, since the time path of growing discounted wages will eventually overtake any path of stagnant or declining discounted wages. If, on the other hand, $s/c < a$, then the present value of future wages will decline for any positive r and workers are best off highly militant, with immediate wage increases as large as possible.

The intuitive meaning of this theorem is apparent. Since s/c is the rate of increase of output per unit of profit, it constitutes the maximal rate at which wages could grow under a compromise. If the maximal conceivable growth of wages is lower than the rate at which workers discount their wage increases, then workers will be worse off if they consent to the appropriation of profits. But if output grows faster than workers discount the future, then workers will be better off choosing a strategy of compromise and waiting for future wage gains.

Figure 15 shows some illustrative functions $W^*(r,s)$ for $h = 30$. The lower segment portrays W^* when $a > s/c$ and the upper segment when $a < s/c$. When $a > s/c$, W^* is a monotonically increasing function of r, but when $a < s/c$, W^* has a maximum at a compromise level of militancy.

Figure 16 presents the numerically derived function $r^*(s)$, that is, the level of militancy which maximizes W^* given workers' risk and the saving behavior of capitalists. As long as $a > 1/c$, this function will be larger than $(1 + s/c)$ for all s. If we assume $c = 4$, then at $a = 0.24$, the rate of saving must be as large as 0.96 for the workers' best reply to be a compromise value of r; at $a = 0.01$, a rate of saving equal to 0.04 will suffice.

The results do not yet constitute a prediction about workers' behavior, however, since the strategies that workers will choose depend upon the behavior of capitalists. Capitalists may be unwilling to increase their rate of saving to levels necessary for a compromise even when one is possible. In fact, capitalists can respond to each threat of workers with a threat of their own: if workers threaten to increase militancy, capitalists may threaten to lower their rate of saving. This, then, is what remains to be investigated.

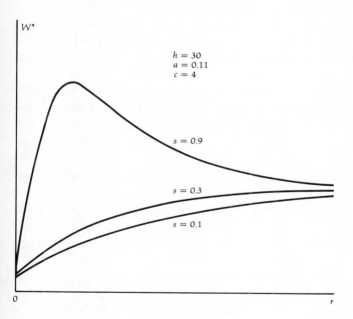

Figure 15.

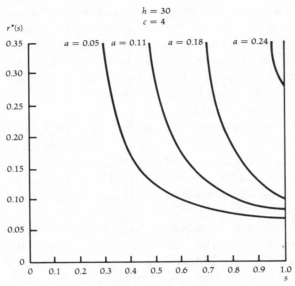

$h = 30$
$c = 4$
$r^*(s)$

Figure 16.

What would be the objective of capitalists in making compromises with workers? Clearly their chief preoccupation would be to maintain profits as the form in which a part of the product is withheld from current consumption. Yet the defense of the institution of private property is not sufficient: actual profits must be obtained. Furthermore, it seems unreasonable to assume that capitalists are nothing but "rational misers." Ultimately they are concerned not only about being able to reinvest profits but also being able to consume them. Capitalists are not simply workers' investing machines: they do have particularistic interests of their own. It seems reasonable, therefore, to assume that capitalists attempt to maximize their consumption, $C(t) = (1 - s)P(t)$, over a period of h years. Moreover capitalists would discount future consumption in accordance with the uncertainty they face.

If the rate of discount for capitalists is b, then the problem faced by capitalists is to choose the value of the rate of saving s, which maximizes the current value of their discounted future consumption given that workers choose the level of militancy, or

$$\max_{s} C^* = (1 - s) \sum_{t = 0}^{t = h} (1 + b)^{-t}\hat{P}(t), \tag{7}$$

where the anticipated path of compromise profits, $\hat{P}(t)$, is given by (5). The rate of saving, s, is the strategic variable of capitalists and $s^*(r)$ is their best-reply strategy, that is, the value of *s* that maximizes C^* given a particular value of *r*, under conditions given by *h*, *b*, and *c*.

The best-reply strategy of capitalists is given by the following theorem. When their horizon is sufficiently long, capitalists' best reply will be to invest as long as the rate at which they discount the future is lower than their return on investment; otherwise they will disinvest. The capitalists' rate of return on investment is equal to the productivity of capital or the increase of output per unit of invested profits, $1/c$, minus the proportion of this unit of profit paid to workers, *r*. Hence, capitalists will find it best to invest at a positive rate if and only if $b < (1/c - r)$. Stated formally:

Capitalists' Best-Reply Theorem

For all $h > H$, where *H* is the same number as in the workers' best-reply theorem,

$s^*(r) < 0$ if $b > 1/c$ for any r,
$s^*(r) < 0$ if $b > (1/c - r)$ or $r > (1/c - b)$,
$s^*(r) > 0$ if $b < (1/c - r)$ or $r > (1/c - {}^1b)$.

When the horizon is infinite, capitalists' best-reply strategy is a bang-bang function, equal to maximal investment or maximal disinvestment according to whether capitalists' discount rate, *b*, is less than or greater than $(1/c - r)$. For finite horizons, the capitalists' best-reply function must be derived numerically. For $h > 12$ (when $c = 4$), $s^*(r)$ is a continuous, monotonically decreasing function with $0 < s^*(r) < 1$ when $r < (1/c - b)$. The greater the restraint of workers' militancy below the quantity $(1/c - b)$, the higher the best-reply rate of saving by capitalists.

The intuitive meaning of the capitalists' best-reply theorem can be seen as follows. The quantity $(1/c - r)$ represents the maximal rate at which profits, and therefore consumption from profits, can grow given the level of militancy, *r*, stipulated under a particular compromise. If the maximal conceivable rate of growth of profits is less than the rate at which capitalists discount the future, capitalists are better off disinvesting. But if the maximal possible rate of growth of profits exceeds the capitalists' discount rate, a strategy of positive investment is optimal.

Figure 17 portrays some illustrative functions $C^*(s, r)$ for an $h = 30$, $c = 4$; Figure 18 shows the positive segment of the function $s^*(r)$ under the same conditions.

Thus far we have examined the best reply of each class to the behavior of the other class, that is, the solution to the maximizing problem facing each class when its opponent behaves in a fixed manner. The best-reply strategy is the optimal strategy if one's opponent is not acting strategically, but both classes do act strategically, and it is only reasonable to assume that each anticipates that the

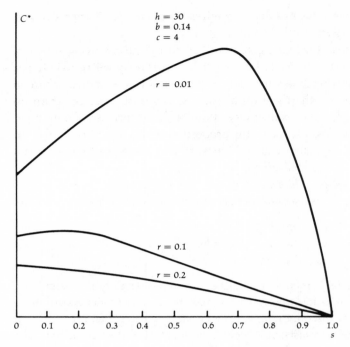

Figure 17.

other will behave strategically. Each class must take into account not only the other's actions but also its reactions, not only the other's current strategy but also the likely response to its own choice of strategy. If, for example, workers' best-reply strategy to some positive rate of saving is to become highly militant, they cannot expect capitalists to continue saving if the workers' best-reply strategy is pursued. Workers must take into account that capitalists' best reply to high levels of militancy is to disinvest.

A pair of strategies (r,s) is a solution to the game if neither class could do better with an alternative strategy given the anticipated response of its opponent. Hence, a solution is a pair (r,s) that, once chosen, will be stable as long as conditions remain unchanged. Note that the intersection of the best-reply functions $(r^*(s^*), s^*(r^*))$ constitutes a solution. Both classes are responding optimally to the current strategy of their opponent. This is the Nash equilibrium. In the model this solution occurs only when compromise breaks down.[5] The capitalists' best reply to high levels of militancy is to disinvest, and the workers' best reply to disinvestment is to be highly militant.

[5] There is an exception. In the limiting case when $a = b = 0$, there is another Nash equilibrium at a point of compromise.

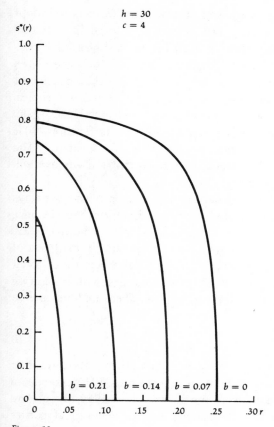

Figure 18.

Suppose, however, that workers anticipate that capitalists will respond to any *r* with their best-reply strategy $s^*(r)$. Now the problem facing workers is to choose the level of militancy which maximizes the function $W^*(r,s^*(r))$, that is, one that maximizes workers' welfare given that capitalists will respond with $s^*(r)$ to any *r* workers might choose. Let this maximizing value of *r* be r^{**}. The pair $(r^{**},$ $s^*(r^{**}))$ is also a solution to the game. The level of militancy r^{**} is the optimal choice of workers given the anticipated response by capitalists and $s^*(r^{**})$ is by definition the capatalists' optimal response to the workers' strategy r^{**}. This is the Stackelberg (1952) solution with workers as the dominant player. Note that r^{**} is not necessarily in the workers' set of best-reply strategies, $r^*(s)$. The *function* $r^*(s)$ is defined as the maximum with respect to *r* of the function $W^*(r,s)$, each value of *s* constant, whereas the *number* r^{**} is defined to be the maximum with respect to *r* of the function $W^*(r,s^*(r))$, where $s = s^*(r)$ is a function of *r*.

Suppose now that it is the capitalists who anticipate that workers will adopt their best-reply strategy $r^*(s)$ to any rate of saving, s, capitalists choose. Capitalists would then seek to maximize $C^*(s, r^*(s))$. Let the maximizing value of s be s^{**}. The pair of strategies $(r^*(s^{**}), s^{**})$ is another solution of the game. Given their anticipations of the workers' response, the capitalists have chosen their best strategy, and the workers are responding optimally to the capitalists' choice. This is the Stackelberg solution with capitalists as the dominant player. Again, s^{**} need not be in the set of capitalists' best-reply strategies. The function $s^*(r)$ is the capitalists' best response to the workers' current level of militancy. The number of s^{**} is the capitalists' optimal choice given that the workers will respond to any s with their best reply, $r^*(s)$.

The Nash equilibrium, which represents absence of compromise, is always possible. What remains to be investigated are the conditions for the existence of compromise, Stackelberg solutions. If the horizon is too short, $h < 12$, no compromise solutions exist. For any $h > 12$, however, the existence of compromise solutions depends entirely upon the relations between the discount rates a and b and the productivity of capital, $1/c$. In the subsequent discussion we assume $h > 12$. (In the numerical illustrations $h = 30$.) There are four cases to consider.

$$a > 1/c, \; b > 1/c. \tag{i}$$

Both workers and capitalists face a large degree of uncertainty about whether any compromise would hold. The situation in France in 1936 provides a prototype: in France few workers were organized before 1936, there were almost no traditions of collective bargaining, several unions and parties competed for workers' support, and the very Matignon agreement was concluded under the pressure of spontaneous occupations of factories. Hence neither workers nor capitalists could expect that the agreement would last and, indeed, six weeks after it was concluded both parties began to undermine it: capitalists by dragging their feet in complying with the wage terms (specifically those concerning minimal wages and paid vacations), and by raising prices, and workers by striking and occupying factories again.

Under these circumstances workers find it best to be highly militant regardless of the saving rate chosen by capitalists, whereas capitalists find it optimal to disinvest regardless of workers' militancy. No compromise is possible. All three solutions collapse into one, the Nash equilibrium, at which $r^*(s) > 1 + s/c$ and $s^*(r) < 0$.

$$a > 1/c, \; b < 1/c. \tag{ii}$$

Workers bear most of the risk, whereas capitalists are relatively certain they would obtain the profits specified by any compromise. This is the case when the degree of unionization is low or several unions compete with each other, capital–labor relations are weakly institutionalized, and workers have little influence over the state. The United States today would provide a prototypical case.

When $b < 1/c$, the best-reply strategy of capitalists is to invest at a positive rate as long as workers are not highly militant: $s^*(r) < 0$ if $r < (1/c - b)$. The best-reply strategy of workers, however, is to increase their militancy regardless of the rate of saving, since $a > 1/c$. One possibility is that workers would follow their best-reply strategy and capitalists would respond by disinvesting, a scenario that ends again without a compromise. But an alternative solution is also possible. Suppose that workers begin their current decision-making process by considering a nonmilitant value of r, say $r = r_0$. (Consult Figure 19 while following this argument.) If the workers choose r_0, then capitalists will choose $s_0 = s^*(r_0)$. Since the workers' best reply to any s is to increase their militancy, they will now consider moving to a new level $r = r_1$. Capitalists, in turn, will respond to the increase of militancy by lowering the rate of investment to $s_1 = s^*(r_1)$. The effect of the capitalists' adjustment will be to drop workers to a function $W^*(r,s_1)$, which is inferior to $W^*(r,s_0)$. If, however, r_1 is only slightly higher than r_0, capitalists will respond (see Figure 18) with a small reduction in their rate of investment, and workers will find that they are better off at the new point $(r,s^*(r_1))$ than they were before. Since workers' best reply to s_1 is again

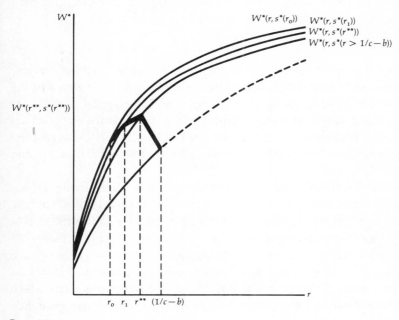

Figure 19.

maximal militancy, workers will now consider raising their militancy further to $r = r^{**}$. Capitalists will lower their rate of saving to $s = s^*(r^{**})$, yet workers will still find they are better off at $(r^{**}, s^*(r^{**}))$ than at any lower value of r. Now as the workers consider increasing their militancy past the level $r = r^{**}$, they discover that the capitalists' best reply is to lower their rate of investment quite sharply, so that workers are worse off at an r slightly higher than r^{**} than they would be at r^{**}. Even though the workers' best response to any fixed rate of saving, including $s^*(r^{**})$, is maximal militancy, the capitalists' threat of disinvestment is effective in the region in which r is somewhat higher than r^{**}. Indeed, the workers discover that if they keep increasing r gradually past r^{**}, they will be successively worse off as $W^*(r, s^*(r))$ keeps decreasing with higher levels of militancy. The threat of disinvestment will not be effective, however, in the entire range of $r > r^{**}$. As r reaches the value $r = 1/c - b$ capitalists will be disinvesting at the greatest possible rate, and their threat will be exhausted. If workers choose an $r > 1/c - b$, the compromise breaks down, workers seek to nationalize capital stock, and capitalists disinvest. Figure 20 presents a graph of the function $W^*(r, s^*(r))$, which is the array of choices facing workers when capitalists respond according to their best reply. There is a maximum at r^{**} which constitutes a compromise solution and a minimum at $1/c - b$.

Will the compromise $(r^{**}, s^*(r^{**}))$ constitute the solution? Unfortunately no answer can be given without additional assumptions. The compromise will be the solution if workers have good reasons to fear the political consequences of a breakdown of compromise, a topic to which we return below.

$$a < 1/c, \ b > 1/c. \tag{iii}$$

Workers are relatively certain to obtain the wages specified by any compromise while capitalists bear the brunt of uncertainty. This would be the case when workers are monopolistically organized, labor–capital relations are institutionalized, and workers are represented by parties that exert electoral influence. The Weimar Republic between 1924 and 1928, Italy between 1969 and 1976, and Great Britain at various times after 1951 would constitute good examples.

When $a < 1/c$, the workers' best-reply strategy is low or moderate militancy as long as the capitalists invest at a sufficient rate: $r^*(s) < (1 + s/c)$ if $s > ac$. The capitalists' best-reply strategy, however, is to disinvest regardless of the level of militancy. But capitalists must consider the workers' response. Figure 21 illustrates the function $C^*(s, r^*(s))$, the anticipated consequence of choosing each positive level of savings given that workers respond according to their best reply. The capitalists' choice is between $s^* < 0$, that is, disinvestment, which entails a breakdown of compromise (not shown) or the best compromise they

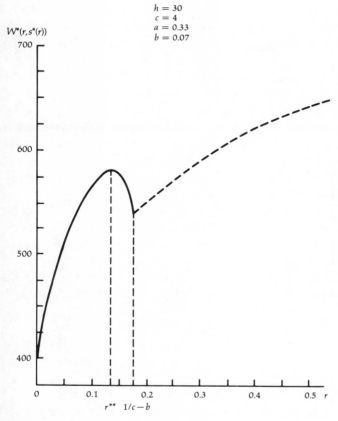

Figure 20.

can achieve, s^{**}. If the breakdown of compromise is sufficiently dangerous politically to capitalists, the solution $(r^*(s^{**}), s^{**})$ will be chosen. Given s^{**}, workers reach a global maximum (under capitalism) at $r^*(s^{**})$, and this value represents a compromise strategy since $s^{**} > ac$. And for capitalists, the payoff from s^{**} is the most that can be gained from any compromise.

$$a < 1/c, \ b < 1/c. \tag{iv}$$

Both capitalists and workers are quite certain they would obtain what would be expected under any compromise. There is a high degree of bilateral monopoly; capital–labor relations are highly institutionalized; the economy is well situated in the international system. Sweden after 1936 and before the mid-1970s would be a prototype. In Sweden, collective agreements began to be concluded at the turn of the century, and by 1905 a significant proportion of

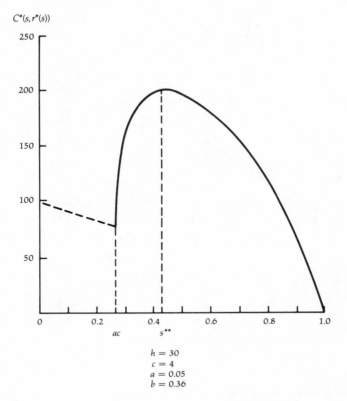

$h = 30$
$c = 4$
$a = 0.05$
$b = 0.36$

Figure 21.

workers was covered by them. These agreements were made binding in a series of decisions by the Supreme Court which first enforced agreements among capitalists and then collective bargains in 1916. In 1920, Labor Courts were established and by 1926 parties could be sued in these courts for unfair bargaining practices. In 1938, a system of collective bargaining was centralized at the countrywide scale, a system that has continued with some modifications up to the present.

In this case, neither the adoption by workers of their best-reply strategy nor by capitalists of theirs would necessarily lead to conflict. Both solutions — $(r^{**}, s(r^{**}))$, where the compromise is enforced by the threat of disinvestment, and $(r^*(s^{**}), s^{**})$, where it is enforced by the threat of militancy — are feasible. Each class would prefer the other to depart from its best-reply strategy. Workers do better threatening capitalists with militancy to the solution $(r^*(s^{**}), s^{**})$, whereas capitalists are better off threatening workers to the solution $(r^{**}, s^*(r^{**}))$. The class which is forced to depart from its best-reply strategy ends up, in effect, paying the costs of the compromise. If both of the compromise solutions are superior for both players to the outcome that would result if they both obstinately pursued their best-reply strategies, workers and capitalists face a coordination problem (Schelling, 1960). I will not pursue this topic further.

To summarize, when both classes are highly uncertain whether a compromise would hold, a compromise cannot be established. Workers become highly militant, regardless of the rate of saving, and capitalists seek to disinvest, regardless of militancy.

When workers are highly uncertain and capitalists relatively certain, a compromise may be established at a point at which workers are kept from increasing their militancy by capitalists' threat of disinvestment, whereas capitalists' optimal rate of investment is positive.

When the workers are relatively certain and the capitalists bear high risk, a compromise may be concluded at a point at which the capitalists are forced to save by the threat of militancy, whereas the workers' optimal level of militancy is not high.

When the workers and capitalists both face only moderate amounts of uncertainty, both a compromise concluded under the capitalists' threat of disinvestment and one reached under workers' threat of militancy are feasible. Either may be concluded.

Beyond Capitalism

What is the alternative to class compromise? I have referred to the breakdown of compromise without specifying what might occur in its stead. Indeed, our results concerning the conditions of class compromise are ultimately unsatisfying in that they are inconclusive. The decision to compromise depends, in the end, on a comparison of the best compromise that can be obtained with the consequences of no compromise. The question of the balance of political power becomes paramount; the outcome highly uncertain. I believe that any analysis based upon rational calculations of expected benefits is of limited value in moments of crisis. Conflicts are inherently laden with uncertainty, and this uncertainty is difficult to evaluate, not only for us but also for the protagonists of our story. Nevertheless I will seek to elucidate the choice that is involved in considering the transition to socialism as an alternative to either compromise or economic militancy under capitalism.

First let us clarify the outcomes that may occur in the absence of compromise. Generically, these are threefold.

(1) Workers have the political power to nationalize the means of production and to organize accumulation on a new basis. Profit is abolished as an economic and legal category and capitalism with it.

(2) Capitalists have the political power to impose a non-democratic solution. Recent experiences of Brazil, Chile, and Argentina demonstrate that profits grow under such regimes simultaneously with a dramatic fall in wages. Economic deprivation of workers as well as widespread physical repression are the hallmark of authoritarian regimes.

(3) Capitalists do not have the power to impose an authoritarian solution nor workers to impose socialism. In this case, the democratic capitalist system continues without compromise but rather with an uneasy stalemate, a prolonged "catastrophic" crisis described by Gramsci (1971: 210 ff.) with specific reference to the MacDonald government in Great Britain. This was perhaps the situation in several Western European countries after the defeats of general strikes fought on economic issues: Sweden in 1909, Norway in 1921, France in 1920, Great Britain in 1926. These situations are characterized by high strike intensity and a fair amount of repression: they constitute a tug-of-war. Wages and profits oscillate sharply.

I will not investigate these alternatives any further but only specify the structure of choice involved in considering the socialist alternative. How would workers choose a strategy of transition to socialism?

Note first that workers may embark upon the strategy of socializing the capital stock under two distinct conditions. The first has been described: compromise is impossible, workers make economic demands, provoke a political crisis, and in this crisis the only choice may come to be between socialism and authoritarian capitalism. This scenario, in which the transition to socialism originates from an economic crisis under capitalism, is the one typically envisaged by marxists as the road to socialism. This is a scenario that leads to the *politique de pire*: in this view, the worse the economic situation under capitalism, the more likely socialism becomes. I am persuaded that this strategy of crisis-mongering is unfeasible and irresponsible. As Varga warned in 1927,

If the working class creates conditions in which the profits of capitalists become impossible but at the same time the bourgeoisie is not defeated politically and the doctrine of the proletariat has not been established, the bourgeoisie, by means of implacable terror, crushes the working class in order to maintain the economic basis of the capitalist system and make possible the exploitation of labor. (Pirker, 1965: 133–4; translated by David Abraham)

Workers may, however, find socialism to be the attractive alternative under the same conditions under which they can conclude an attractive compromise under capitalism. If workers have political power that enables them to enforce compromises under capitalism, would they not use this power to transform the society into socialism? If socialism is preferable under the same conditions under which workers are able to conclude a compromise under capitalism, no compromise would ever be concluded by rational workers. Hence, the conditions of capitalist compromise must always include the superiority of such a compromise to the socialist alternative.

Let us speculate about the following scenario. Suppose that at some time $t = 0$ workers decide to nationalize the entire capital stock. At some later time $t = T$ the final nationalization bill is passed and the entire capital stock is socialized. During the remaining period, from $t = T$ to $t = h$, the institution of profit no longer exists and investment decisions are made by the entire society through some reasonable voting mechanism.

During the period $0 \leqslant t < T$, that is, until socialization is complete, the private ownership of capital remains intact. Faced with imminent nationalization, capitalists will disinvest as rapidly as possible. They cannot be prevented from disinvesting, and they cannot be taken by surprise: even Lange (1964), the foremost advocate of the "one stroke" nationalization strategy, admitted that some disinvestment would occur before capital stock is nationalized. Let $S^*(T)$ be the current value of discounted wages between $t = 0$ and $t = T$ when workers pursue a strategy of socialization and capitalists respond by disinvesting. It is likely that $S^*(T)$ will not be the most that workers could obtain between $t = 0$ and $t = T$. If $W^*(T)$ is the best they could do under capitalism, then the difference between these quantities is the cost of the transition strategy during this period.

At $t = T$ the capital stock becomes entirely nationalized and henceforth the economy operates in the following manner. The entire society now joins in the program of determining the optimal rate of saving out of total output, s_w, and the volume of investment is given by $\Delta K(t) = s_w Y(t)$.[6] Let q be the risk inherent in investment facing the socialist society. Then the problem to be solved would be:

$$\max_{s_w} S^* = (1 - s_w)Y(T) \sum_{t=T}^{t=h} (1 + q)^{-(t-T)} (1 + s_w/c)^{(t-T)}.$$

Let the rate of saving which solves this problem be s^*, and the resulting welfare of workers under socialism be $S^*(h - T)$.

The total value of socialism to workers making a strategic choice at $t = 0$

---

[6] We hope that the reader will not mistake this model of socialism for a description of the Soviet Union or other Eastern European countries. In those countries investment decisions arise out of a game between central planners and managers, with a known effect of investing at a level higher than the preference of the population.

would also depend, however, upon the risk that the socialist transition would be aborted or subverted under the pressure of the armed forces, foreign governments, foreign firms, or even by the workers themselves, if they object to the costs that have to be borne during the period $0 \leqslant t < T$. (See Kolm, 1977, for some of these considerations.) Even if a nationalization law is passed by a parliament in accordance with all of the constitutional requirements, capitalists have numerous ways to fight back. If the probability that the socialist transition would be accomplished is $(1 - f)$ and the probability that the final outcome would be a capitalist dictatorship is f, then we can think of $kS^*(h - T)$, $k < 1$, as the expected value of the revolutionary attempt, where $kS^*(h - T) = (1 - f)S^*(h - T) + f$ (material welfare under capitalist dictatorship). Note that k is likely to be closer to unity the greater the proportion of the capital stock is already publicly owned and the greater the electoral strength of the socialist parties.

The total value of pursuing a strategy of transition to socialism to workers at $t = 0$ can be thus thought of as: $S^* = S^*(T) + kS^*(h - T)$, where $S^*(T)$ and $S^*(h - T)$ are as given above. Note that this is again the current value of the socialist transition to workers at $t = 0$ when they decide whether or not to embark on this road. Hence, this value would be compared to the best workers can do under the particular conditions of democratic capitalism, $W^*(r,s)$, where (r,s) represents either a compromise or a tug-of-war.

I will not carry this discussion any further, mainly because I believe that this calculation involves too many imponderables to be taken seriously in practice. I wanted to clarify the nature of this decision, but I do not intend this to be a description of how the decisions to embark or not to embark upon the socialist path are in fact made.

Class Conflict and the State

Suppose for a moment, as did Marx, that the conflict over material interests is irreconcilable and that workers' pursuit of material interests leads them inevitably to the realization that these interests can be advanced if and only if the institution of profit is abolished altogether. Given this assumption, the reproduction of capitalist relations becomes problematic. Even if all the conditions for expanded reproduction of capital are fulfilled "of itself," "by the mere repetition of isolated acts of production" (Marx, 1967, I: 577–8), the survival of capitalist relations is no longer guaranteed when workers organize collectively to abolish them. One must then look beyond the system of production for the mechanisms by which capitalism is maintained. Hence a functionalist account of capitalist reproduction follows necessarily from this model of class conflict. For, if an irreconcilable conflict over the realization of material interests is characteristic of any capitalist society and if capitalism withstood this conflict during at least one hundred years, then some mechanisms external to class relations must be evoked to explain this durability. Whenever class conflict happens to generate a threat to the reproduction of capitalist relations, some mechanism, most often thought to be the state, must come to the rescue by repressing, organizing ideological domination, or coopting.

The gradual rejection of instrumentalist theories of the state (Miliband, 1970) and their replacement by a model in which the state is viewed as relatively autonomous from class relations did not alter this functional logic. In the instrumentalist version, the state was acting predictably in defense of the interests of capitalists or like-capitalists. In the structuralist version, the state is seen as autonomous from particularistic interests of capitalists and as based on popular support: "the popular class state" (Poulantzas, 1973). Yet somehow this state still manages to repress, to organize ideological domination, and to inter- vene where and when needed in ways designed to and having the effect of maintaining capitalism in the face of conflicts. Both the instrumentalist and autonomous theories of the state are functionalist theories, and although the instrumentalist theory is clearly at odds with the facts, it has at least the logical virtue of explaining why the state — concrete people functioning in concrete institutions — does all that is necessary to reproduce capitalist relations.

In fact, ultimately even the state as an institution disappears from this functionalist analysis. Since, by assumption, the state invariably responds to the functional requirements of capitalist reproduction and since its policies have, by assumption, the function of fulfilling these requirements, one can proceed from requirements to reproduction without bothering with the state at all. The very concept of the state is based on a reification. The state is ready-to-wear; it is tailored before class conflicts, as if in anticipation of those conflicts, appearing fully clothed whenever these conflicts threaten the reproduction of capitalist relations. The state is always given, already in its functional garb, before any conflicts occur, before any problems call for resolution.

Indeed, the perennial difficulty of any functionalist perspective is to account for the reasons why conflicts among specific groups under concrete historical circumstances would regularly result in the state performing its functions. It is quite true that once the manner in which a society responds to variations of historical conditions has been institutionalized, much of this response is automatic. To put it differently, each society organizes the mechanisms of its reproduction as a system. Yet it is equally apparent that the activity of institutions and the institutions themselves are the continual outcome of conflicts. Under concrete historical circumstances, particular groups enter into conflicts over particular issues, and the outcome of these conflicts is a particular organization and a specific set of policies of the state. What is not clear is why this policy would be predictably one that would have the function of reproducing capitalist relations. Clearly the answer to this question cannot be that the state reproduces capitalist relations because this "is" its function. This answer can be twofold: either the capitalist system is organized in such a manner that it is reproduced regardless of all conflicts, and then these conflicts, including class conflict, acquire the status of a superfluous ritual, as in Sahlins, or outcomes of conflicts do in fact determine the policies that the state pursues, in which case the burden of explanation is shifted to these conflicts and any concept of function becomes redundant.

These problems – an implausible account of reproduction, the inability to explain why the state pursues particular policies, and the reification of the state – are inherent in any functionalist perspective. Our claim, however, is that this perspective is made necessary by an incorrect model of class conflict in democratic capitalist societies. The very problem of reproduction appears as a functional one because the model of irreconcilable class conflict leads to the conclusion that capitalism could not have survived as a choice of the working class. Indeed, the working class appears in this model as a passive victim of repression, a perpetual dupe of ideological domination, or, at best, as repeatedly betrayed by its leadership.

If our model of class conflict is valid, then the need for this kind of a construction disappears. The policies pursued by the state in capitalist societies – the policies designed to invigorate and strengthen the capitalist system of social organization – are no longer viewed as functions of an autonomous state facing the threat of a revolutionary working class. These policies – and the state itself – now appear as an expression of a compromise: they are quite instrumental with regard to the interests of a class coalition that includes both capitalists and organized workers. When workers pursue strategies that lead to a compromise, the state does what appears necessary to reproduce capitalism because this is the choice of the workers as well as the capitalists. The organization of the state as an institution and the policies pursued by this institution constitute an expression of a specific class compromise.

Class compromise implies a particular organization of political relations, a particular relation between each class and the state, a particular set of institutions, and a particular set of policies. The state must enforce the compliance of both classes with the terms of each compromise and protect those segments of each class that enter into a compromise from non-cooperative behavior of their fellow class members. The state must induce individual capitalists to make the decisions required by the class compromise, shifting the terms of choice which they confront to produce the requisite aggregate effects as capitalists compete with each other. Finally, since the state of class compromise is a democratic state, it must see to it that the class coalition that forms the compromise can win popular support in elections, which implies that interests of those excluded from the particular coalition must also be taken into account. All of these indications lead, therefore, to the kind of a state that was envisioned by Keynes when he claimed that "It is not the ownership of the instruments of production which it is important for the state to assume. If the state is able to determine the aggregate amount of resources devoted to augmenting the instruments and the basic rate of reward to those who own them, it will have accomplished all that is necessary". (1964: 378) Necessary, that is, to organize class compromise.

6. Democratic Capitalism at the Crossroads*

The Choices We Face

The ideology that orients the current right-wing offensive is in many ways a ghost of the 1920s: antistatist, emphasizing the hegemony of the entrepreneur, portraying popular consumption as inimical to national interests, and based on the belief in the rationality of the market and in the autonomous importance of money. Yet what is new in this ideology is the dominant role played by technical economic theory. In the 1920s, deflationary policies and the principles of the gold standard and of balanced budgets were justified as an accumulated wisdom derived from experience. The only abstract basis for these principles was the quantity theory of money. The ideological appeal was couched in terms of popular values, such as thrift, responsibility, and common sense. The spokesmen for this ideology were typically officials of the Treasury and the bankers. In the 1970s, in contrast, the justification is derived from seemingly technical theories: "monetarism," "*la nouvelle économie*," and "rational expectations" are all being offered as scientific reasons why everyone will be better off if the state withdraws from the economy and capitalists are allowed to accumulate without distributional considerations. Even the most naked program for an upward distribution of income – Reagan's economic policy – is masked as a "supply-side theory," with a concocted Laffer curve as its main theoretical mainstay.

It was Keynes who transformed macro-economics from a frame of mind into a theory: a deductive method for analyzing the determinants of national income and for evaluating alternative policies. His followers constructed mathematical models of capitalist economies and described statistically particular economies in terms of these models. The new theory became the framework within which particular groups presented their interests as universal. It became the vehicle for the articulation of claims to hegemony and the language of economic policy. It is

* This chapter was written jointly with Michael Wallerstein

a lasting legacy of the Keynesian revolution that the terrain of ideological conflict has been conquered by technical economic theory.

While many people have subsequently claimed that the central principles of Keynesian economics had been presaged by Marx and some of his followers, in fact marxist economic theory has never been of economic importance for the left. Marx's theory provided a useful threefold analysis: first, capitalism is based on exploitation (the source of profit is surplus value); second, the private property of the means of production is the source simultaneously of the injustice and the irrationality of capitalism; third, the falling rate of profit is the source of crises. The theory has been politically useful only as a justification of revolutionary goals, specifically of the program of nationalization of the means of production. Marx's economics, even its most sophisticated version, is not a helpful tool for addressing workers' distributional claims within capitalism and it is useless as a framework for administering capitalist economies. It is easy to say "so what," but the fact is that all mass movements of the Left historically have had to face precisely these tasks.

As a result, it has been the understanding of the capitalist economy and the policy recommendations provided by Keynesian economics that the Left has embraced. But Keynesian economics is now badly tarnished. Two phenomena that have characterized much of the developed capitalist world since the early 1970s, a gradual increase in the rate of inflation and a gradual decline in the rate of growth, have proved remarkably unresponsive to the traditional interventions prescribed by Keynesian theory. Yet this deeply ingrained tradition perseveres, providing the basis for much of the Left's current reactions to the conservative offensive. Many continue to insist that the supply of savings is not problematic, that demand is chronically insufficient, and that a redistribution of income, full-employment policies, and social spending are the only ways to get out of the current crisis. The problem is that such a response is no longer convincing. It represents a reaction of clinging to old ideas and old policies that the Right claims, with some justification, have been tried and found wanting. An obstinate defense of policies associated with past failures abdicates the ideological terrain to the Right and, we believe, is not necessary.

What, then, are the choices we face? At one level we are discussing a question about an economic project that would constitute a reasonable and appealing alternative both to the policies of demand management and to the current wave of right-wing supply-oriented economics. But economic theories are rationalizations of the political interests of conflicting classes and groups, and should be treated as such. Behind economic alternatives lurk visions of society, models of culture, and thrusts for power. Economic projects entail political and social ones.

The Keynesian Revolution as a Compromise

The combination of democracy and capitalism constitutes a compromise: those who do not own instruments of production consent to the institution of the private ownership of capital stock while those who own productive instruments consent to political institutions that permit other groups to effectively press their claims to the allocation of resources and the distribution of output. It may be worth recalling that this compromise was deemed unfeasible by Marx, who claims that the "bourgeois republic" is based on a contradiction that renders it inherently unstable as a form of social organization. A combination of private ownership of the means of production with universal suffrage, Marx argued, must lead either to "social emancipation" of the oppressed classes utilizing their political power or to "political restoration" of the oppressing class utilizing its economic power. Hence, Marx held, capitalist democracy is "only the political form of revolution of bourgeois society and not its conservative form of life," "only a spasmodic, exceptional state of things ... impossible as the normal form of society."

It was Keynesianism that provided the ideological and political foundations for the compromise of capitalist democracy. Keynesianism held out the prospect that the state could reconcile the private ownership of the means of production with democratic management of the economy. As Keynes himself put it: "It is not the ownership of the instruments of production which it is important for the state to assume. If the state is able to determine the aggregate amount of resources devoted to augmenting the instruments and the basic reward to those who own them, it will have accomplished all that is necessary." (1964: 378) Democratic control over the level of unemployment and the distribution of income became the terms of the compromise that made democratic capitalism possible.

The problem of the 1930s was that resources lay fallow: machines stood idle while men were out of work. At no time in history was the irrationality of the capitalist system more blatant. As families starved, food – already produced food – was destroyed. Coffee was burned, pigs were killed, inventories rotted, machines rusted. Unemployment was the central political problem of society.

According to the economic orthodoxy of the time, this state of affairs was simply a given and the only recourse was to cut the costs of production, which meant cutting wages and transfers. Some relief measures to assist the employed were obviously urgently required, but whether such measures were advisable from an economic point of view was at best controversial. In Great Britain the Labour government in fact proposed to reduce unemployment compensations: this was the condition for being bailed out by the I.M.F. of the time, where "M."

stood for the Morgan Bank. But in Sweden the Social Democratic Party, having won the election of 1932, broke the shell of the orthodox monetary policy. As unemployment climbed sharply with the onset of the Great Depression, they stumbled upon an idea that was truly new: instead of assisting the unemployed, the Swedish Social Democrats employed them. It was the beginning of the marriage of the Left and Keynesian economics.[1]

Keynesianism provided the foundation for class compromise by supplying those political parties representing workers with a justification for holding office within capitalist societies. And such a justification was desperately needed. Ever since the 1890s, social democrats had thought that their irreversible electoral progress would culminate in an electoral majority that would allow them one day to enter into office and legislate their societies into socialism. They were completely unprepared for what ensued: in several countries social democratic, labor, and socialist parties were invited to form governments by default, without winning the majority that would have been necessary to pursue the program of nationalization, because the bourgeois parties were too divided to continue their traditional coalitions. Indeed, the first elected socialist government in the world was formed by the Swedish Social Democrats in 1920 just as they suffered their first electoral reversal. And once in office, socialists found themselves in the embarrassing situation of not being able to pursue the program of nationalization and not having any other program that would distinguish them from their bourgeois opponents. They could and did pursue ad-hoc measures designed to improve conditions for their electoral constituency: the development of public housing, the institution of unemployment relief, the introduction of minimum wages, income and inheritance taxes, and old age pensions. But such measures did not differ from the tradition of conservative reforms associated with Bismarck, Disraeli, or Giolitti. Socialists behaved like all other parties: with some distributional bias toward their own constituency but full of respect for the golden principles of the balanced budget, deflation, gold standard, etc.

Keynesianism suddenly provided working-class political parties with a reason to be in office. It appeared that there was something to be done, that the economy was not moving according to natural laws, that economic crises could be attenuated and the waste of resources and the suffering alleviated if the state pursued anticyclical policies of demand management. If the economy was producing at a level below its capacity, given the existing stock of capital and labor, a proper government policy could increase output until it approached the economy's full potential. The government had the capacity to close the "full-

---

[1] In fact, the question whether the Swedish policies were an application of the ideas of Keynes or were developed autonomously, from Marx via Wicksell continues to evoke controversy. See Gustafsson (1973).

employment gap," to insure that there would be no unemployment of men and machines. Full employment became a realistic goal that could be pursued at all times.

How was this to be done? Here again Keynesian economics provided a technical justification for class compromise. The answer it provided was to increase consumption. In the Keynesian diagnosis, the cause of unemployment was the insufficiency of demand. Hence any redistribution of income downwards to people who consume most of it and any expansion of government spending will stimulate production and reduce unemployment.[2] Given the existing capital stock, the actual output can always be raised by increasing wages, transfers to the poor, and government spending, or by reducing taxes. Since raising output means augmenting the rate of utilization of resources, the same policies will diminish unemployment. Thus the distributional bias of the Left toward their electoral constituency found a rationalization in a technical economic theory. As Léon Blum put it, "a better distribution . . . would revive production at the same time that it would satisfy justice."

But more was at stake. In the orthodox thinking, any demands by workers or the unemployed for higher consumption appeared as a particularistic interest, inimical to future national development. To increase wages or social services was to raise costs of production and to divert resources from the investment necessary for growth, accumulation of capital, and improved productivity. The welfare of the poor was a matter of private charity, not of economics. But in the Keynesian framework it is consumption that provides the motor force for production, and suddenly workers and the poor turned out to be the representatives of the universal interest. Their particularistic interest in consumption coincided with the general interest in production. The "people" became the hegemonic force in society. As Bertil Ohlin stated in 1938, "In recent years it has become obvious that . . . many forms of 'consumption' – food, clothing, housing, recreation –. . . represent an investment in the most valuable productive instrument of all, the people itself." (1938: 5) The terms of discourse became transformed.

Not all "Keynesian" positions are the same. One policy direction – warmly embraced by the radical Left – focused on the redistribution of income toward wages and transfers. This is what happened in France in 1936. A more cautious and more successful, policy consisted of manipulating government spending,

---

[2] In theory there is another Keynesian instrument: increasing investment expenditure – and thus aggregate demand – by lowering interest rates. But the effect of nominal interest rates upon the level of investment proved empirically to be the weakest link of the Keynesian approach, a conclusion reached by Tinbergen in 1939. Therefore monetary policy was used in practice mainly to accommodate fiscal policy, that is, to prevent government deficits from driving up interest rates or to control inflation, but not to stimulate demand, at least not intentionally.

taxation, and the money supply. The Swedish policy of 1932 was exclusively an "employment policy": it consisted of productive public employment financed by deficits and increased taxation. Wage rates did not increase in Sweden until 1938, well after the economy was out of the slump. In fact, the simple formal framework of Keynesian economics, as is found in modern macro-economic textbooks, favors government spending over redistribution of income: the "multiplier" for government spending is greater than unity, while for wages and transfers it is less than unity. Hence, at least in principle, government spending more than pays for itself in increased production, while distribution of income partially hurts other components of demand.

In all of its forms, the Keynesian compromise consisted of a dual program: "full employment and equality," where the first term meant regulation of the level of employment via the management of demand, particularly government spending, and the latter consisted of the net of social services that constituted the "welfare state." The Keynesian compromise, therefore, came to consist of more than an active role for the government in macro-economic management. As the provider of social services and regulator of the market, the state acted in mulitiple social realms. Governments developed manpower programs, family policies, housing schemes, income assistance nets, health systems, etc. They attempted to regulate the labor force by mixing incentives and deterrents to participation in the labor market. They sought to alter patterns of racial and regional disparities. The result is that social relations are mediated through democratic political institutions rather than remaining private.

At the same time, the Keynesian compromise became increasingly dependent upon economic concessions granted to groups of people organized as nonmarket actors. Politics turned into an interplay of coalitions among such groups, giving rise to corporatist tendencies of direct negotiation, either between organized groups – particularly labor and capital – under the tutelage of the government or between each group and the government. The allocation of economic resources became increasingly dominated by relations of political forces.

The compromise was tenable as long as it could provide employment and material security. Indeed, by most criteria of economic progress the Keynesian era was a success. Whether or nor this was due to the efficacy of Keynesian economic policies or was merely fortuitous is a matter of debate. Nevertheless, output grew, unemployment was low, social services were extended, and social peace reigned. Until the late 1960s, Keynesianism was the established ideology of class compromise, under which different groups could conflict within the confines of a capitalist and democratic system. And, with the possible exception of Karl Rehn's 1951 program in Sweden and the Italian Communist Party's short-lived austerity policy of the mid-1970s, Keynesianism provided the only framework for such a compromise. The crisis of Keynesianism is a crisis of democratic capitalism.

Economic Alternatives

Keynesian economics is demand economics. The supply of capital and the supply of labor are assumed to be constant. The supply of savings is determined endogenously: it always equals investment. As demand is stimulated, whether by government policies or exogenous events, production expands to match demand, income increases and so do savings until a new equilibrium is reached where savings again equal investment at a higher level of capacity-utilization. The level of output shifts to maintain the equality of savings and investment. Moreover, since the Keynesian problem is to bring the actual output to the potential level of the already existing capital stock, the accumulation of capital is ignored altogether, to the point where new investment is assumed to be nonnegative at the same time that the total stock of capital is assumed to be constant.

Keynesian economics is the economics of the "short run," where the short run is a situation rather than a period of time, in which cumulative changes of capital stock can be ignored. Given the Keynesian problem, this assumption is not unreasonable, but the effect is that this framework has nothing to say about the determinants of the potential level of output, about capital accumulation, or about productivity. The problem for Keynesian policies is always to close the gap between actual output and potential output, whatever the potential might happen to be.

Suppose for the moment that this problem has been solved and the economy is producing at its full potential. Since the already installed capital stock is now fully utilized, output cannot be increased without investment, that is, without new additions to the capital stock. In the demand view of the world, no longer Keynes' own but nevertheless very much "Keynesian," demand stimulation will still have the effect of increasing output, this time by "accelerating" investment.[3] Investors are assumed to make their investment decisions in order to increase production to match the expected future aggregate demand. Hence, the same government policies – spending, distribution of income, reduction of taxation – will continue to be effective, since by stimulating demand past the level of potential output the government will stimulate investment and economic growth.

[3] This theory of investment was first suggested by Clark (1917). Its modern form is due to Chenery (1952).

212 Democratic Capitalism at the Crossroads

But things look different when the supply of productive inputs is no longer taken to be fixed or passive. Now the question of whether the supply of savings is sufficient becomes problematic. The supply of savings available for investment is what is left from the total output after wages, transfers, and government expenditures have been subtracted. Hence the very measures designed to stimulate demand have the effect of reducing potential savings, that is, the savings that are available when the economy is running at its full potential.

As long as the economy operates below the full potential level there is no contradiction involved. The output determined by the level of aggregate demand is assumed not to be greater than the level possible given the already existing capital stock, and the supply of savings is not a constraint. Indeed, in such circumstances, savings are too high and the Keynesian remedies all involve a reduction of savings as a proportion of output. But when the economy is close to full employment the measures meant to increase aggregate demand and therefore to decrease aggregate saving have the effect of limiting the rate of growth of potential output. And since potential output is the ceiling for actual output, short-run demand stimulation turns out to have perverse effects for the long run. When we encounter symptoms of insufficient investment – the stagnation of real wages, the decline of productivity, the obsolescence of plant and equipment – demand management provides no solution. Indeed, the stimulation of demand accentuates the problem when the problem is the shortage of capital.

The supply side is the kingdom of the bourgeoisie. Here the bourgeoisie appears hegemonic: the realization of its interest in profits is a necessary condition for the improvement of the material conditions of everyone. Increased output requires investment, investment is financed by savings, savings are financed by profits. Hence profits are the condition for growth. From the supply side it is savings that provide the motor for accumulation and, as all studies show, workers do not save much. Increases in wages and transfers as well as "welfare" spending appear, therefore, as hindrances to growth. So does taxation of the wealthy and any form of government intervention that restricts profitability, even if such restrictions reflect social costs and negative externalities.

Clearly, such a rendition of the economic system is not particularly appealing to those who consume most of their incomes. The natural response of the Left is to claim that the very problem of the supply of savings is a false one.[4] This is a response embedded in the Keynesian framework in which investment and growth are constrained by insufficient demand, not by available savings. But the

[4] See, for example, Perlo (1976), Sweezy and Magdoff (1980): or, most recently, Rothschild (1982).

response is wrong. The inadequate rate of investment in the U.S. did not suddenly appear in the recessions of the last ten years. Investment, capital accumulation, and growth of output per worker have been lower in the U.S. than in any major advanced capitalist economies, except for Great Britain, throughout the postwar period.[5] What is fallacious in the claims of right-wing economists is not the assertion that the supply of savings is insufficient to finance the desirable level of investment, but the argument that savings are insufficient because profits are too low.

True, the mere fact that the level of investment is inadequate does not imply that savings must be increased – at least if we accept the possibility that most of current investment may be socially wasteful, superfluous, or otherwise undesirable. The aggregate balance always hides qualitative alternatives. One bomber absorbs as much savings as would a modern mass-transit system for the city of Chicago. If investment is insufficient, there are many places to look for waste, and nonmilitary public expenditures would not necessarily be the first place selected by a rational observer.

But such a qualitative response is not sufficient. Moreover, it is not synonymous with an indiscriminate cry for a continued expansion of government spending, for supporting obsolete industries, and for an obstinate stimulation of demand. The problem of the supply of savings must be faced as such.

The historical experience of several countries demonstrates that growth can be generated without pernicious effects upon the distribution of income when governments actively influence the rate and the direction of investment and the supply of labor. The postwar German "miracle," the rapid growth of Japan, and the apparent success of the Swedish Social Democrats in combining relatively fast growth of productivity with the most egalitarian distribution of income in the West demonstrate that there exists an alternative to demand-management as well as to profit-oriented, right-wing supply policies.

Although they have been pursued in somewhat different forms in several countries, these alternative supply-oriented policies have never been formalized in a theoretical framework. Indeed, the Swedish Social Democrats seem to have stumbled upon them in 1951 in a manner reminiscent of their discovery of deficit spending in 1932: mainly as a remedy to the problem of maintaining price stability under conditions of full employment (Rehn, 1952). Of the German post-1949 policies it is typically said that they were a discovery of bankers who behaved as if Keynes had never existed. Yet both the Germans and the Swedes, along with a number of other countries, successfully pursued sustained

---

[5] For a recent study, see John Kendrick (1981).

programs consisting of public control over investment, elimination of inefficient industries, manpower policies designed to reduce structural unemployment, and expansion of the welfare system.

In order to understand abstractly these investment-oriented supply strategies, one must note first that in advanced capitalist economies productive investment is financed largely out of profit incomes. This implies that the rate of accumulation, that is, the ratio of the change in capital stock over total capital stock, is approximately equal to the product of two quantities: the rate of saving out of profits and the after-tax rate of profit.[6] For example, a 6 percent rate growth could be accomplished by a saving rate of 60 percent combined with a rate of profit of 10 percent or, equivalently, by a saving rate of 30 percent combined with a rate of profit of 20 percent.

The crucial question is whether firms can be made to invest when the rate of profit is low. The argument of the Right is that this situation is unfeasible, since without sufficient future rewards capitalists will not abstain in the present. Big business and the political forces that represent it always claim that the only way the volume of savings can be increased is by raising the after-tax rate of profit, an increase that is supposed to have two effects. First, given a constant rate of saving out of profits, either directly by firms or by the recipients of profit income, the aggregate volume of savings will rise in proportion to the increase in the aggregate volume of profits. Second, a higher rate of return is promised to induce a higher propensity to save out of profits. Giving more money to "those who save," in the words of the *Wall Street Journal*, will encourage them to save at a higher rate. Indeed, the central tenet of the new economics is that a redistribution of income in favor of profits is a necessary cost the society must bear in order to produce a higher rate of investment and economic growth. The policies of the Right, therefore, are designed to increase the effective rate of profit by sharply reducing nominal rates of taxation of incomes derived from property, by cutting down nonmilitary public expenditures, by eliminating all of the profit-constraining regulation, and by limiting the right of workers to organize and strike. They offer in return the promise of increased investment, improvement of productivity, and an acceleration of growth.

Yet there are countries — those mentioned above among them — in which the rate of investment has been relatively high while the after-tax rate of profits has been relatively low. These are the countries in which governments sought to alter the terms of choice of private decision-makers between consumption and investment through taxes, credits, and direct subsidies.

Let us concentrate on the use of the tax system. Consider all taxes levied on

---

[6] Formally, $\Delta K / K = sP/K$, where K is the capital stock and ΔK its change, s is the rate of saving out of profit, P is the volume of profits, and P/K is the rate of profit.

incomes derived from the ownership of capital. They typically include a personal income tax on earned income ("salaries" of top executives), a personal income tax on property income, a tax on wealth, and a corporate profit tax. Given any mixture of these incomes there exists some average nominal rate of taxation of the aggregate property income. At the same time, all Western countries use the tax system as an instrument for stimulating investment: by a preferential treatment of capital gains, depreciation write-offs, investment credits, and grants. Given a mix of these different manners of investing, there exists again an average rate of investment relief, a rate that depends upon the rate of investment. Hence, the effective tax rate – the rate at which incomes from profits are in fact taxed – will be determined by the difference between the nominal rate of taxation and the rate of investment relief.

Let us now compare different tax systems. When the nominal tax rate on profits is low, the tax system has the effect of keeping the after-tax rate of profit high – independent of the rate of investment. Such a tax system rewards wealth, not investment. It may – although the evidence is at best mixed (New York Stock Exchange, 1981) – provide an incentive to invest, but it provides no assurance. It imposes no penalties on unproductive uses of profits. Hence, lowering the nominal rate of taxation of profits is the program of business. Owners of capital are then free to do whatever they find in their self-interest without any control.

But suppose that the nominal tax-rate on profits is high – *very* high – and the marginal rate of investment tax relief is also high, at least for some chosen types of investment.[7] Unproductive uses of profits are now being punished. People and firms that do not invest do not receive tax breaks. The terms of choice facing the owners of capital are altered, presenting the choice of investing in publicly designated directions or paying taxes. It is now in the interests of firms to invest.

Consider, again, the example of two societies that add to their capital stock and output at the rate of 6 percent per year: one with the after-tax rate of profit of 20 percent and the rate of investment of 30 percent, the other with the after-tax rate of profit of 10 percent and the rate of investment out of profits of 60 percent. As is illustrated in Table 8, the distributional implications of these alternative patterns of growth are quite staggering. When accumulation is financed by a high rate of investment with a low rate of profit, Case B, the share of wages and government spending is much higher and the rate of consumption out of profit incomes much lower than Case A where accumulation is financed with a high rate of profit and a low rate of investment. The choice is brutally clear. The same rate of growth can be obtained in different ways. The question is simply who

[7] As Shonfield put it, referring to Germany, "To make the trick work, tax rates had to be high. They were." (1969: 282) And so were tax credits for investments: see his Appendix IV.

Table 8. *Two Hypothetical Patterns of Capital Accumulation at 6 Percent Per Year (Net incremental capital–output ratio is 2)*

	CASE A	CASE B
	%	%
Rate of growth of output		
and capital stock	6	6
Net investment/output	12	12
Rate of profit	20	10
Rate of saving out of profits	30	60
Share of profits in output	40	20
Share of wages and government	60	80
Share of consumption out of profits	28	8
Investment + Wages and government + Consumption out of profits = 100%		

will pay the cost of accumulation: the wage-earners and unemployed or the owners of capital.

Hence, the problem of the supply of capital, that is, of investment and productivity, can be addressed without redistributing incomes upwards and dismantling government services – if the tax system is used to reward investment and discourage consumption of profit incomes. This kind of tax system satisfies three criteria. First, it delivers investment. Second, it does not place the burden of sacrifice on wage-earners and those dependent upon the government for survival. Third, if applied with qualitative criteria, it allows society to choose the directions of investment on the basis of criteria other than private profitability.

None of the above is intended to suggest, however, that democratic control over investment, exercised through the tax system, is a panacea. Decisions over the allocation of investment involve a number of trade-offs that are painful, as trade-offs are. We do not have consensual criteria by which to evaluate the choices presented by considerations of social effects, environment, health and safety, depletion of natural resources, and profitability. And in the absence of such criteria qualitative control over investment could lead to whimsical rule by government bureaucrats responding to political pressures. The exercise of discretion in investment policy makes it possible for firms (private and public) to succeed on the basis of influence within government bureaucracies rather than on the strict merits of their undertakings. And as long as market rationality remains the international criterion of efficiency in the allocation of resources, market criteria tend to ultimately prevail under the pressure of international competition.

Moreover, the goals of economic growth and increased productivity are in conflict with the goal of protecting existing jobs. A policy that encourages labor-saving innovations, that refuses subsidies to inefficient producers or protection to obsolete industries, must be coupled with Swedish-style manpower programs of job-retraining and subsidies for labor mobility. But, as the Swedes dicovered, such manpower policies are socially costly and may be politically intolerable.[8] Measures designed to make people move according to the shifting patterns of industry imply that families are uprooted, social ties are fractured, and even entire communities may die deserted by the breadwinners.

Yet a comprehensive, consistent system of public control over investment and income distribution opens the possibility for the realization of the original goal of the socialist movement, the goal that has been abandoned and perverted in its history, namely, reduction of the necessary labor time. It is ironic that, since the 1930s, full employment has been the predominant concern for the Left. What in the middle of the nineteenth century used to be called "wage slavery" became the condition to be made universal. The working class traveled a long road from seeking to abolish the wage relation to attempting to insure that none are excluded from it. As Rosa Luxemburg observed in 1906, workers had become an obstacle to technical change that would make possible their own liberation. Defense of obsolete plants and inefficient industries for the sake of maintaining jobs has been an almost irresistible stance to the Left, with inevitable detrimental effects for economic welfare. The maintenance of full employment has turned into a major barrier to investment that would improve productivity, increase output, raise wages, and/or reduce working time.

The priority that the Left has given to the creation of jobs is inevitable so long as a decent standard of living is contingent upon being employed. Only when a sufficient minimum income is guaranteed to all will the maintenance of full employment no longer be a necessary object of economic policy. A substantial degree of equality, then, is a precondition for a working-class-supported macro-economic policy that would allow jobs to be lost for the sake of productivity growth, that would not protect technologically backward plants and industries, that would encourage rather than block labor-saving innovations. But consider the rewards. At an annual rate of productivity growth of less than 3 percent, output per worker doubles in twenty-five years: within one generation we could reduce labor time by one-half. Whether people would opt to use productivity gains to increase consumption or free time we do not know. But once the maintenance of full employment ceases to be a fetish, once decent life conditions are assured for everyone, this choice will be open.

---

[8] For discussions of the problem encountered by the Swedish Social Democrats in the most ambitious attempt to date in a capitalist economy to shape the supply of both labor and privately owned capital through government policies, see Ohlin (1977) and Heilbroner (1980).

Market Economics as a Political Project

In any society some decisions have a public impact while others have a private, or limited, effect. And in any society some decisions are made by the public while others are restricted to the private realm. Investment decisions – decisions to withhold a part of society's resources from current consumption and to allocate them to replace or augment the instruments of production – have an impact that is both general and long-lasting, that is, public. Yet the very institution of private property implies that they are a private prerogative. Control over investment is the central political issue under capitalism precisely because no other privately made decisions have such a profound public impact.

The program of the Right is to let the type and quantity of investment be determined by the market. The market, after all, is an institution that coordinates private decisions and aggregates preferences. If the market is undistorted by monopolies, externalities, etc., and consumers are sovereign, the market aggregates private decisions in a way that corresponds to preferences of individuals as consumers. The decisions made by profit-maximizing investors will respond to the preference of consumers concerning the atemporal and intertemporal allocation of resources. But the preferences to which the market responds are weighted by the amount of resources each individual controls. That an idealized "perfect" market matches aggregated consumer preferences for private goods efficiently is the first lesson of welfare economics. That aggregated consumer preferences reflect the distribution of income and wealth is an often neglected corollary.

A democratic political system constitutes another mechanism by which individual preferences are aggregated. If political competition is free of coercion and if voters are sovereign, then government policies will reflect the aggregated preferences of individuals as citizens. But as citizens individuals are weighted equally. Hence, the same set of individual preferences, for private as well as public goods, will normally yield a demand for a different allocation of resources when they are aggregated by political institutions rather than by the market.

Further, the market provides no guarantee that those whose consumption is most restrained in the present will reap the rewards of investment in the future. In any society some part of the current output must be withheld from consumption if production is to continue and consumption is to increase. What distinguishes capitalism is that investment is financed mostly out of profits, the part of the product withheld from wage-earners. It is upon profits that the renewal and enlargement of the capital stock depend. Hence, under capitalism, the presence of profits is a necessary condition for the improvement of material conditions of any group within the society. But it is not sufficient. Profits may be hoarded, consumed, exported, or invested badly. Even if capitalists are abstemious, efficient, and prescient, their market relation with workers ends as the cycle of production is completed and the wages are paid, and there is nothing in the structure of the capitalist system of production that would guarantee that wage-earners would be the ones to benefit from the fact that a part of the product is currently withheld from them as profit.

Any class compromise must, therefore, have at least two aspects: one concerning the distribution of income and the second concerning investment. If those who do not own capital are to consent voluntarily to the private property of the instruments of production, they must have a reasonable certainty that their material conditions would improve in the future as the result of current appropriation of profit by capitalists. Until recently, this compromise was rarely stated explicitly, for it is basically institutional: workers consent to the institution of private property of the instruments of production and owners of these instruments consent to political institutions through which other groups can effectively process their demands. Today, as trust in the compromise is eroding, workers are demanding more explicit commitments. As a recent report commissioned by the European Trade Union Confederation declared: "To accept the level of profits required for investments and to give companies a sound financial basis, workers will increasingly demand a say in decisions about investments and a fairer share of the income they generate." (Köpke, 1979: iv)

The current period, however, is the first moment since the 1920s in which owners of capital have openly rejected a compromise that involves public influence over investment and the distribution of income. For the first time in several decades, the Right has an historical project of its own: to free accumulation from all the fetters imposed upon it by democracy. For the bourgeoisie never completed its revolution.

Just as it freed accumulation from the restraint of the feudal order, the bourgeoisie was forced to subject it to the constraint of popular control exercised through universal suffrage. The combination of private property of the means of production with universal suffrage is a compromise, and this compromise implies that the logic of accumulation is not exclusively the logic of private actors.

What is involved in the current offensive of the Right is not simply a question of taxes, government spending, or even the distribution of income. The plans for relaxing taxation of profits, abolishing environmental controls, eliminating welfare programs, removing government control over product safety and conditions of work, and weakening the labor unions add up to more than reorientation of the economic policy. They constitute a project for a new society, a bourgeois revolution.

It is thus necessary to consider the following question: what kind of a society would it be in which accumulation would be free from any form of political control, free from constraints of income distribution, from considerations of employment, environment, health of workers, and safety of consumers? Such hypothetical questions have no ready-made answers, but let us speculate.

It would be a society composed of households and firms, related to each other exclusively through the market. Social relations would become coextensive with market relations and the role of the political authority would be reduced to defending the market from attempts by any group organized as nonmarket actors (i.e. other than households and firms) so alter the rationality of market allocations. Since social and political relations would be depoliticized, demands by nonmarket actors would find no audience. The tension between accumulation and legitimation would be overcome: accumulation would be self-legitimizing for those who benefit from it and no other legitimacy would be sought. As it has been said, "the government does not owe anybody anything."

Household income would depend solely upon the market value of the labor performed. Reproduction of the labor force would be reprivatized and the traditional division of labor within the household — between earners and nurturers — would be restored. Persons excluded from participation in gainful activities would have no institutional guarantee of survival. They might be isolated on "reservations," whether inner cities or depressed regions, where they could be forgotten or ignored.

Workers would be disorganized as a class. If wage bargaining is decentralized by law to the level of the firm (as it is now in Chile) and if the process of internationalization of production continues, the monopoly power of unions would be effectively broken. Workers would be controlled by a combination of decentralized co-optation by some firms, by repression oriented against monopoly power, and — most importantly — by the threat of unemployment.

All of these changes would represent a reversal of trends that we are accustomed to see as irreversible. Indeed, the picture we drew can be easily obtained by combining the trends of contemporary capitalism described by, say, E. H. Carr or Jurgen Habermas, and reversing them. Economic relations would be depoliticized. Government economic planning would be abandoned. Legitimation would be left to the market. The "economic whip" would be reinstated as the central mechanism of political control.

Is such a society feasible? The Chilean experience demonstrates that it is feasible when accompanied by brutal repression, the destruction of democratic institutions, the liquidation of all forms of politics. At least in Chile — most observers agree — such a restructuring of the society could not have succeeded under democratic conditions, without the military dictatorship. But is it feasible without destroying formal democracy, without a "Chileanization" of capitalist democracies?

Where electoral participation has traditionally been high, where working-class parties enjoy electoral support, and where access to the electoral system is relatively open – in most Western European countries – the project of the Right seems doomed to failure under democratic conditions. But in the United States, where about 40 percent of adults never vote, where parties of notables have a duopolistic control over the electoral system, and where the barriers to entry are prohibitive, one must be less sanguine about the prospects. For suppose that the project is economically successful, even if for purely fortuitous reasons, and beneficial for a sizeable part of the electorate, that the Right captures both parties, and the offensive enjoys the support of the mass media. . . . Such a prospect is not totally far-fetched.

7. Exploitation, Class Conflict, and Socialism: The Ethical Materialism of John Roemer

Introduction

John Roemer's general theory of exploitation provides an analytical framework for the fundamental problem of any theory of revolution: under what conditions would anyone living under a particular organization of society rationally opt for an alternative? Specifically, Roemer explains why workers living under capitalism should prefer socialism. I believe that his formulation is incorrectly specified and that the answer is erroneous.

In order to get to this issue, some preliminary steps are needed. I begin by summarizing Roemer's two theories of exploitation, that is, those sections of his article that define exploitation, assert its existence, and explain its origins.[1] Then I examine his claim that while class struggle can be understood in terms of, and only in terms of, the exploitation of labor, accumulation of capital is a "technical fact," not related uniquely to labor exploitation. I argue that the consequence of this formulation is to foreclose a priori the possibility that class conflicts would have any effect on the material well-being of workers under capitalism. Roemer's workers face the stark choice of individually maximizing their wages or collectively struggling for socialism. Unable to struggle for any change under capitalism, they are thus condemned, by his assumptions, to be revolutionary. Roemer fails to demonstrate that anyone living under capitalism, including workers, would have good reasons to prefer socialism. I also believe that I know a valid answer to Roemer's question: for workers, socialism is preferable to capitalism not because it would increase their consumption at the cost of capitalists but because in a socialist society everyone could jointly decide to which needs societal resources should be allocated.

[1] In addition to the article by John E. Roemer, "New Directions in the Marxian Theory of Exploitation and Class" (1982a), I consulted at times Roemer's book, *A General Theory of Exploitation and Class* (1982b), which contains proofs of the theorems summarized in the article. However, I did not study these proofs systematically.

Exploitation and Its Origins

What do we need a theory of exploitation for? Roemer's views are so original that they force us to rethink this basic question. And we must be careful to define the object of the theory accurately. Roemer's article, which bears the title of "Theory of Exploitation", is, I believe, ultimately intended as a theory of something else.[2]

A theory of exploitation would define exploitation such that the phenomena denoted by it could be said to exist (at least contingently) and, further, the theory would explain why these phenomena exist and why they assume particular historical forms. Roemer begins by defining exploitation as a transfer of labor time, and using this definition, he proves a startling theorem about the origins of exploitation.

What makes this theorem so startling is that never before has a marxist logically demonstrated that the cause of exploitation is the (unequal) private property of the means of production. Marxists before classified people by their relation to the ownership of the means of production, by whether they sold or bought labor power, and by the relation between the values of their labor power and their labor, that is, exploitation. From Marx on, they asserted that these three ways of looking at a society are equivalent, that is, that the owners of the means of production are the purchasers of labor power and the appropriators of surplus labor. They have never shown this theorem to be true. Roemer did.

Roemer shows first that even if everyone owns the means of production necessary to produce their subsistence and even if there is no surplus and no exchange of labor, exploitation will still exist, as long as the initial endowments in the means of production ("wealth," for short) are unequal. This proof, to be found in Roemer's book, demonstrates that exploitation can be meaningfully defined in a market economy even without any wage relations or, to put it differently, that the inequality of wealth (alienable) endowments is a sufficient condition for exploitation to occur. This result is startling in two ways.[3] First, it shows, against neoclassical economists, that gains from trade and exploitation are not mutually exclusive. Second, it demonstrates that the concept of exploitation can be applied to international economic relations where direct wage relations are absent.

Roemer then introduces wage relations, and he proves two theorems. The

[2] Much of what passes for marxist theory of the state is in fact a state theory of capitalist reproduction, that is, a theory that explains the reproduction of capitalist relations in terms of the role played by the state. Similarly, the so-called dependency theory is typically not a theory of dependency at all but a theory that accounts for certain types of development in terms of dependency.
[3] Roemer thinks that he is also demonstrating that the source of exploitation cannot be the extraction of surplus labor at the point of production. This claim is false, however, as shown below.

first one asserts that people ordered by magnitudes of their wealth endowments will order themselves into classes, defined by the sale or purchase of labor power, as they seek to maximize their objectives. Here again some new results appear. The class structure turns out to consist of five classes, rather than the customary three, since Roemer distinguishes pure capitalists (rentiers who do not work for themselves) from mixed capitalists (entrepreneurs who work for themselves and hire others) and pure proletarians (who work only for others) from mixed proletarians (who work with their own means of production as well as sell their labor power).[4] Having worked for years on squeezing census materials into marxist class categories, I find these distinctions useful. For example, as many as one-fifth of industrial workers owned and operated their own land in some capitalist societies.[5]

The second theorem, one that Roemer treats as fundamental for his proof, is that exploitation (net transfer of labor time embodied in commodities) is determined solely by class positions. All those who sell labor power work more for what they get than all those who purchase labor power (or, equivalently, those who borrow and loan capital). Hence embodied labor time is transferred in exchanges from those who sell labor power to those who purchase it.

Put together, the Wealth–Class Correspondence Theorem and the Class–Exploitation Correspondence Theorem assert that (1) exploitation can be said to exist under very general institutional and technological conditions and (2) exploitation results from unequal ownership of the means of production. Moreover, exploitation exists under capitalism even if everyone gains all that is possible to gain from the exchanges of labor power and of produced commodities.

For a number of reasons, however – some of them related to the alleged deficiencies of labor theories of value – Roemer is led to an alternative, "general" view of exploitation. While the exploitation defined and explained thus far was, in spite of its abstract definition, a model of capitalist appropriation of surplus labor, Roemer, who is very concerned with explaining exploitation under what he calls "socialism," develops a meta-theory of exploitation designed to apply to any mode of production. To paraphrase his formulation: exploitation exists in a given society if and only if some group within this society could improve its material welfare by "withdrawing" in a specific way from this society. The notion of "withdrawing" is not to be interpreted literally, since the comparisons of the welfare of groups within and without a particular economy are based

---

[4] What I do not understand is how pure capitalism appear in the accumulation model in which everyone would presumably use up their labor constraint. Perhaps a more thorough reading of Roemer's book would make this more clear.

[5] Roemer's classification does not allow, however, for people who sell their own labor and power and hire others to work their capital while not working it themselves.

exclusively on the properties of static equilibria. In Roemer's words, a group is to "be conceived of as exploited if it has some *conditionally feasible alternative* under which its members would be better off." (1982a: 276)

This new, what I shall refer to as the "contingent withdrawal," definition of exploitation entails as well a casual explanation, which Roemer thinks is different from the one entailed by the "surplus labor" definition. Roemer contrasts what he calls the property-relations approach to the surplus-value approach to exploitation. I think, however, that he confuses some issues. One issue is whether exploitation can be satisfactorily defined in general terms by reference to labor values, his claim being that it cannot be. A separate issue is what causes exploitation to exist, whether in the contingent-withdrawal sense or in the labor-value sense, where labor value can be meaningfully defined. Finally, some of the controversy is diffused by Roemer's own proof that under capitalism the two definitions turn out to be equivalent.

What Roemer seems to be showing, I believe, is that exploitation is a result of unequal ownership of the means of production (alienable and inalienable) both if we use the general definition of contingent withdrawal and if we use the labor-value definition. Indeed, the Class–Exploitation Correspondence Principle is not where the explanation of labor exploitation lies. It is the unequal distribution of wealth that generates classes. Indeed, Roemer's explanation of labor exploitation could be constructed without any reference to class, as it was originally constructed by Roemer himself. The cause of labor exploitation is still the unequal distribution of wealth. Hence, if the contingent-withdrawal definition is superior to the surplus-value definition it is not because it provides a better causal explanation. Rather, it is because the surplus-value definition is deficient, or, as Roemer also claims, it is because the contingent-withdrawal definition makes clear "the ethical imperatives" of marxian theory.

Exploitation and Class Struggle

Once we have a theory (theories) of exploitation, what are we to use it for? Since Roemer states his answer explicitly, I will let him speak for himself: the purpose of a theory of exploitation is to explain class struggle (Ibid.: 274). But what is class struggle, between whom and about what? "We look at history," Roemer observes, "and see poor workers fighting rich capitalists. To explain this, or to justify it, or to direct it and provide it with ideological ammunition, we construct a theory of exploitation in which the two antagonistic sides become classified as the exploiters or exploited." (Ibid.: 274–5) Moreover, Roemer continues, this is "a particular theory of capitalism that corresponds to the interpretation of capitalism as a class struggle between poor workers and rich capitalists, which, according to historical materialism, is the most informative historical interpretation of capitalism." (Ibid.: 275)

Thus Roemer's concept of exploitation appears in a triad with class struggle and inequality. Let us first distinguish the two steps in Roemer's connection, the relation between inequality and exploitation and between exploitation and class struggle, working backwards.

Roemer believes that we need a theory that will "produce the decomposition of society into exploiters and exploited that corresponds to the class struggle of capitalism." (Ibid.: 275) Indeed, we were already told that when we look at history we see workers fighting capitalists. This is a threefold claim: that the subjects of history are necessarily and invariably the exploited and exploiters; that these collective actors necessarily and invariably "fight" or constitute "antagonistic sides" in their relation to each other, and, finally, that all historical change is due to the fight between the exploited and the exploiters. I will argue that Roemer does not establish any logical correspondence between exploitation and class struggle, that no such correspondence is here to establish, and that his historical assertions are entirely rhetorical.

I will not comment on this aspect of Roemer's views in any detail; to do so would be to repeat what many, including myself, have already said many times: that the organization of classes as historical subjects, collectivities-in-struggle, is not determined by the places occupied by individuals within the realm of property relations. There is no relation to be deduced here. The history of capitalism need not be a history of class struggle between the exploited and the exploiters, although it may happen to be that if workers and capitalists organize as such and if everyone struggles only in their capacity of workers or capitalists. The history of capitalism may be a history of struggle *among* exploiters; it may be a history of struggle among women, nations, races, or religious groups. If we were to construct a theory of exploitation and class struggle we would have to begin by abandoning any belief that they "correspond" to each other. Indeed, as I read some of Roemer's passages, I am reminded of the kind of "marxism" George Marchais offers the French public on television: "There are the rich and the poor, the exploiters and the exploited. . . ."

Moreover, even if the exploited and the exploiters appeared as such to move the history of capitalism, it yet remains to be shown that they would necessarily and invariably "fight" with each other. This issue is complex and important for the subsequent discussion, so let us introduce some distinctions.

Why do Roemer's workers necessarily fight his capitalists? The reason is to be found in the very way Roemer formulates his analysis. His capitalism works entirely in isolated cycles of exchange–production – exhange and his method of analysis is based entirely on comparisons of the properties of static equilibria resulting from such cycles. At the beginning of each cycle all actors trade their initial endowments, then production occurs, and then they trade again and evaluate the results. The final result of each cycle is an equilibrium solution (at which all markets clear) and associated with each solution is a distribution of income (or leisure). Indeed, note that the entire history of capitalism is exhausted in Roemer's models by one cycle in which everything is determined by the initial distribution of wealth endowments.

Given this formulation, the economic actors involved must be myopic about the future. Everyone seeks to maximize his or her objectives instantaneously and does not look beyond the particular cycle. Hence, Roemer's workers cannot compare, for example, what would happen if they forsook the maximization of *current* income and allowed capitalists to accumulate at a fast pace with the strategy imposed upon them by Roemer's assumptions, which is the maximization of current income (or leisure).

Furthermore, the equilibrium distribution of current income is determined in each cycle by the initial distribution of wealth (that is, of income that has been either accumulated previously or is given exogenously) in such a way that those who are poorer in the initial wealth are exploited and obtain less current income than those who are richer in initial wealth and exploit. This feature of Roemer's construction has, I believe, profound consequences for his understanding of class struggle. Before, however, we analyze these consequences let us examine in detail how and why Roemer constructs his framework in this way.

Note first that "poor workers" (like "rich capitalists") can refer to two different conditions: those who are poor (in initial wealth) and who therefore become workers or those who are workers (and thus exploited) and who therefore become poor (in current income). Indeed, Roemer is saying both: the Wealth–Class Correspondence Theorem asserts the first and the Class–Exploitation Correspondence Theorem asserts the second. Together these theorems assert that the final distribution of income is determined solely by the initial distribution of wealth: we end up with the poor worker poor and the rich capitalist rich.

There are at least two reasons why this correspondence between initial wealth and current income might not be as tight as it appears in Roemer's formulation. The first concerns the extraction of labor at the point of production; the second concerns unequal labor endowments.

The extraction of labor at the point of production plays no role in Roemer's exploitation. His analysis, he says, "challenges those who believe that the process of labor exchange is the critical moment in the genesis of capitalist exploitation."[6] (Ibid.: 266–7) In fact, this is an understatement, since his analysis has no place whatsoever for exploitation at the point of production. But, I think, Roemer misinterprets his own argument, mistaking an assumption for a conclusion.

Roemer argues the point as follows. First, he demonstrates that exploitation exists in the absence of labor exchange. He thus challenges – correctly so, I should add – those who believe in the crucial importance of the labor process. Then he introduces labor exchange, without modifying any of the other original assumptions. In the economy in which there is no labor exchange, everyone using the same production technique works with the same intensity, and Roemer transports this assumption to "Labor Market Island," where people work for others as well as for themselves. It makes no difference whether one is operating with one's own capital or somebody else's. Thus the problem of extracting labor out of labor power is simply assumed out of existence: it is an assumption, not a conclusion, and, I believe, it is an unreasonable assumption. Roemer reasons from an "even if" (there is no labor exchange) case to an "if" (there is labor exchange) case, treating the latter as simply less general than the former. They are different.

The second reason initial wealth does not always correspond to current income concerns unequal labor endowments. Roemer insists that any "proper" theory of exploitation must classify "the poor as exploited and the rich as exploiters," and his theory is thus a "proper" one since it yields such a classification (Ibid.: 274). Furthermore, he wants the relation between exploitation and inequality to work both ways: not only must the rich – more correctly, the wealthy – turn out to be exploiters, but only exploiters can be allowed to be rich. Note how Roemer reasons. Suppose we look at a distribution of income in the United States today, and we discover that lawyers employed by big corporations are rich (in income) in comparison to small capitalists. (In fact, in Sweden a few years ago the average income from employment was higher than the average income from property.) Roemer says in effect that whatever theory of exploitation we settle upon, it should not allow for this observation. Hence the choice we face is between a theory that assumed a uniform distribution of labor endowments and is thus "proper" but patently false and a theory that allows for unequal labor endowments and thus is not proper because it dissociates the distribution of current income from the initial distribution of wealth. Faced with this dilemma – and it *is* a dilemma if one wants a theory that is both proper and true – Roemer abandons the labor theory of exploitation altogether in favor of the contingent-withdrawal theory (Ibid.: 286).

---

[6] According to Robert Paul Wolff, for example, "the capitalist's political domination of the worker in the production process is the key to the extraction of a surplus from the workers." (1980: 119)

We have seen two reasons why the distribution of current income might not be as directly determined by the initial distribution of wealth as Roemer insists it must be. If we allow for the possibility that people may not use a particular technique of production as efficiently when they work for others as they do when they work for themselves, then the distribution of income among capitalists will depend not only upon their initial endowments but also upon their success in extracting surplus labor at the point of production. If we allow for unequal labor endowments then the distribution of income will depend not only upon alienable but also upon inalienable endowments. Hence, the magic circle linking initial wealth to current income to accumulated wealth would break.

Let us now consider why Roemer's workers must necessarily fight capitalists. Suppose that Roemer is correct in claiming that the distribution of income is fixed once and for all, given the initial wealth endowments. This would imply that the only alternative states of the world that economic agents could compare, evaluate, and struggle for would be the equilibrium distributions of income, each associated with a particular mode of production. Workers are born under capitalism; their preferences are fixed; they inherit an initial distribution of wealth; and thus, in Roemer's world, their fate *under capitalism* is sealed. There is nothing they can do to alter their lot under capitalism. All they can do is to maximize their objectives (current income or leisure) under the initial distribution of wealth and arrive at the highest income compatible with their initial wealth, from being poor to being poor. The only way they could improve their material conditions is by redistributing wealth. But in Roemer's formulation they cannot redistribute wealth under capitalism: wealth is accumulated income, income is given by initial wealth, and no other way of redistributing wealth exists. Hence, workers can only turn to socialism: if they want to improve their material conditions they must be revolutionary.

This is not a credible theory in my view and, I would claim, not a particularly relevant one politically. Any reasonable theory that would seek to explain, justify, or direct workers' struggle for socialism – the tasks for a theory of exploitation according to Roemer – would have to (1) allow for the possibility that workers can individually or collectively improve their conditions under capitalism, (2) recognize that this is what most organized workers have been trying to do during the history of capitalism, and only then (3) specify the conditions under which workers would struggle for socialism. If workers are to rationally opt for socialism it must be because socialism is preferable to the best outcome they can achieve under capitalism, not just to their current situation under capitalism. For Roemer, the "ethical imperative" is that exploitation "correspond" to class struggle and the "withdrawal" correspond to socialism, but the reason for this ethical imperative is that his workers are never given a chance.

Exploitation, Class Struggle, and Accumulation

Having argued that the purpose of a theory of exploitation is to explain class struggle, Roemer maintains that the exploitation of labor cannot explain the accumulation of capital. Since the relevant passage lends itself to alternative interpretations, I cite it in extenso:

> In contrast, the choice of a labor theory of exploitation cannot be to explain the accumulation of capital, as is sometimes maintained. Such a claim would be sound if labor power were the only exploited commodity under capitalism. But as mentioned above, every commodity is exploited in a surplus-producing economy − labor power is not special in this regard, contrary to what Marx implied. The accumulation of capital can therefore be explained, as a technical fact, by choosing any commodity as value numéraire. But class struggle between proletarians and capitalists can only be explained by choosing labor as the value numéraire. (Ibid.: 275)

I will read this passage as follows: No theory of exploitation formulated in terms of labor values can explain the accumulation of capital. The accumulation of capital is just a "technical fact" that can be explained in a variety of equivalent ways as opposed, presumably, to being a social process. If one wants to preserve a labor-value conception of exploitation, one should join Roemer in the project of explaining the class struggle between poor workers and rich capitalists.

Let me restate the claims Roemer makes. One is that no labor-value theory of exploitation can explain the accumulation of capital. Another one is that such a theory and only such a theory can explain class conflict. The third one seems to be that class struggle is what is worth explaining, while explaining accumulation is rather trivial. And note immediately one startling implication of these assertions: since labor exploitation cannot explain accumulation and only exploitation can explain class struggle, accumulation and class struggle cannot be explained within the same theory of exploitation.

At this moment it becomes useful to compare Roemer's views with those of Marx. Marx, as all the interpreters seem to agree, did intend his theory of labor exploitation to explain the origins of profit and thus accumulation. But, claims to the contrary notwithstanding, he never developed a theory that would relate the social processes of accumulation and class struggle. Marx's theory of accumulation, in *Capital*, has no logical place for class struggle: class conflicts can in his theory accelerate or retard accumulation and all the tendencies associated with it, but they cannot transform this process. To be blunt, all the references to class conflict in *Capital* are just lip-service. Class conflict results in Marx's analysis in temporary and transitional deviations but cannot affect the laws of capitalist development, and theories are about laws, not about deviations. Marx's views of accumulation ignored the effects of class organization, by workers as well as by capitalists. Some interpreters, beginning with Lindsay, through Sweezy, to the Poznan Philosophical School, defend this theory by saying that it is a valid analysis of the capitalist development at this level of abstraction.[7] But abstractions from processes that affect predictions are bad abstractions.

Nevertheless, I think that a theory that would systematically relate the exploitation of labor, class struggle, and accumulation of capital is possible in principle on the condition that we modify four assumptions that Marx and Roemer share. Thus the model of the conflict of interests between workers and capitalists must be modified by introducing time preferences. The assumption of competition must be modified to allow for imperfections due to the collective organization of workers and capitalists. The notion that income distribution is determined endogenously, by purely economic factors, must be abandoned in favor of a conflict model of distribution. And, finally, the state must be introduced explicitly as an actor. Unless we make these modifications, we will continue to separate "marxist economics" from the "marxist theory of the state," as we have been doing during the past twenty years or so. Indeed, the most striking feature of the vigorous development of contemporary marxism is that the worlds of "economics" and of "politics" have been hermetically sealed from each other. Since the state is "autonomous," politics is studied without any reference to economic dynamic. Since economic actors never organize collectively, economic dynamic can be studied without any reference to politics. Economic actors behave strategically but only as individuals seeking to maximize their wages or profits. Political actors are not actors at all: they are automata struggling with each other over ill-defined or completely conjured "long-term" interests.

Let me just cite one example outside the scope of Roemer's article.[8] A heated

---

[7] "Really the whole controversy is beside the point. The period under review saw the development of capitalism . . . but it also saw the rise and development of quite another system, that of social control as exercised through trade unions and social legislation. What has actually happened is not the outcome of capitalism but the outcome of social control and capitalism acting on one another. But when Marx talked of increasing misery, he was talking of what would be the outcome of unmodified capitalism." (Lindsay, 1925: 25)

[8] Let me emphasize that my target in this section is not "marxist economics" in the sense of everything written by people who see themselves or are seen as marxists. My target is the "theory of production," whether written by marxists or not. For a textbook that reviews all the developments, see Pasinetti (1977). Recently, there has appeared a number of marxist articles that incorporate the full range of strategic behaviors of workers and capitalists into their very assumptions, joining the observation of Joan Robinson that "everyone can see that his relative earnings depend upon the bargaining power of the group he belongs to." (1972: 199) My favorite formulation is by the economist John Hale, who wrote in the 1920s: "All incomes . . . are not 'products' created by the recipients: they are payments derived from the rest of the community by the exertion of some sort of pressure."

debate has been going on among marxist economists about the secular tendencies of the rate of profit. The orthodox argument is that competing capitalists are compelled to invest in a way that brings down the average rate of profit, and the revisionist argument is that the rate of profit in a competitive economy is indeterminate. This debate does elucidate the dynamic of competitive capitalism, but suppose that the rate of profit does indeed fall when capitalists compete. Would not their first step be to organize collectively to mitigate this ruinous competition? Marx did not study this possibility systematically because he seemed to believe that, by the time capitalists organize collectively, conditions will have been created for socialism and the problem will be irrelevant. But we have now been living for a good many years in a world in which capitalists have been organized, albeit not always successfully, in a variety of ways – economic, corporative, and political. Why go on with competitive models of expanded reproduction if today's economic actors are organized collectively and behave strategically as political forces?

A marxist economic theory – and by marxist I do not mean someone who accepts Marx's assumptions or even his problems but someone who seeks to understand the relation between conflicts and developments in search of a universal emancipation – must be a theory that builds the full range of strategic alternatives into the very core of its assumptions. It must be a theory that would give economic actors a chance to organize, to struggle collectively, to exert influence over the state, and to have effects upon the economy. It must be a theory that would treat the particular structures of the capitalist market, the particular forms of the organization of classes and of the state, and the particular patterns of exploitation and accumulation as contingent consequences of strategic behaviors of actors pursuing their goals in all the ways they can pursue them under capitalism. It cannot be a theory that poses for workers a false choice between individual pursuit of economic well being under autonomatically operating capitalism or a collective pursuit of revolutionary goals.

The developments in marxist economics during the past years have consisted almost exclusively of assimilating marxism into the mainstream of bourgeois economics. The task of the "revisionists" is to show that Marx's economic theory can be cleaned out logically to conform to the general framework of equilibrium growth. The resistance of the "obscurantists," to use Steedman's apt characterization, was in turn to claim that no such cleaning is needed since Marx's theory is logically clean the way it is. But it is what Marx and modern growth theorists have in common – that is, the framework in which accumulation takes place "of itself" as economic actors pursue their goals exclusively as market actors – that makes Marx's theory irrelevant to the understanding of contemporary capitalism and of the political choices inherent within it. Production models specify the technical relations among economic quantities, for example, the technical relations between the rate of exploitation and the (maximum) rate of accumulation. But the system of production must not be viewed as a self-operating automaton. Rather, it is a source of *constraints* under which workers and capitalists, individually or collectively, enter into conflicts or compromises, within and between the various classes, in pursuit of their goals. A marxist economic theory, to end this lengthy outburst, must be a political theory of the economy, a theory in which the actors who determine the rate of exploitation, the rate of accumulation, the distribution of income, the rate of unemployment, or the level of prices are, or at least can conceivably appear as, collective actors who pursue their goals in a variety of ways, not simply by moving their capital or their bodies from sector to sector. And this means that marxist economic theory must free itself of Marx, or at least that Marx for whom the reproduction of capital takes place "of itself," "by a mere repetition of isolated cycles of production."[9] Only then are we going to have a theory, as distinct from the marxism done in departments of economics and political science, and only then are we going to have a theory that would say something about the world around us and the choices it presents.

A cynical reader will have undoubtedly noticed that I advocate that we abandon the attempts to link Marx to one bourgeois theory and that we instead link him to another. I do. I am persuaded that we should fully embrace the game-theory approach to the understanding of economic phenomena and that we should limit the role of production models to the specification of technical relations that constitute constraints of game models.

I am, therefore, most sympathetic to the turn Roemer takes in passing to the "general" theory of exploitation. His general theory is formulated in the language of collective strategic behavior, and, I believe, is the correct formulation. The problem, however, is that Roemer abandons the analysis of the internal dynamics of capitalism (or for that matter of any mode of production) altogether. Revolution is not the entire game workers play, capitalism is also a part of this game. Having dissociated accumulation from class struggle, Roemer sees accumulation as a "technical fact" and class struggle as limited to conflicts over modes of production. Under capitalism there is only accumulation; class struggle is only between modes of production. This formulation, I believe,

---

[9] Or the Marx who wrote, "the rise of wages therefore is confined within limits that not only leave intact the foundations of the capitalist system, but also secure its reproduction on a progressive scale" (1967, 1: 582), and "the tendency of the rate of profit to fall is bound up with a tendency of the rate of exploitation to *rise* . . . Nothing is more absurd, for this reason, than to explain the fall in the rate of profit by a rise in the rate of wages, although this may be the case by way of exception". (1967, 3: 240) Even if the rate of profit were to fall as the rate of exploitation rose, this would in no way preclude the rate of profit from falling as the rate of exploitation fell. However, it is the very notion that the economy operates automatically that is at issue.

makes Roemer unable to explain either the dynamic of capitalism or the transition to socialism. Indeed, I will now seek to demonstrate that it is because Roemer does not reserve a place for class struggle within capitalism that he fails to provide a credible theory of the transition to socialism.

Exploitation and the Transition to Socialism

We might concede that Roemer's general theory of exploitation provides workers with better "ideological ammunition" than the highly abstract and obtuse surplus labor theory. At least, one could argue, Roemer's preferred definition says to workers directly "Take your share of society's resources and you will be better off," while the surplus-value interpretation only informs them that they are getting paid less than they produce. However, we shall not concede this superiority, for a number of reasons.

Roemer's model of "withdrawal" from capitalism is a purely Leninist one: the factories are here, workers have been taught how to operate them, and all we have to do is to change the owners (George, 1973; Santamaria and Manville, 1976). It is a model of what Korsch called a "capitalist socialization" of the means or production, as distinguished from a "socialist socialization," which changes the objectives of accumulation, not only the owners (1975: 60–82). In Roemer's socialism, alienable resources (the means of production as opposed to labor endowments) are equally distributed, presumably in the sense that each citizen has one vote to influence the allocation of society's resources.[10] The withdrawal from capitalism is thus based on a comparison of the welfare of workers (the income with which to purchase produced goods) under the capitalist-unequal and the socialist-equal distribution of the means of production.

Note first that in Roemer's formulation the total output of the economy is not affected by the structure of property. Since withdrawal is instantaneous (involving comparisons of static equilibria), neither the total mass of wealth endowments, nor the technology, nor the autonomous labor productivity are affected by the withdrawal into socialism. The socialist system satisfies the same needs as before.

Second, note that those who are better off by "withdrawing" are always a group within a society, less than all. Specifically, when a society moves from capitalism to socialism those people who were exploited as workers under

---

[10] I am not certain whether Roemer intends this description to apply to Eastern European socieites. I hope not. These societies are not socialist in Roemer's sense. The equality of all individuals there with regard to the ownership of society's inalienable resources is at most an empty formality, with the effective capacity to dispose of these resources being monopolized by party bureaucracies. Roemer's socialism is not possible without some kind of political democracy. Yet these are obviously not capitalist societies in Roemer's sense, and the question arises where they fit into his typology.

capitalism gain, and those people who were exploiting as capitalists lose, both the means of production and their current income. Hence for the society as a whole the "withdrawal" is not Pareto superior to the previous arrangements. Workers gain, capitalists lose, and the total remains the same.

Now, it may be objected that history is a history of class struggle and that to speak about "the society as a whole" is to ignore its class character, fall into the bourgeois trap, and so forth. But I have counter-arguments. This time I will even seek support from Marx, who certainly believed that revolutions are always improvements in the Pareto sense (even if they may have horrible distributional effects, as in the industrial revolution). Revolutions, Marx maintained, always carry the banner of universal interest, not of class self-interest, and this universalism is no empty talk: revolutions occur only when the ascending class is a true representative of universal interests against the old society. Moreover, I would claim that Marx's "ethical imperatives," if he had any, were also universalistic, not particularistic.

Marx's beliefs are not binding on anyone else, however, so let us approach the issue analytically. Thus Roemer assumes that socialism is not more efficient than (Pareto superior to) capitalism in satisfying material needs. Since workers gain in the passage from capitalism to socialism, capitalists must necessarily lose. Capitalists would therefore not prefer socialism to capitalism. But would workers? Remember that Roemer further assumes that workers are motivated exclusively by their material needs: they seek to maximize current revenue. While, in reality, workers under capitalism would be better off under socialism than in their current position under capitalism, within Roemer's assumptions, workers would do better not by withdrawing from capitalism but by becoming capitalists. While being exploited under capitalism would be the last preference of workers, socialism would be less desirable than a system in which they would become the exploiters and someone else the exploited. Roemer's "ethical imperative" might thus be to withdraw from capitalism, a system of exploitation of men by men, to the kind of socialism in which, as the old joke has it, it is "vice versa."

In sum, if everyone is motivated exclusively by his material needs and if socialism is not more efficient than capitalism – two assumptions Roemer uses – then socialism is not the most preferred alternative for anyone, including those who are exploited under capitalism. Roemer's formulation may explain a lot of history of capitalism, but it does not justify a preference for socialism.

One might be tempted to defend Roemer's formulation by arguing explicitly what Roemer himself assumes implicitly, namely, that no major redistribution of wealth endowments under capitalism is feasible. After all, Roemer restricts the set of choices available to workers to "conditionally feasible alternatives." But is such a redistribution any less feasible than socialism? Historically, I would claim, it does not appear less feasible.[11] But the burden of proof should rest with Roemer, and he never defines what "feasible" means. Instead he offers us a unilinear conception of history.

Roemer seems unable to decide whether he is an ethical socialist or a historical materialist, whether his Marx is Kant or Newton, and he produces a strange mixture in which "ethical imperatives" turn out to order themselves according to the laws of a necessary succession of modes of production. Feudalism is to be morally criticized from the standpoint of its juridical inequality, and the only way of withdrawing from it is to capitalism. Capitalism is to be ethically rejected because of its economic inequality, from which one can withdraw only to socialism. Socialism is based on the inequality of labor endowments. Both the notion that each type of society engenders a particular critique of itself and the notion that all ethical judgments must specify feasible historical alternatives are important. But Roemer's specification of the model of "withdrawal" is simply too mechanical to be reasonable. Any model of this kind must, in my view, permit both the transformations that alter the welfare of particular groups within the confines of a specific type of society ("reforms") and a multiplicity of critiques and "withdrawals" (a feminist critique of capitalism, for example, need not be identical with a workers' critique).

I do not want to deviate too far from Roemer's own concerns, but I do wish to clarify the source of my objections. Specifically, I am not inviting Roemer or the reader to grant that the visible hand of socialism is more efficient in satisfying consumption needs than the profit-driven mechanism of capitalism. Indeed, I am not persuaded that socialism would be more efficient. However, unless socialism would be more efficient, the justification for socialism is not persuasive if the only need this system is to serve is consumption. Moreover, even if socialism were more efficient in this sense, rational workers motivated exclusively by their consumption needs would not move in the direction of socialism in any reasonably well-functioning capitalist system because of the temporary loss of welfare that capitalists would be able to inflict upon them as a retribution. Hence the question of the superiority of socialism may simply be moot. It seems to me, therefore, that if we still wish to find reasons why socialism would be preferable and the transition to it feasible, we must abandon the narrowly economicist view of historically invariant material interests altogether.

Indeed, I am now prepared to claim that socialism would be superior because

[11] According to Henri Pirenne, "from the beginning of the Middle Ages to our times . . . for each period into which our economic history may be divided, there is a distinct and separate class of capitalists. In other words, the group of capitalists of a given epoch does not spring form the capitalist group of the preceding epoch. At every change of economic organization we find a breach of continuity . . . there are as many classes of capitalists as there are epochs in economic history." (1914: 494–515)

it would permit the society as a whole, by which I mean all individuals through a democratic process, to decide collectively which needs should be satisfied in the process of accumulation. This choice is not available under capitalism, where the economic mechanism can only maximize the production of commodities, independently of anyone's will. To put it differently, capitalist accumulation must be directed toward the production of commodities, while under socialism the process of accumulation could be organized to realize other goals. These goals, in principle, could be any goals a society would choose. In this sense socialism would be superior to any alternative social organization. However, at the same time, the notion of "the" socialism, socialism in singular, becomes untenable. We may arrive at a socialism in which the outcome of political conflicts – and there would be conflicts – would be to direct societal resources to maximize free time; we may arrive at one that would maximize employment, one in which people would seek beauty, one in which they would not leave the capitalist rationality of maximizing consumption, and also one in which they would devote all the resources to armaments. The instrinsic feature of a socialist organization of society is the capacity of the society as a whole to choose in a democratic way the mix of needs to be satisfied in the allocation of resources. How the society would allocate these resources cannot be determined a priori since we do not know what people would do if they were free to choose.

Postscript: Social Democracy and Socialism

Three conclusions do not follow from the arguments developed in this book. These arguments do not lead to a rejection of social democracy. They do not assert that reforms are impossible. They do not imply that workers would never opt for socialism. And, since popular wisdom teaches that pessimism is but informed optimism, I do not even consider my views pessimistic, only informed.

This clarification seems necessary because such conclusions tend to be attributed to the analyses developed above by writers who are more sanguine than I am about the transformative potential of the European Left, particularly the Swedish Social Democracy. In fact, I think that social democrats have done about as well as they could have under historical circumstances not of their choosing and I am quite sympathetic to their unenviable predicaments. I only doubt that they would lead their societies to socialism. I am sure that reforms are possible, but that does not mean that reformism is a viable strategy of transition to socialism. I do not know under what conditions workers and other people would prefer socialism over capitalism, but I think I have demonstrated that they are unlikely to opt for socialism in an exclusive pursuit of their economic interests. And since I see the combination of capitalism with political democracy as a form of society that is highly conducive to the pursuit of immediate economic interests, I am skeptical about the possibilities of bringing about socialism by a deliberate action of trade-unions, political parties, or governments.

I do not see my views as implying a rejection of social democracy or, more broadly, reformist socialism because I do not see acceptable historical alternatives.[1] In retrospect, the crucial decision was to seek political power. When Marx criticized in 1864 all those who sought to build a socialist society autonomously and independently of the existing institutions, he claimed that their project was unfeasible without first conquering political power. This is why

[1] It takes either an entrenched habit or ill will to interpret my views as an endorsement of Leninism, as does Siriani (1984). I suspect that the syllogism which leads to this conclusion must be that anyone who is a socialist critical of reformism ergo must be a revolutionary, that is, a Leninist. Personally, I feel free of the mental prison in which this alternative has been perpetuated. I see myself as a follower not of Vladimir Ilyich but of that other great Russian socialist thinker, Georgij Konstantinowich Pessim.

"the great duty" he defined for the working class was to struggle for power. Reformists, specifically Bernstein, eventually translated this task into competition for the control of the existing government institutions, while revolutionaries, notably Lenin, wanted to conquer power in order to destroy these institutions. But in either case the struggle for socialism became politicized; it became a struggle for political power. True, this power was to be used eventually as an instrument for realizing all the goals socialists sought but at the same time all goals which they sought became subordinated to one centralized thrust for political power. Whether at stake were working conditions at the local mill, a neighborhood school, a cultural center, wages, or the situation of women, everything became merged into one big struggle, "the class struggle," that required the conquest of political power. Wanting to improve conditions under which one worked, militating to win equality, forming a consumer cooperative, struggling to free sexuality, or organizing to plant flowers in a local park would be related to socialism by becoming all intertwined into an electoral campaign (or an insurrectionary conspiracy) designed to win control over the government. One could not struggle for socialism in one's personal life, every day; one would not be struggling for it when transforming relations within one's family, work group, or neighborhood. Socialist practice required a unique repository in political parties because they were the institutions that related everything to the "great duty of the working class."

Was the alternative possible? Could the movement for socialism remain independent of the existing political institutions? Could it have developed autonomously, in a decentralized, spontaneous, polymorphous manner? Was it feasible for the cooperatives, unions, and clubs of the 1860s and the 1880s to remain autonomous and to pursue their own goals? Ironically, the first movement in one hundred years which attempted such a "self-limitation" was born under the "communist" rule, in Poland. Yet Arato (1983) is right that the limited character of the goals creates a strategic dilemma. This is the same dilemma that socialists and anarchists faced in Western Europe. When confronted with a hostile and repressive state, no movement can stop short of reaching for political power − even if it has most limited objectives; just to protect itself. Socialists had no choice: they had to struggle for political power because any other movement for socialism would have been stamped out by force and they had to utilize the opportunities offered by participation to improve the immediate conditions of workers because otherwise they would not have gained support among them. They had to struggle for power and they were lucky enough to be able to do it under democratic conditions. Everything else was pretty much a consequence.

Once socialists had decided to struggle for political power and once they began to compete within the existing representative institutions, everything that followed was narrowly constrained. Most of the original fears about deleterious effects of participation did materialize: masses could not struggle for socialism but had to delegate this task to leaders–representatives, the movement became bureaucratized, tactics were reduced to electoralism, political discussions were limited to issues that could be resolved as a result of victory in the next elections, any project of society that would not help win elections was denounced as a utopia. Since socialists still could not win elections with majorities necessary to pursue the socialist program – the program with which they originally sought to conquer political power – they had to do what was possible. They became committed to employment, equality, and efficiency. They did do much: socialists strengthened political democracy, introduced a series of reforms in favor of workers, equalized the access to education, provided a minimum of material security for most people. It is moot whether some of the same reforms would not have been introduced by others and the general gist of evidence indicates that social democratic tenure in office does make a difference for efficiency and equality. Where they have been successful, social democrats institutionalized a relatively solid compromise between organizations of workers and of capitalists.

Social democrats brought about a number of reforms: a sufficient proof that reforms are possible. In fact, capitalism was being reformed even before first socialists came to office: there was Disraeli, Bismarck, Giolitti. The issue is not whether reforms are possible but reformism. Those who conclude that reforms are to be expected as the result of the governmental tenure of the Swedish Social Democrats (for example, Stephens, 1979; Esping-Anderson, 1984) or as an eventual consequence of implementing the Alternative Economic Strategy in Great Britain (for example, Hodgson, 1982) are most likely correct. But they claim to have demonstrated the possibility of reforms leading to socialism – and that is not the same.

Reforms would lead to socialism if and only if they were (1) irreversible, (2) cumulative in effects, (3) conducive to new reforms, and (4) directed towards socialism. As we have seen, reformist socialists since the 1890s thought that reforms would indeed satisfy all these conditions and thus gradually cumulate in socialism. So far at least they have not.

Reforms are reversible. The recent series of right-wing electoral victories resulted in denationalizations of industries, eliminations of welfare programs, reductions of protection from unemployment, restrictions of civil liberties and of the right to organize, and so forth. Moreover, as Martin (1975) has shown, in many cases it is sufficient that the government does nothing for previously introduced reforms to become undone.

Reforms do not necessarily cumulate even if they are not reversed. Reforms would cumulate if each new reform were a step to some state of the world we would recognize as socialism. But life constantly generates new problems that call for resolution, whether these problems result from past reforms or occur independently. Contamination of the environment, proliferation of dangerous products, bureaucratization of the state apparatus, erosion of the private sphere, complication of policy issues beyond the comprehension of most citizens, the growth of administrative control − all these phenomena have arisen since socialists entered the path of reforms. True, many old ills were overcome or at least mitigated, but quite a few new ones emerged. Indeed, lists of problems to be resolved are not any shorter in the socialist programs of today than they were at the turn of the century. The most striking impression one gets from looking at the way in which socialists see their mission today − an exchange of letters among Brandt, Kreisky, and Palme (1976) is most revealing − is that they think of themselves as standing ready to cope with whatever problems that are likely to appear, rather than to transform anything. And coping with problems is not reformism.

Not all reforms are conducive to new reforms. This is the thrust of the oldest doubts about the reformist strategy, particularly by Luxemburg. In several situations reforms which satisfy immediate demands of workers undermine future possibilities. "Insofar as trade unions can intervene in the technical department of production," Luxemburg noted, "they can only oppose technical innovation. . . . They act here in a reactionary direction." (1970a: 21) The issue which continues to occupy the center of controversies concerns the effect of reforms upon the working-class movements. Luxemburg was again the most articulate proponent of the view that reforms demobilize − a view for which I find much historical support. Yet several students of the Swedish Social Democracy, notably Korpi (1978, 1983), muster empirical evidence to support the argument that each new wave of reforms has had a mobilizing impact upon the Swedish working class. The success of the Swedish Social Democrats is often contrasted to the failure of the British Labour Party to achieve similar reforms and to maintain working-class mobilization (Higgins and Apple, 1983). All that can be said at this time is that there is enough evidence on both sides of the argument to call for a more systematic empirical investigation than the issue has received thus far.

What does seem clear is that compressing reforms into a single moment does not resolve but intensifies the difficulties. There are still some writers who believe that the enthusiasm of socialist transition will make everyone so productive that no economic crisis would ensue (Hodgson, 1982). Thus far, however, socialist governments which tried to combine nationalizations, redistribution of income, and acceleration of growth invariably discovered that stimulation of demand through redistribution of income does not work when it becomes a part of such a package. Eventually not only investment falls but even capacity utilization; wage gains become eroded; economic constraints become unbearable, and the reform program collapses.

Finally, even if reforms were irreversible, cumulative, and mobilizing, where do they lead? Do they lead to socialism? This is a more controversial issue, since we can no longer avoid saying something about the meaning of "socialism."

If socialism consists of full employment, equality, and efficiency, then the Swedish Social Democrats are reasonably close to the goal and not likely to go too far back from it. If they succeed in addition in socializing a large part of industry under popularly elected public boards of directors and in continuing to run the economy in a fairly efficient manner, many will consider that at least the Swedish ship would have completed the voyage described by Jaures, having floated unnoticeably but unmistakably into socialist waters.

Suppose then that the Swedish strategy does work: industries are socialized without an investment strike, public ownership continues to be supported by voters, workers are disciplined, and the economy enjoys an advantageous position in the international system. Profit is pursued efficiently, an almost full employment is maintained, inequality is reduced to a minimum. Everyone works, everyone works profitably, and everyone is equal. This is certainly an attractive vision.

But one could also describe this society differently. Here is a society in which blind pursuit of profit has become the exclusive principle of rationality, to the point that even the socially owned enterprises are guided by this principle. Wage slavery has become universalized to the point that everyone is subjected to toil. Alienation reigns: individuals are forced to sell their labor power and even the society as a whole cannot control the process of accumulation, which obeys criteria of private profitability. Families and schools are organized and regulated to prepare for production. Young people are forced into molds so that they would fit into places in this system. It would be trivial to go on.

This is not a caricature but a description in terms of the socialist project of one hundred years ago; in terms of that socialist movement that set itself to abolish the pursuit of profit, wage slavery, and the divisions they entail; that was to bring emancipation, liberation. Socialism was to be a society in which people individually would acquire control over their lives because their existence would no longer be an instrument of survival and people would collectively acquire control over shared resources and efforts because their allocation would be a subject of joined deliberation and rational choice. Socialism was not a movement for full employment but for the abolition of wage slavery; it was not a movement for efficiency but for collective rationality; it was not a movement for equality but for freedom.

Socialists gave up these goals when they discovered that they could not realize them in the foreseeable future. Economic conditions were not ripe and political support insufficient. Seeking to advance the immediate interests of their constituents, socialists thus opted for the pursuit of efficiency, employment, and equality – a second-best and the best that was possible.

The simultaneous pursuit of higher wages and full employment placed socialists in a dilemma. The response of profit-maximizing firms to wage pressure is to reduce employment and under capitalism people who are not fully employed are typically much worse off materially. Hence socialists have to struggle to increase employment and to protect those who are not employed, in either case inducing firms to employ more people than they would have otherwise. When socialists push for higher wages, they induce firms to utilize techniques of production which save labor and generate unemployment. When they force firms to employ or to bear the costs of unemployment, they induce firms to utilize techniques which are labor-intensive. Thus either people are unemployed and suffer material deprivation or they labor unnecessarily. Indeed, the struggle for full employment results in retarding the possibilities of liberation of labor.

Since the efforts to secure full employment are becoming increasingly quixotic, socialists are stumbling onto the program of reducing labor time and redistributing work. This program is not popular among fully employed sectors of the working class as well as among socialist politicians and managers who are concerned about efficiency and competitiveness. Yet this program does constitute a way out of the dilemma. Reduction of labor time without a corresponding reduction of wages forces firms to seek labor-saving techniques and thus to create possibilities of subsequent reductions of labor time. These possibilities are constrained by international competition which divides workers in different countries and which prevents governments from legislating reductions of working hours. These possibilities are also limited by the availability of techniques of production. Yet techniques of production are not given. They become available as the "existing" techniques among which firms choose because a society actively seeks the particular kinds of techniques. We all know how many people would have been working today in banks had computers not been invented and introduced. I.B.M. is right: "Machines should work, people should think."

Let us engage in some utopian fantasies. With Marx, imagine first a society where labor in which a human being does what a machine could do has ceased. All processes of production, maintenance, and distribution are performed by machines unassisted by direct labor. Machines are produced by machines according to instructions of meta-machines, which are programmed to produce a basket of goods while minimizing physical resources. Labor time necessary to produce these goods (including machines and meta-machines) is negligible. Some human activities ("indirect labor") eventually enter this production process but they need not occupy us at the moment.

Secondly, suppose that this process operates in such a way that the output (measured as a vector of physical quantities) can always be strictly larger than it was previously.

Thirdly, all individuals, regardless of their characteristics and contributions, obtain what they need.

These three features – automation, accumulation, and independence of want-satisfaction from labor – constitute the necessary conditions for the liberation of labor, a double liberation simultaneously from toil and from scarcity. A socialist society would be a society organized on two principles. First, production would be organized so as to generate the capacity for an almost instantaneous satisfaction of material wants of everyone while reducing direct labor to a historically feasible minimum. Secondly, besides a historically necessary minimum of mutual claims and guarantees no other institutions would exist. Scarcity, toil, and socially organized repression would be abolished. Free time is a necessary and sufficient condition for socialism because it constitutes freedom from want, labor, and socially induced constraint.

Without going into details, let us see what free time implies. First, note that several problems of capitalism become simply irrelevant. "Unemployment" is no longer the fate of free labor power. Conditions of work lose their importance as work under such conditions disappears. Equality ceases to be a meaningful term: it is an issue only in an unfree society. Freedom from scarcity and labor means that needs become qualitatively heterogeneous, and their satisfaction no longer reducible to a single dimension. Under socialism those people are rich who have rich needs (Heller, 1974). Even democracy is less problematic: democratic participation in the making of binding decisions loses its urgency when few decisions made by anyone are binding upon others. A democratic family is a family where all members are equal; a socialist family is one in which they are free. The problem is no longer one of extending democracy from the political to the social realm – the quintessence of social democracy under capitalism – but of reducing mutual constraint. Hence, of the needs and problems of capitalism little if anything remains. "Free time – which is both idle time and time for higher activity – has *naturally* transformed its possessor into a different subject." (Marx, 1973: 712)

Time free from labor is free. While certain ways of dividing activities may emerge as a result of freely formulated choices, this division is no longer an institution. Choices are not only freely made: they are freely formulated. When direct labor is not necessary, places-to-be-occupied in the division of labor no longer exist. We are no longer born, as Sartre put it, in the image of our dead grandfather (1960: 15). The choice is no longer "what will I become," where the "what" is prior and given as "a pilot," "a nurse," or "a garbage collector." The "what" itself becomes the object of individual making; it is continually reinvented by each individual for him- or herself.

These choices may result in specialization of activities, as some people push the frontiers of molecular biology while others push those of tennis. Some people may like to teach others while other people may be captivated by watching trees grow. This freedom obviously poses the question upon which Carr reflected in the seclusion of his Oxford study (1961: ch. 3): would labor (indirect, that is, scientific and direct to the extent to which it is still necessary) happen to be performed as a result of free choice? I do not know; we are too far away to speculate.

Free time, from labor and scarcity, also implies that the society, to coin a horror, becomes "defunctionalized." A particular manner of organizing one activity would no longer be necessary for reproducing other activities. Socialist society, to follow Sartre again, would be organized without being institutionalized. "The family" is no longer an institution: people organize cohabitation as and if they cohabit. Since functions of the family are no longer given when labor is no longer necessary, sex, nurture, and maintenance need not be associated according to any prior pattern (Mitchell, 1966). Sexual repression loses its social basis (Marcuse, 1962).

Needs no longer assume the form of "interests," that is, the limits of their satisfaction are no longer objectifications of human activity. Their dynamic is driven and restricted only by their internal structure. Objectification occurs if and only if it responds to a need for objectification: I paint or split genes because I like to see painting or the truth of hypotheses. No "end of history" occurs here, as is sometimes supposed in the argument that Marx was inconsistent when he posited simultaneously that needs are dynamic and that scarcity can be abolished. We must think dialectically: scarcity is abolished because the capacity to satisfy material needs asymptotically converges to their dynamic path.[2] Whether material needs would continue to grow under socialism I again do not know. As long as the satisfaction of needs is externally constrained, we cannot tell what human needs are.

Speaking of the Paris Commune, Marx emphasized that the working class has

---

[2] Differential calculus is only an application of the dialectical method to mathematics — at least this is what Engels said somewhere in *The Anti-Duhring*.

no ready-made ideals to realize, it has only to set itself free (in McLellan, 1977: 545). This statement should not be taken as an injunction against utopian fantasies and even less as one against utopian analyses. All it asserts is that we cannot tell today what a socialist society would be like precisely because we do not know what human beings would want and what they would do if they were free. Socialism is not yet another social order, it is the end of all social orders: this statement should be taken seriously. "Socialism" in singular is thus a contradiction in terms, for socialism means freedom and thus variety. It means freedom, not democracy, equality, creativity, or happiness. Socialism is not a new form of coercion to make everyone "creative."[3] A free individual may be uncreative; "realization of human potential" may show that it would have been better if this potential remained dormant. Freedom may turn into universal misery; it may bring forth the truly human sources of repression, if indeed the finite nature of life underlies the aggressive and repressive forces (Brown, 1959). We do not know. Socialism is not a millennium, not a guarantee of happiness. It is a society free of alienation – if this term can still be restored to its meaning rather than be used as a generalized lament – a society in which objective conditions have been abolished, in which people are at every moment free, in which nothing is prior and given, in which life is not an instrument of survival, and things not instruments of power, in which all values are autonomous, in which the relation between a person and oneself is not mediated by things. Abolition of capitalism is a necessity not because such are the laws of history or because socialism is superior to it in any way, neither for reasons of Newton or Kant, but only because capitalism prevents us from becoming whatever we might become when we are free.

Having arrived at an unknown destination we must, unfortunately, return to the very first step. We have seen that capitalism develops the conditions for liberation but it cannot free. We have seen that freedom is necessary and sufficient for socialism. But does capitalism generate the need for freedom, a need that could underlie a political transition toward socialism?

This is not a question to be resolved theoretically. The only way to know is by practice, a political practice in the broadest, Greek, sense of the word "political." Unity of theory and practice does not have a unique repository in political parties. The need for freedom is integral. Socialist democracy is not something to be found in parliaments, factories, or families: it is not simply a democratization of capitalist institutions. Freedom means de-institutionalization; it means individual autonomy. Socialism may perhaps become possible, but only on the condition that the movement for socialism regains the integral scope that characterized several of its currents outside the dogmas of the Internationals,

[3] See Marcuse's splendid polemic against Fromm in the epilogue to *Eros and Civilization* (1962: 216–51).

only on the condition that this movement ceases to make the socialist project conditional upon the continual improvement of material conditions of the working class. It may become possible when socialism once again becomes a social movement and not solely an economic one, when it learns from the women's movement, when it reassimilates cultural issues.

The time is not near. There is every reason to expect that capitalism will continue to offer an opportunity to improve material conditions and that it will be defended by force where and when it does not, while conditions for socialism continue to rot. This is why dreams of a utopia cannot be a substitute for the struggle to make capitalism more efficient and more humane. Poverty and oppression are here, and they will not be alleviated by the possibility of a better future. The struggle for improving capitalism is as essential as ever before. But we should not confuse this struggle with the quest for socialism.

References

Abraham, David. 1982. Review Essay: The S.P.D. from Socialist Ghetto to Post-Godesberg Cul-de-Sac. *Journal of Modern History*. 54: 417–50.

Ajam-Bouvier, Maurice and Gilbert Mury. 1963. *Les Classes Sociales en France*. Paris.

Alford, Robert. 1963. *Party and Society*. Chicago: Rand McNally.

   1967. Class Voting in the Anglo-American Political Systems. In S. M. Lipset and Stein Rokkan (eds), *Party Systems and Voter Alignments*. New York: Free Press.

Allardt, Erik. 1964. Patterns of Class Conflict and Working Class Consciousness. In Erik Allardt (ed.), *Cleavages, Ideologies, and Party Systems*. Helsinki: Westermack Society.

   and Pertti Pesonen. 1967. Cleavages in Finish Politics. In S. M. Lipset and Stein Rokkan (eds), *Party Systems and Voter Alignments*. New York: Free Press.

   and Włodzimierz Wesołowski (eds). 1978. *Social Structure and Change. Finland and Poland in Comparative Perspective*. Warszawa: Polish Scientific Publishers.

Almond, Gabriel and Sidney Verba. 1965. *The Civic Culture*. Boston: Little, Brown.

Althusser, Luis. 1970. *For Marx*. New York: Vintage Books.

   1971. Ideology and Ideological State Apparatuses. In *Lenin and Philosophy*. New York: Monthly Review Press.

Anderson, Perry. 1977. The Antinomies of Antonio Gramsci. *New Left Review*. 100: 5–78.

Arato, Andrew. 1973. The Second International: A Reexamination. *Telos*. 18: 2–53.

   1983. The Democratic Theory of the Polish Opposition: Normative Intentions and Strategic Ambiguities. Unpublished paper.

Arrow, Kenneth J. 1962. The Economic Implications of Learning by Doing. *Review of Economic Studies*. 29: 155–73.

Balibar, Etienne. 1970. Fundamental Concepts of Historical Materialism. In Luis Althusser and Etienne Balibar, *Reading Capital*. New York: Pantheon Books.

Barber, Benjamin. 1970. Review of Ralph Miliband, *State in Capitalist Society*. *American Political Science Review*. 64: 928–9.

Bauer, Otto. 1919. *Der Weg zum Sozialismus*. (Wien). Translated into French by F. Calissy as *La Marche au Socialisme*. Paris: Libraire de l'Humanité.

Beer, Samuel. 1969. *British Politics in the Collectivist Age*. 2nd edn. New York: Vintage Press.

Bergier, J. F. 1973. The Industrial Bourgeoisie and the Rise of the Working Class. In C. M. Cippola (ed.), *The Industrial Revolution*. London: Penguin.

Berglund, Sten and Ulf Lindstrom. 1978. *The Scandinavian Party System(s)*. Lund: Studentlitteratur.

Bergounioux, Alain and Bernard Manin. 1979. *La Social-Démocratie ou le compromis*. Paris: P.U.F.

Bernstein, Eduard. 1961. *Evolutionary Socialism*. New York: Schocken.

Birnbaum, Pierre. 1979. La question des élections dans la pensée socialiste. In Pierre Birnbaum and J. M. Vincent (eds), *Critique de pratique politique*. Paris: Gallileo.

Bobbio, Norberto. 1967. Gramsci e la concezione della società civile. In *Gramsci e la cultura contemporanea*. Roma: Editori Riuniti.

Bologna, Sergio. 1972. Class Composition and the Theory of the Party at the Origin of Workers-Council Movement. *Telos*. 13: 3–28.

Bonomi, Giorgio. 1975. La théorie gramscienne de l'Etat. *Les Temps Modernes*. 343: 976–98.

Borre, Ole. 1977a. Recent Trends in Danish Voting Behavior. In Karl H. Cerny (ed.), *Scandinavia at the Polls. Recent Political Trends in Denmark, Norway, and Sweden*. Washington, D.C.: American Enterprise Institute.

  1977b. Personal communication.

Bottomore, Thomas B. 1966. *Classes in Modern Society*. New York: Vintage Books.

Boulding, Kenneth. 1970. *A Primer on Social Dynamics. History as Dialectics and Development*. New York: Free Press.

Bourdieu, Pierre. 1976. Marriage Strategies as Strategies of Social Reproduction. In Robert Forster and Orest Ranum (eds), *Family and Society*. Baltimore: The Johns Hopkins University Press.

Braga, Giorgio, 1956. *Il Comunismo fra gli Italiani*. Milan: Comunità.

Brandt, Willy, Bruno Kreisky, and Olof Palme. 1976. *La Social-Démocratie et l'avenir*. Paris: Gallimard.

Braud, Philippe. 1973. *Le Comportement électoral en France*. Paris: P.U.F.

Briggs, Asa. 1961. The Welfare State in Historical Perspective. *European Journal of Sociology*. 2: 221–58.

Brody, Andras. 1970. *Proportions, Prices, and Planning: A Mathematical Restatement of the Labor Theory of Value*. Budapest: Akademiai Kiado.

Brown, Norman O. 1959. *Life against Death. The Psychoanalytical Meaning of History*. New York: Vintage Books.

Bull, Edvard. 1955. Industrial Workers and Their Employers in Norway Around 1900. *Scandinavian Economic History Review*. 3: 64–84.

Burawoy, Michael. 1976. The Functions and Reproduction of Migrant Labor: Comparative Material from Southern Africa and the United States. *American Journal of Sociology*. 81: 1050–87.

Canbareri, Serafino. 1973. Il concetto di egemonia nel pensiero di A. Gramsci. In Instituto Gramsci, *Studi Gramsciani*. Roma: Editori Riuniti.

Cardoso, Fernando H. 1973. Althusserianismo o Marxismo? In R. B. Zenteno (ed.), *Las Clases sociales en América Latina*: Mexico. Siglo XXI.

Carillo, Santiago, 1974. *Demain l'Espagne*. Paris: Seuil.

Carr, Edward H. 1961. *The New Society*. London: Oxford University Press.
   1966. *The Bolshevik Revolution*. London. Volume I.
Castels, Manuel. 1975. Immigrant Workers and Class Struggles in Advanced Capitalism: The Western European Experience. *Politics and Society*. 5: 33–66.
Chenery, Hollis. 1952. Overcapacity and the Acceleration Principle. *Econometrica*. 20: 1–28.
Chiaràmonte, Gerardo. 1975. Report to the Central Committee of the P.C.I. October 29–30. *The Italian Communist*.
Chodak, Szymon (ed.) 1962. *Systemy Partyjne Wspólczesnego Kapitalizmu*. Warszawa: Ksiaźka i Wiedza. 1917.
Clark, Maurice J. 1917. Business Acceleration and the Law of Demand: A Technical Factor in Economic Cycles. *Journal of Political Economy*. 25: 217–35.
Claudin, Fernando. 1975. *The Communist Movement from Comintern to Cominform*. Part One. New York: Monthly Review Press.
Cole, G. D. H. 1919. *Guild Socialism*. London.
Colletti, Lucio. 1972. Bernstein and the Marxism of the Second International. In *From Rousseau to Lenin*. New York: Monthly Review Press.
Colton, Joel. 1953. Léon Blum and the French Socialists as a Government Party. *Journal of Politics*. 15: 517–43.
   1969. Politics and Economics in the 1930s: The Balance Sheet of the 'Blum New Deal'. In Charles K. Warner (ed.), *From the Ancien Régime to the Popular Front*. New York: Columbia University Press.
Coser, Lewis. 1959. *The Functions of Social Conflict*. Glencoe: Free Press.
Craig, F. W. S. (ed.). 1969. *British Parliamentary Election Results, 1918–1949*. Glasgow: Political Reference Publications.
Cripps, Sir Stafford. 1933. Democracy or Dictatorship – The Issue for the Labour Party. *Political Quarterly*. 467–81.
Dahrendorf, Ralf. 1959. *Class and Class Conflict in Industrial Society*. Stanford: Stanford University Press.
   1964. Recent Changes in the Class Structure of European Societies. *Daedalus*. 93.
Damgaard, Erik. 1974. Stability and Change in the Danish Party System Over a Half Century. *Scandinavian Political Studies*. 9: 103–25.
Derfler, Leslie. 1973. *Socialism Since Marx: A Century of the European Left*. New York: St. Martin's Press.
Dogan, Mattei. 1967. Political Cleavage and Social Stratification in France and Italy. In S. M. Lipset and Stein Rokkan (eds), *Party Systems and Voter Alignments*. New York: Free Press.
Droz, Jacques. 1966. *Le Socialisme démocratique*. Paris: Armand Colin.
Edel, Matthew. 1979. A Note on Collective Action, Marxism, and the Prisoner's Dilemma. *Journal of Economic Issues*. 13: 751–61.
Edwards, Stewart. *Selected Writings of Pierre-Joseph Proudhon*. Garden City, N. J.: Anchor Books.
Elster, Jon. 1975. Optimism and Pessimism in the Discussion of the Standard of Living

During the Industrial Revolution in Britain. Paper presented at the 14th International Congress of Historical Sciences, San Francisco.

Elvander, Nils. 1979. *Scandinavian Social Democracy: Its Strengths and Weaknesses.* Stockholm: Almquist & Wiksell.

Engels. 1942. *The Origins of the Family, Private Property, and the State.* New York: International Publishers.

1958. *The Condition of the Working Class in England.* New York: Macmillan.

1959. Socialism: Utopian and Scientific. In L. S. Feuer (ed.), *Marx and Engels. Basic Writings on Politics and Philosophy.* Garden City: Doubleday.

1960. Introduction (1895) to Karl Marx's *The Class Struggles in France, 1848 to 1850.* Moscow: Progress Publishers.

No date. *A Contribution to the Critique of the Social Democratic Draft Programme of 1891.* Moscow: Foreign Languages Publishing House.

and Karl Marx. 1935. *Correspondence 1846–1895.* New York: International Publishers.

Ensor, R. C. K. 1908. *Modern Socialism as Set Forth by the Socialists in Their Speeches, Writings, and Programmes.* New York: Charles Scribner's Sons.

Esping-Anderson, Gösta. 1979. Comparative Social Policy and Political Conflict in Advanced Welfare States: Denmark and Sweden. *International Journal of Health Services.* 9: 269–93.

1984. *The Social Democratic Road to Power.* Princeton: Princeton University Press.

Fiechtier, Jean-Jacques. 1965. *Le Socialisme français: de l'affaire Dreyfus à la Grande Guerre.* Genève: Librairie Droz.

Fiori, Giuseppe. 1973. *Antonio Gramsci: Life of a Revolutionary.* New York: Schocken Books.

Frölich, Paul. 1972. *Rosa Luxemburg: Her Life and Work.* New York: Monthly Review Press.

Fromm, Erich. 1961. *Marx's Concept of Man.* New York: Frederick Ungar.

Furet, François. 1963. Pour une définition des classes inférieures à l'époque moderne. *Annales: Economies, Sociétés, Civilisations.* 18

Fusilier, Raymond. 1954. *Le Parti Socialiste Suédois. Son Organisation.* Paris: Les Editions Ouvrières.

Gay, Peter. 1970. *The Dilemma of Democratic Socialism.* New York: Basic Books.

George, François. 1973. Oubliant à Lenin. *Les Temps Modernes.*

Geras, Norma. 1976. *The Legacy of Rosa Luxemburg.* London: New Left Books.

Glyn, Andrew and Bob Sutcliffe. 1972. *British Capitalism, Workers and the Profit Squeeze.* London: Penguin.

Godelier, Maurice. 1972. *Rationality and Irrationality in Economics.* London: New Left Books.

Goldberg, Samuel P. 1973. *Introduction to Difference Equations.* New York: John Wiley & Sons.

Goldthorpe, John and David Lockwood. 1963. Affluence and the British Class Structure. *The Sociological Review.* 11: 133–63.

Gornick, Vivian. 1977. *The Romance of American Communism.* New York: Basic Books.

Gough, Ian. 1972. Marx's Theory of Productive and Unproductive Labour. *New Left Review*. 76: 47–72.

Gramsci, Antonio. 1971. *Prison Notebooks*. Edited by Quintin Hoare and Geoffrey Nowell Smith. New York: International Publishers.

Green, Nathaniel. 1971. Introduction to *European Socialism Since World War I*. Chicago: Quadrangle Books.

Griffuelhes, Victor. 1910. L'infériorité des capitalistes français. *Mouvement Socialiste*. 226: 329–32.

Guerin, Daniel. 1970. *Anarchism. From Theory to Practice*. New York: Monthly Review Press.

Gustafsson, Bo. 1973. A Perennial of Doctrinal History: Keynes and the 'Stockholm School'. *Economy and History*. 17: 114–28.

1978. A New Look at Bernstein: Some Reflections on Reformism and History. *Scandinavian Journal of History*. 3: 275–96.

Habermas, Jurgen. 1975. *Legitimation Crisis*. Boston: Beacon Press.

Harcourt, G. C. 1972. *Some Cambridge Controversies in the Theory of Capital*. Cambridge: Cambridge University Press.

Harrod, R. F. 1970. Dynamic Theory. In Amartya Sen (ed.), *Growth Economics*. London: Penguin.

Harsanyi, John C. 1977. *Rational Behavior and Bargaining Equilibrium in Games and Social Situations*. Cambridge: Cambridge University Press.

Haupt, Georges. 1980. *L'Historien et le mouvement social*. Paris: François Maspero.

Heidar, Knut. 1977. The Norwegian Labour Party: Social Democracy in a Periphery of Europe. In William E. Paterson and Alastair H. Thomas (eds), *Social Democratic Parties in Western Europe*. London: Croom Helm.

Heilbroner, Robert. 1980. Swedish Promise. *New York Review of Books*. December 4: 33–6.

Heller, Agnes. 1974. *The Theory of Need in Marx*. London: Allison & Busby.

Henderson, Arthur. 1918. *The Aims of Labour*. 2nd edn. New York: B. W. Heubsch.

Hentila, Seppo. 1978. The Origins of the *Folkheim* Ideology in Swedish Social Democracy. *Scandinavian Journal of History*. 3: 323–45.

Higgins, Winton and Nixon Apple. 1983. How Limited is Reformism? A Critique of Przeworski and Paritch. *Theory and Society*. 12: 603–30.

Hill, Keith. 1974. Belgium: Political Change in a Segmented Society. In Richard Rose (ed.), *Electoral Behavior: A Comparative Handbook*. New York: Free Press.

Hobsbawm, Eric. 1962. *The Age of Revolution*. New York: New American Library.

1973. *Revolutionaries*. New York: New Amerian Library.

1978. The Forward March of Labour Halted? *Marxism Today*. September: 279–86.

Hodgson, Geoff. 1982. On the Political Economy of Socialist Transition. *New Left Review*. 133: 52–67.

Horkheimer, Max. 1973. The Authoritarian State. *Telos*. 15: 3–24.

Howard, Dick. 1973. Re-reading Luxemburg. *Telos*. 18: 89–107.

Hunt, Richard N. 1970. *German Social Democracy 1918–1933*. Chicago: Quadrangle Books.

Jacobsen, John K. 1980. *Chasing Progress*. Ph.D. Dissertation. University of Chicago.

Jaffré, Jerome. 1980. The French Electorate in March 1978. In Howard R. Penniman (ed.), *The French National Assembly Election of 1978*. Washington, D.C.: American Enterprise Institute.

Jaures, Jean. 1971. *L'Esprit de socialisme*. Paris: Denoel.

Joll, James. 1966. *The Second International, 1889–1914*. New York: Harper & Row.

Kaldor, Nicolas. 1970. Model of Distribution. In Amartya Sen (ed.), *Growth Economics*. London: Penguin.

1972. Marginal Productivity and Macroeconomic Theories of Distribution. In G. C. Harcourt and N. F. Laing (eds), *Capital and Growth*. London: Penguin.

Kalecki, Michal. 1936. The Lesson of the Blum Experiment. *Economic Journal*. 48: 26–41.

Kautsky, Karl. 1919. *Terrorisme et communisme*. Paris: Ed. Povolozky.

1925. *La Révolution prolétarienne et son programme*. Bruxelles: L'Eglantine.

1971. *The Class Struggle*. New York: W. W. Norton.

Kendrick, John. 1981. Sources of Growth in Real Product and Productivity in Eight Countries, 1960–1978. Paper prepared for the Office of Economic Research, The New York Stock Exchange. New York.

Keynes, John Maynard. 1964. *The General Theory of Employment, Interest, and Money*. New York: Harvest Books.

Kolm, Serge-Christophe. 1977. *La Transition socialiste*. Paris: CERF.

Konopnicki, Guy. 1979. *Vive le centenaire du P.C.F.* Paris: Editions Libres.

Korpi, Walter. 1978. *The Working Class in Welfare Capitalism: Work, Unions, and Politics in Sweden*. London: Routledge & Kegan Paul.

1983. *The Democratic Class Struggle*. London: Routledge & Kegan Paul.

Korsch, Karl. 1975. What Is Socialization? *New German Critique*. 6: 60–82.

Kramer, Gerald. 1971. Short-Term Fluctuations in U.S. Voting Behavior, 1896–1964. *American Political Science Review*. 65: 131–43.

Kuczynski, Jurgen. 1967. *The Rise of the Working Class*. New York: McGraw-Hill.

Kuhn, Thomas. 1970. *The Structure of Scientific Revolutions*. 2nd edn. Chicago: University of Chicago Press.

Lafferty, William A. 1971. *Economic Development and the Response of Labor in Scandinavia*. Oslo: Universitetforlaget.

Lancaster, Kevin. 1973. The Dynamic Inefficiency of Capitalism. *Journal of Political Economy*. 81: 1092–109.

Landauer, Carl. 1959. *European Socialism*. 2 volumes. Berkeley: University of California Press.

1961. The Guesdists and the Small Farmer: Early Erosion of French Marxism. *International Review of Social History*. 6: 212–25.

Lange, Oskar. 1964. *On the Economic Theory of Socialism*. Edited by B. E. Lipincott. New York: McGraw-Hill.

Laski, Harold. 1935. *Democracy in Crisis*. Chapel Hill: University of North Carolina Press.

Lasswell, Harold. 1936. *Politics: Who Gets What, When, and How*. New York: McGraw-Hill.

Lenin, V. I. 1949–52. *Sochineniya*. Moscow. Volume 29.

1964. *What Is To Be Done*. Moscow: Progress Publishers.

Leser, Norbert. 1976. Austro-Marxism: A Reappraisal. *Journal of Contemporary History*. 11: 133–48.

Lewin, Leif. 1975. The Debate on Economic Planning in Sweden. In Steven Koblik (ed.), *Sweden's Development from Poverty to Affluence, 1750–1970*. Minneapolis: University of Minnesota Press.

Bo Jansson, and Dag Sorbom. 1972. *The Swedish Electorate 1887–1968*. Stockholm: Almquist & Wiksell.

Lichtheim, George. 1965. *Marxism*. New York: Praeger.

Lindsay, John. 1925. *Karl Marx's Capital*. London: Oxford University Press.

Lipset, Seymour M. 1960. *Political Man*. Garden City, N. J.: Doubleday.

Luce, R. D. and Howard Raiffa. 1958. *Games and Decisions*. New York: John Wiley.

Luhmann, Niklas. 1975. *Legitimation Durch Verfahren*. 2nd edn. Darmstadt: Luchterhand.

Lukacs, Georg. 1970. *Lenin: A Study of the Unity of his Thought*. Cambridge, Mass.: M.I.T. Press.

1971. *History and Class-Consciousness*. Cambridge, Mass.: M.I.T. Press.

Luxemburg, Rosa. 1967. *The Russian Revolution and Leninism or Marxism?* Ann Arbor: University of Michigan Press.

1970a. *The Mass Strike, the Political Party, and the Trade Unions*. In M. A. Waters (ed.), *Rosa Luxemburg Speaks*. New York: Pathfinder Press.

1970b. *Reform or Revolution*. New York: Pathfinder Press.

Lyman, Richard. 1957. *The First Labour Government. 1924*. London.

1965. The British Labour Party: The Conflict Between Socialist Ideals and Practical Politics Between the Wars. *Journal of British Studies*. 5: 140–52.

Mabille, Xavier and Val R. Lorwin. 1977. The Belgian Socialist Party. In W. E. Paterson and A. H. Thomas (eds), *Social Democratic Parties in Western Europe*. London: Croom Helm.

McDonald, Ian M. and Robert M. Solow, 1981. Wage Bargaining and Employment. *American Economic Review*. 71: 896–908.

MacIver, R. M. 1947. *The Webb of Government*. New York: Macmillan.

McKibbin, Ross. 1974. *Evolution of the Labour Party, 1910–1924*. London: Oxford University Press.

McLellan, David. 1977. *The Thought of Karl Marx*. New York: Harper & Row.

Maddison, Angus. 1964. *Economic Growth in the West*. New York: Norton.

Magri, Lucio. 1970. Problems of the Marxist Theory of the Revolutionary Party. *New Left Review*. 60: 97–128.

Maier, Charles S. 1975. *Recasting Bourgeois Europe*. Princeton: Princeton University Press.

Mandel, Ernest. 1971. *The Formation of the Economic Thought of Karl Marx*. New York: Monthly Review Press.

Marcus, Steven. 1975. *Engels, Manchester, and the Working Class*. New York: Vintage Books.

Marcuse, Herbert. 1962. *Eros and Civilization*. New York: Vintage Books.

Marglin, Steven. 1974. What do Bosses Do? *Review of Radical Political Economy*.

Martin, Andrew. 1975. Is Democratic Control of Capitalist Economies Possible? In Leon Lindberg (ed.), *Stress and Contradiction in Modern Capitalism*. Lexington, Mass.: Lexington Books.

Martin, Penny Gil. 1972. *Party Strategy and Social Change: The Norwegian Labour Party*. Ph.D. Dissertation. Yale University. University Microfilm # 72–31450.

Marx, Karl. 1934. *The Eighteenth Brumaire of Louis Bonaparte*. Moscow: Progress Publishers.

1952a. *The Class Struggles in France, 1848 to 1850*. Moscow: Progress Publishers.

1952b. *Wage Labour and Capital*. Moscow: Progress Publishers.

1967. *Capital*. 3 volumes. New York: International Publishers.

1967. *The Communist Manifesto*. Edited by Harold Laski. New York: Pantheon Books.

1971. *Writings on the Paris Commune*. Edited by Hal Draper. New York: International Publishers.

1973. *Grundrisse*. Edited by Martin Nicolaus. New York: International Publishers.

1974. Inaugural Address of the International Working Men's Association. In David Fernbach (ed.), *The First International and After*. London: Penguin.

No date. *The Poverty of Philosophy*. Moscow: Progress Publishers.

and Frederick Engels. 1962. *On Britain*. 2nd edn. Moscow: Foreign Language Publishing House.

1964. *The German Ideology*. Moscow: Progress Publishers.

1969. *Selected Works in Three Volumes*. (MESW). Moscow: Progress Publishers.

Matin, Le. 1978. *Le Dossier des Législatives 1978*. Numéro Hors Serie.

Menil, George De. 1971. *Bargaining: Monopoly Power vs. Union Power*. Cambridge, Mass.: Harvard University Press.

Mercurio, El. 1970. September 5.

Michelat, Guy et Michel Simon. 1975. Catégories socio-professionnelles en milieu ouvrier et comportement politique. *Revue Française de Science Politique*. 25: 291–316.

Michels, Roberto. 1962. *Political Parties: A Sociological Study of the Oligarchical Tendencies of Modern Democracy*. New York: Collier Books.

Miliband, Ralph. 1970. *The State in Capitalist Society*. New York: Basic Books.

1975. *Parliamentary Socialism: A Study in the Politics of Labour*. 2nd edn. London: Merlin Press.

1977. *Marxism and Politics*. Oxford: Oxford University Press.

Mitchell, Juliet. 1966. Women: The Longest Revolution. *New Left Review*. 40: 11–37.

Mobil Oil Company. 1976. Paid advertisement. *New York Times*, May 6.

Möller, Gustav. 1938. The Unemployment Policy. *Annals of the American Academy of Political and Social Science*. 197: 47–72.

Monde, Le. 1973. *Les Forces Politiques et les Elections de Mars 1973*.

1977. *Le Dossier des Nationalisations*.

Morishima, Michio. 1973. *Marx's Economics*. Cambridge: Cambridge University Press.

Musgrave, Richard A. 1971. Provision for Social Goods in the Market System. *Public Finance*. 26: 304–20.

Nettl, Peter. 1969. *Rosa Luxemburg*. London.

New York Stock Exchange. 1981. *U.S. Economic Performance in a Global Perspective*, New York.

Nicolaus, Martin. 1967. Proletariat and the Middle Class in Marx: Hegelian Choreography and the Capitalist Dialectic. *Studies on the Left*. 7: 22–49.

Nomad, Max. 1966. The Anarchist Tradition. In M. M. Drakovitch (ed.), *The Revolutionary Intellectuals, 1864–1943*. Stanford: Stanford University Press.

Nuti, Domenico M. 1972. 'Vulgar economy' in the theory of income distribution. In E. K. Hunt and Jesse Schwartz (eds), *A Critique of Economic Theory*. London: Penguin.

O'Connor, James. 1973. *The Fiscal Crisis of the State*. New York: St Martin's Press.

1976. Productive and Unproductive Labor. *Politics and Society*. 5.

O'Donnell, Guillermo. 1976. Modernization and Military Coups: Theory, Comparisons, and the Argentine Case. In A. F. Lowenthal (ed.), *Armies and Politics in Latin America*. New York: Holmes & Meier.

1977. Apuntes para una teoria del Estado. Buenos Aires: CEDES.

1978. Notas para el estudio de la burguesia local, con especial referencia a sus vinculaciones con el capital transnacional y el aparato estatal. Buenos Aires: CEDES.

Offe, Claus and Volker Runge. 1975. Theses on the Theory of the State. *New German Critique*. 6: 137–48.

and Helmuth Wiesenthal. 1980. Two Logics of Collective Action: Theoretical Notes on Social Class and Organizational Forms. In Maurice Zeitlin (ed.), *Political Power and Social Theory*.

Ohlin, Bertil. 1938. Economic Progress in Sweden. *The Annals of the American Academy of Political and Social Science*. 197: 1–7.

Ohlin, Göran. 1977. The Changing Role of Private Enterprise in Sweden. In Karl Cerny (ed.), *Scandinavia at the Polls*. Washington D.C.: American Enterprise Institute.

Paggi, Leonardo. 1977. Gramsci's General Theory of Marxism. *Telos*. 33: 27–70.

Pappi, Franza U. 1973. Parteiensystem und Sozialstruktur in der Bundesrepublik. *Politische Vierteljahresschrift*. 14: 191–213.

1977. Sozialstruktur, Gesseleschaftliche Wertorientierungen und Wahlabsicht. *Politische Vierteljahresschrift*. 18: 195–230.

Parti Communiste Français. 1971. *Traité marxiste d'économie politique: Le Capitalisme monopoliste d'état*. Paris: Editions Sociales. 2 volumes.

Parti Socialiste Français, Parti Communiste Français. 1972. *Programme Commun du Gouvernement*. Paris.

Pasinetti, Luigi. 1970. Profit and Growth. In Amartya Sen (ed.), *Growth Economics*. London: Penguin.

1977. *Lectures in the Theory of Production*. New York, Columbia University Press.

Paterson, William E. 1977. The German Social Democratic Party. In W. E. Paterson and A. H. Thomas (eds), *Social Democratic Parties in Western Europe*. London: Croom Helm.

Perlo, Victor. 1976. The New Propaganda on Declining Profit Shares and Inadequate Investment. *Review of Radical Economics*. 8: 53–64.

Pesonen, Pertti. 1968. *An Election in Finland: Party Activities and Voter Reactions*. New Haven: Yale University Press.

Petersson, Olaf and Bo Särlvik. 1975. The 1973 Election. *General Elections 1973*, vol. 3. Stockholm: Central Bureau of Statistics.

Piccone, Paul. 1975. Korsch in Spain. *New German Critique*. 6.

    1977. Beyond Lenin and Togliatti: Gramsci's Marxism. *Telos*.

Pirenne, Henri. 1914. The States in the Social History of Capitalism. *The American Historical Review*. 19: 494–515.

Pirker, Theo (ed.). 1965. *Komintern und Faschismus*. Stüttgart: Deutsche Verlags-Anstalt.

Plekhanov, Georgij V. 1965. *Sochynenya*. Vol. XI. Moscow.

Poulantzas, Nicos. 1973. *Political Power and Social Classes*. London: New Left Books.

    1974a. *Fascism and Dictatorship*. London: New Left Books.

    1974b. *Les Classes sociales dans le capitalisme aujourd'hui*. Paris: Seuil.

Przemiany w strukturze klasy robotniczej w krajach kapitalistycznych. 1963. Warszawa: Ksiaźka i Wiedza.

Przeworski, Adam. 1975. Institutionalization of Voting Patterns, or Is Mobilization the Source of Decay? *American Political Science Review*. 69: 49–67.

    1976. Sociological Theory and the Study of Population. Paper presented at the Workshop on Population and Development, CLACSO, Oaxtapec, Mexico.

    and Michael Wallerstein. 1982. The Structure of Class Conflict in Democratic Capitalist Societies. *American Political Science Review*. 76: 215–38.

Rabier, Jean-Claude. 1978. On the Political Behavior of French Workers. *Acta Sociologica*. 21: 355–70.

Rehn, Gösta. 1952. The problem of Stability: An Analysis and Some Policy Proposals. In Ralph Turvey (ed.), *Wages Policy Under Full Employment*. London: William Hodge.

Robinson, Joan. 1972. Prelude to a Critique of Economic Theory. In E. K. Hunt and Jesse Schwartz (eds), *A Critique of Economic Theory*. London: Penguin.

Roemer, John. 1978. Neoclassicism, Marxism, and Collective Action. *Journal of Economic Issues*. 12: 147–61.

    1979. Divide and Conquer: Microfoundations of a Marxian Theory of Wage Discrimination. *Bell Journal of Economics*. 10: 695–705.

    1982a. New Directions in the Marxian Theory of Exploitation and Class. *Politics and Society*. 11: 253–87.

    1982b. *A General Theory of Exploitation and Class*. Cambridge, Mass.: Harvard University Press.

Rokkan, Stein and Henry Valen. 1982. The Mobilization of the Periphery. In Stein Rokkan (ed.), *Approaches to the Study of Political Participation*. Bergen: Michelsen Institute.

Rose, Richard and Derek Urwin. 1969. Social Cohesion, Political Parties and Strains in Regimes. *Comparative Political Studies*. 2: 7–67.

Rosenberg, Arthur. 1965. *Democracy and Socialism*. Boston: Beacon Press.

Rothschild, Emma. 1982. The Philosophy of Reaganism. *New York Review of Books*. April 15: 19–26.

Salvadori, Massimo. 1979. *Karl Kautsky and the Socialist Revolution, 1880–1938*. London: New Left Books.

Samuelson, Paul A. 1966. The Pure Theory of Public Expenditure. In *The Collected Scientific Papers of Paul A. Samuelson*. Edited by Joseph E. Stieglitz. Cambridge, Mass.: M.I.T. Press.

Santamaria, Ulysses and Alain Manville. 1976. Lenin and the Problem of Transition. *Telos*, 27: 79–97.

Särlvik, Bo. 1960. Swedish National Election Survey. ICPSR # 7366.

1964. The Determinants of Voting in Sweden. ICPSR # 7339.

1966. Political Stability and Change in the Swedish Electorate. *Scandinavian Political Studies*. 1: 188–222.

1967. Party Politics and National Opinion Formation: A Study of Issues in Swedish Politics, 1956–1960. *Scandinavian Political Studies*. 2: 167–202.

1974. Sweden: The Social Bases of the Parties in a Developmental Perspective. In Richard Rose (ed.), *Electoral Behavior: A Comparative Handbook*. New York: Free Press.

1977. Recent Electoral Trends in Sweden. In Karl Cerny (ed.), *Scandinavia at the Polls*. Washington, D.C.: American Enterprise Institute.

Sartre, Jean-Paul. 1960. *Critique de la raison dialectique*. Paris: Gallimard.

1968. *The Communists and the Peace*. New York: George Braziller.

1973. Elections, piège à cons. *Les Temps Modernes*. 318: 1099–108.

Scase, Richard. 1977. *Social Democracy in Capitalist Societies*. London: Rowman & Littlefield.

Schelling, Thomas. 1960. *Strategy of Conflict*. Cambridge, Mass.: Harvard University Press.

Schiller, Berndt. 1975. Years of Crisis, 1906–1914. In Steven Koblik (ed.), *Sweden's Development from Poverty to Affluence, 1750–1970*. Minneapolis: University of Minnesota Press.

Schorske, Carl E. 1955. *German Social Democracy 1905–1917: The Development of the Great Schism*. New York: Harper & Row.

Schumpeter, Joseph. 1942. *Capitalism, Socialism, and Democracy*. New York: Harper.

Shonfield, Andrew. 1969. *Modern Capitalism*. Oxford: Oxford University Press.

Skidelski, Robert. 1970. 1929–1931 Revisited. *Bulletin of the Society for the Study of Labour History*. 21: 6–8.

Sombart, Werner. 1909. *Socialism and the Social Movement*. London: J. M. Dent.

1976. *Why is there no socialism in the United States?* White Plains, N.Y.: International Arts and Sciences.

Sondages. 1960 and 1973.

Spriano, Paolo. 1967. *Storia del Partito Comunista Italiano. I. Da Bordiga a Gramsci*. Torino: Einaudi.

Stacklelberg, H. von. 1952. *The Theory of the Market Economy*. Translation and introduction by A. T. Peacock. London: William Hodge.

Stephens, John D. 1979. *The Transition from Capitalism to Socialism*. London: Macmillan.

1981. The Changing Swedish Electorate. Class Voting, Contextual Effects, and Voter Volatility. *Comparative Political Studies*. 14: 163–204.

Stigler, George. 1973. General Economic Conditions and National Elections. *American Economic Review*. 33: 160–7.

Sweezy, Paul. 1942. *The Theory of Capitalist Development*. New York: Monthly Review Press.

and Harry Magdoff. 1980. Are Low Savings Ruining the U.S. Economy? *Monthly Review*. 7: 1–17.

Taylor, Michael. 1976. *Anarchy and Cooperation*. London: John Wiley and Sons.

Terray, Emmanuel. 1972. Prolétaire, salarié, travailleur productif. *Contradictions*. 2.

Texier, Jacques. 1968. Gramsci, théoricien des superstructures. *Pensée*. 139: 35–60.

Theil, Henri. 1976. *Econometrics*. New York: John Wiley and Sons.

Thomas, Alastair H. 1977. The Danish Social Democratic Party. In W. E. Paterson and A. H. Thomas (eds), *Social Democratic Parties in Western Europe*. London: Croom Helm.

Thompson, Edward P. 1963. *The Making of the English Working Class*. New York: Vintage Books.

Tilton, Timothy A. 1979. A Swedish Road to Socialism: Ernst Wigforss and the Ideological Foundations of Swedish Social Democracy. *American Political Science Review*. 73: 505–20.

Tingsten, Herbert. 1973. *The Swedish Social Democrats*. Totowa: Bedminster Press, 1973.

Touchard, Jean. 1977. *La Gauche en France depuis 1900*. Paris: Seuil.

Toutain, J-C. 1963. La population de la France de 1700 à 1959. *Cahiers de l'Institut de Science Economique Appliquée*. Série AF.3: 3-247.

Toynbee, Arnold. 1956. *The Industrial Revolution*. Oxford: Oxford University Press.

Urry, John. 1973. Towards a Structural Theory of the Middle Class. *Acta Sociologica*. 16: 175–87.

Uusitalo, Hannu. 1975. *Class Structure and Party Choice: A Scandinavian Comparison*. Helsinki: University of Helsinki Research Reports.

Vaisov, Mifhat. 1971. Sui concetti di laboro produttivo e emproduttivo. *Critica Marxista*. 9: 121–35.

Valen, Henry and Willy Martinussen. 1977. Electoral Trends and Foreign Politics in Norway: The 1973 Storting Election and the EEC Issue. In Karl H. Cerny (ed.), *Scandinavia at the Polls*. Washington, D.C.: American Enterprise Institute.

Vylder, Stefan de. 1976. *Allende's Chile: The Political Economy of the Rise and Fall of the Unidad Popular*. Cambridge: Cambridge University Press.

Waldenberg, Marek. 1967. Poczatki, debaty wok rewizjonizmu. *Kultura l'Spół eczenstwo*. 11: 1–54.

Wall, Irwin M. 1970. The Resignation of the First Popular Front Government of Léon Blum, June 1937. *French Historical Studies*. 6: 538–54.

Wallerstein, Michael. 1982. Working-class Solidarity and Rational Behavior. Unpublished manuscript. University of Chicago.

Weill-Raynal, Etienne. 1956. Les obstacles économiques à l'éxperience Blum. *La Revue Socialiste*. 98.

Wiatr, Jerzy J. 1965. *Spoleczenstwo*. Warszawa: PWN.

Wigforss, Ernst. 1924. Industrial Democracy in Sweden. *International Labour Review*. 9: 667–79.

1938. The Financial Policy During Depression and Boom. *Annals of the American Academy of Political and Social Science*. 197: 25–40.

Williams, Gwyn A. 1975. *Proletarian Order: Antonio Gramsci, Factory Councils and the Origins of Communism in Italy, 1911–1921*. London: Pluto Press.

Wolff, Robert Paul. 1980. A Critique and Reinterpretation of Marx's Labor Theory of Value. *Philosophy and Public Affairs*. 10.

Wright, Erik Olin. 1976. Class Boundaries in Advanced Capitalist Societies. *New Left Review*. 98: 3–42.

Name Index

263

Taylor, Michael, 97
Terray, Emmanuel, 84
Texier, Jacques, 135
Theil, Henri, 128
Thomas, Alastair H., 19
Thompson, Edward P., 69, 71
Tilton, Timothy A., 42
Tinbergen, Jan, 209
Tingsten, Herbert, 8, 9, 10, 15, 18, 22, 25,
    26, 29, 30, 32, 33, 35, 42, 50, 55, 103
Touchard, Jean, 109
Toutain, J.-C., 63
Toynbee, Arnold, 86
Trotsky, Lev D., 2

Urry, John, 82, 84, 86
Uusitalo, Hannu, 125, 127

Vaisov, Mifhat, 84
Valen, Henry, 108

Varga, Eugen, 198
Verba, Sidney, 143
Vollmar, Georg von, 30
Vuskovic, Pedro, 45
Vylder, Stefan de, 46

Waldenberg, Marek, 48
Wall, Irwin M., 36
Wallerstein, Michael, 105, 171, 185, 205
Weber, Max, 55, 59, 64
Weill-Raynal, Etienne, 46
Wesołowski, Włodzimierz, 125
Wiatr, Jerzy J., 63
Wicksell, K., 36, 208
Wiesenthal, Helmuth, 97
Wigforss, Ernst, 32, 33, 36, 38, 42
Williams, Gwyn A., 32
Wolff, Robert P., 229
Wright, Erik Olin, 26, 65, 87, 94, 106

Subject Index